D1309446

www.wadsworth.com

www.wadsworth.com is the World Wide Web site for Wadsworth and is your direct source to dozens of online resources.

At *www.wadsworth.com* you can find out about supplements, demonstration software, and student resources. You can also send email to many of our authors and preview new publications and exciting new technologies.

www.wadsworth.com
Changing the way the world learns®

From the Wadsworth Series in Mass Communication and Journalism

General Mass Communication

Anokwa/Lin/Salwen, *International Communication: Issues and Controversies*
Biagi, *Media/Impact: An Introduction to Mass Media,* Seventh Edition
Bucy, *Living in the Information Age: A New Media Reader,* Second Edition
Craft/Leigh/Godfrey, *Electronic Media*
Day, *Ethics in Media Communications: Cases and Controversies,* Fourth Edition
Dennis/Merrill, *Media Debates: Great Issues for the Digital Age,* Third Edition
Fellow, *American Media History*
Gillmor/Barron/Simon, *Mass Communication Law: Cases and Comment,* Sixth Edition
Gillmor/Barron/Simon/Terry, *Fundamentals of Mass Communication Law*
Hilmes, *Connections: A Broadcast History Reader*
Hilmes, *Only Connect: A Cultural History of Broadcasting in the United States*
Jamieson/Campbell, *The Interplay of Influence: News, Advertising, Politics, and the Mass Media,* Fifth Edition
Kamalipour, *Global Communication*
Lester, *Visual Communication: Images with Messages,* Third Edition
Overbeck, *Major Principles of Media Law,* 2005 Edition
Straubhaar/LaRose, *Media Now: Understanding Media, Culture, and Technology,* Fourth Edition
Zelezny, *Communications Law: Liberties, Restraints, and the Modern Media,* Fourth Edition
Zelezny, *Cases in Communications Law,* Fourth Edition

Journalism

Bowles/Borden, *Creative Editing,* Fourth Edition
Chance/McKeen, *Literary Journalism: A Reader*
Craig, *Online Journalism*
Fischer, *Sports Journalism at Its Best: Pulitzer Prize-Winning Articles, Cartoons, and Photographs*
Fisher, *The Craft of Corporate Journalism*
Gaines, *Investigative Reporting for Print and Broadcast,* Second Edition
Hilliard, *Writing for Television, Radio, and New Media,* Eighth Edition
Kessler/McDonald, *When Words Collide: A Media Writer's Guide to Grammar and Style,* Sixth Edition
Laakaniemi, *Newswriting in Transition*
Miller, *Power Journalism: Computer-Assisted Reporting*
Poulter/Tidwell, *News Scene: Interactive Writing Exercises*
Rich, *Writing and Reporting News: A Coaching Method,* Media Enhanced Fourth Edition
Rich, *Writing and Reporting News: A Coaching Method, Student Exercise Workbook,* Media Enhanced Fourth Edition
Stephens, *Broadcast News,* Fourth Edition
Wilber/Miller, *Modern Media Writing*

Photojournalism and Photography

Parrish, *Photojournalism: An Introduction*

Public Relations and Advertising

Diggs–Brown/Glou, *The PR Styleguide: Formats for Public Relations Practice*
Hendrix, *Public Relations Cases,* Sixth Edition
Jewler/Drewniany, *Creative Strategy in Advertising,* Eighth Edition
Newsom/Haynes, *Public Relations Writing: Form and Style,* Seventh Edition
Newsom/Turk/Kruckeberg, *This Is PR: The Realities of Public Relations,* Eighth Edition
Sivulka, *Soap, Sex, and Cigarettes: A Cultural History of American Advertising*
Woods, *Advertising and Marketing to the New Majority: A Case Study Approach*

Research and Theory

Baxter/Babbie, *The Basics of Communication Research*
Baran/Davis, *Mass Communication Theory: Foundations, Ferment, and Future,* Third Edition
Littlejohn, *Theories of Human Communication,* Seventh Edition
Merrigan/Huston, *Communication Research Methods*
Rubin/Rubin/Piele, *Communication Research: Strategies and Sources,* Sixth Edition
Sparks, *Media Effects Research: A Basic Overview*
Wimmer/Dominick, *Mass Media Research: An Introduction,* Seventh Edition

Online Journalism

Reporting, Writing and Editing for New Media

RICHARD CRAIG
San Jose State University

THOMSON
WADSWORTH

Australia • Canada • Mexico • Singapore • Spain
United Kingdom • United States

THOMSON
™
WADSWORTH

Publisher: Holly J. Allen

Assistant Editor: Shona Burke

Editorial Assistant: Laryssa Polika

Senior Technology Project Manager: Jeanette Wiseman

Senior Marketing Manager: Kimberly Russell

Marketing Assistant: Andrew Keay

Advertising Project Manager: Shemika Britt

Project Manager, Editorial Production: Mary Noel

Art Director: Robert Hugel

Print/Media Buyer: Lisa Claudeanos

Permissions Editor: Sarah Harkrader

Production Service: Vicki Moran, Publishing Support Services

Photo Researcher: Sarah Harkrader

Copy Editor: Kay Mikel

Cover Designer: Bill Reuter

Compositor: G & S Typesetters, Inc.

Printer: Webcom

For more information about our products, contact us at:
Thomson Learning Academic Resource Center
1-800-423-0563

For permission to use material from this text or product, submit a request online at
http://www.thomsonrights.com.
Any additional questions about permissions can be submitted by email to
thomsonrights@thomson.com.

Library of Congress Control Number: 2004105788
ISBN 0-534-53146-6

Thomson Wadsworth
10 Davis Drive
Belmont, CA 94002-3098
USA

Asia
Thomson Learning
5 Shenton Way #01-01
UIC Building
Singapore 068808

Australia/New Zealand
Thomson Learning
102 Dodds Street
Southbank, Victoria 3006
Australia

Canada
Nelson
1120 Birchmount Road
Toronto, Ontario M1K 5G4
Canada

Europe/Middle East/Africa
Thomson Learning
High Holborn House
50/51 Bedford Row
London WC1R 4LR
United Kingdom

Latin America
Thomson Learning
Seneca, 53
Colonia Polanco
11560 Mexico D.F.
Mexico

Spain/Portugal
Paraninfo
Calle Magallanes, 25
28015 Madrid, Spain

Contents

||||||

Preface

Did you log on to the World Wide Web this morning? If you did, you're certainly not the only one. With millions of people worldwide surfing the Web every day, the Internet has become the hub of a global marketplace of information and commerce. It has also created thousands of jobs for new college graduates, many of whom find themselves working for news organizations on the Internet—either online versions of existing publications or Web-only publications with their own new audiences. Because of this, and because Web news is a new medium that's still developing, today's students are eager to learn how to operate as online journalists and gain experience in the process.

Plenty of journalism textbooks on the market today can teach you how to write or edit. And a few can teach you about computer-assisted reporting and using the Internet as a resource. But until now there has been no comprehensive textbook to teach you how to report, write and edit for online media.

Online Journalism: Reporting, Writing and Editing for New Media rethinks the notion of teaching journalism. Rather than simply fine-tuning an existing work to include a few online elements, this book has been built from the ground up with the special characteristics of the Internet in mind. The aim is to teach students the most important aspects of journalistic reporting, writing and editing using standards common to the profession while maintaining a constant focus on the unique characteristics and needs of online journalism. With this book and its corresponding Web site, you will learn a mix of new and traditional skills to help you flourish online.

Because the medium is so new, this book works to refocus your existing journalistic knowledge to fit the needs of the online medium. You'll notice that throughout this book the familiar is compared with the unfamiliar, the old with the new. The idea is not only to introduce new concepts but also to tie together elements of journalism and Web usage to prepare you to create a truly unique product—online news.

The book is organized into four parts, each of which teaches you important points about what it takes to be an online journalist:

Part I, Reporting for Online Journalists, teaches students how to gather information using traditional and online means, how to come up with story ideas, and how to prepare for interviews and ask useful, informed questions.

Part II, Writing for Online Journalists, takes the next step and shows budding reporters how to organize information and how to write stories clearly and effectively for the online audience. Special attention is paid to writing effective leads and crafting stories that are both informative and easy to read.

Part III, Editing for Online Journalists, addresses standard editing questions from the unique point of view of online publications. Beginning editors learn about proper story length, proper use of links, multimedia and interactive elements and basic HTML layout in this section.

Part IV, Standards, Laws and Ethical Issues, deals with the laws and issues that are specific to online journalism. Students see how developing standards for online media create both opportunities and pitfalls for online journalists.

Each part of the book has a brief introduction to acquaint you with the subject and put the material in context. Two subjects serve as the main subtext of these introductions—the differences between traditional and online media, and the unique makeup and needs of the online news audience.

In addition, every chapter of the book contains interviews with online journalists. Some of them are well known and work for large media corporations, while others work at smaller outlets but have produced innovative content and use unique approaches to getting the most out of the online medium. Each of these professionals shares insights about putting news online and offers suggestions for beginning online journalists.

Each chapter ends with a list of Related Web Sites, so you can go online to see examples of the concepts being discussed, and a series of exercises, including InfoTrac® College Edition resources. Many of the exercises involve finding material online or in the community, as well as interviewing, writing and editing material for publication online.

Best of all, this book is backed up with a comprehensive Web site—http://communication.wadsworth.com/craig. The site isn't just a rehash of the book—it's an ongoing and vital part of the book's learning experience. Face it—in this day and age, by the time any book is published, it's starting to get out of date. The Web site supplements the book by providing updates, links and unique material that you can use throughout the semester. Here are a few of the features:

- As you follow along in the book, you can visit the actual sites and other items referred to in the text. For example, when the book refers to the way the MSNBC site uses Java applets to spice up its page, you can see it in action yourself.

- Each chapter of the book has its own page on the site, which includes links to items relevant to the chapter's subject matter. This will help you gain a fuller understanding of the book's concepts—for example, particular styles of leads and structures of stories.

- This site provides links to audio content that enriches the book's content. In particular, the site contains audio clips of the online journalists who were interviewed for the book, so you can hear what they have to say in their own voices.

- When big news events happen, the site will be updated to tie different sections of the book to various elements of the coverage of those events and to keep classes consistently on top of the news. For example, coverage of a natural disaster might have elements relating to online databases (Chapter 4), writing styles (Chapter 6), multimedia (Chapter 12) and legal issues (Chapter 15). You can look at the site to find links showing how an event happening right now relates to concepts from the book.

While grounded in the fundamentals of good journalism practice, one important goal of this book is to get you excited about the possibilities of practicing journalism in this new and utterly unique medium. No other medium has allowed journalists to present information so quickly, using so many different types of content. For today's online journalists, the sky's the limit!

ACKNOWLEDGMENTS

On a project of this size, there seems to be an endless list of people to thank, but I'll try to keep this somewhat manageable. First, thanks to Holly Allen, Shona Burke and Karen Austin at Wadsworth / Thomson Learning for their patience and contributions. Thanks also to Mary Noel and Vicki Moran for helping to smooth the production process, and to Kay Mikel for her eagle-eyed editing (and tolerance of my writing style). Nancy Ellickson and Jan Shaw both spent hours reading drafts of the manuscript, providing excellent suggestions and catching numerous mistakes. This book has been greatly enriched by their participation. I'd also like to thank my fellow faculty at San José State University's School of Journalism and Mass Communications for their support and encouragement, particularly Dennis Wilcox, who provided tremendous guidance. I should not forget Janice Lew, Amanda Hilty and Mary Ellen Weitekamp, who have regularly rescued me from my own inadequacies. In addition, I'd like to thank all of the journalism professionals I've interviewed for this book. Their input made the book come alive, adding a currency and relevance it would never have had otherwise.

I would also like to thank the following reviewers: Stephen K. Doig, Arizona State University; Christine D. Harvey, University of Maryland; Kris Kodrich, Colorado State University; Eric Meyer, University of Illinois; Gene Murray, Grambling State University; Jane B. Singer, University of Iowa; Leonard Strazewski, Columbia College Chicago; James Tidwell, Eastern Illinois University; and Ken Waters, Pepperdine University.

Finally, I thank my wife Melissa for all of her love and support during the long process of putting this project together.

PART I

||||||

Reporting for
Online Journalists

Online journalism is an exciting and expanding field, but what makes it different from more traditional media? In this book you will learn the advantages and disadvantages of working in the online environment and how to become a credible journalist in this still evolving medium. Part 1 focuses on gathering information specifically for online media. Once you are familiar with the general landscape of the Internet, you can apply this knowledge in your search for information and statistical data that are useful in online journalism. Here is a brief overview of the topics addressed in Part 1.

1 Why Is Online Journalism Different, and Why Should You Care?

So news stories are posted online these days—so what? Is that really any different from putting them on television or in a magazine or newspaper? Chapter 1 acquaints you with some of the basic notions of online journalism and how it developed. In addition, this chapter raises the major issues that are addressed throughout the book.

2 The Job of the Online Journalist

Being a journalist on the Web is very different from being a traditional journalist—or is it? This chapter examines the traditional skills all journalists, online or offline, must learn. In addition, online news workers discuss the things journalists must learn to succeed in the online medium. Finally, you will learn how to prepare for finding a job in the online medium.

3 Generating and Focusing Story Ideas

Since online journalism can take many forms, formulating story ideas is no longer a routine process. This chapter discusses ways to use the focus of your publication and the characteristics of its audience to generate story ideas and to come up with twists on standard story ideas.

4 Web Resources and Databases

The Web is an ever-expanding ocean of information. How do you navigate through it to explore a particular topic? Chapter 4 focuses on the uses for searches and describes some of the most useful search tools online. A brief tutorial is also included, which describes the most effective ways to maximize the capabilities of the high-tech compass known as a search engine.

5 Sources and Interviewing

Online journalists get information from people, books, databases and from a seemingly limitless number of Web sites. This chapter looks at these sources and resources, examining information outlets of many kinds. Online information is not always as credible as it seems, and it is the responsibility of the journalist to evaluate these sources of information. The chapter also examines the art of interviewing, including elements both traditional (selection of interviewees, interview preparation and so forth) and modern (the use of new technologies to help in securing, researching and recording interviews).

1

1

||||||

Why Is Online Journalism Different, and Why Should You Care?

The changes that have taken place in journalism in the past 100 years are no less staggering than those that have affected most other aspects of human life. Journalists cover news today using techniques and resources unthinkable in the early 1900s, and online journalists do a job that was unknown just 15 years ago. Yet the function of the journalist has largely remained unchanged. This chapter examines how journalism has evolved into the multimedia enterprise we know today.

THE TECHNOLOGICAL EVOLUTION OF JOURNALISM

On September 11, 2001, when hijacked commercial airliners crashed into the World Trade Center and the Pentagon, Americans knew about it within minutes. Television and radio stations ran live coverage, **Internet** outlets updated their information regularly, and many newspapers produced extra editions. TV viewers were alerted so quickly to the first World Trade Center attack that many watched live as the plane struck the second tower. Less than an hour after the first attack, huge worldwide audiences had gathered and witnessed the collapse of each of the two towers. The notion of having to wait to find out news of this magnitude was unthinkable. Two basic human needs—to gain understanding in a time of tragedy and to share that information—drove both news organizations and ordinary citizens to use the Internet at unprecedented levels.

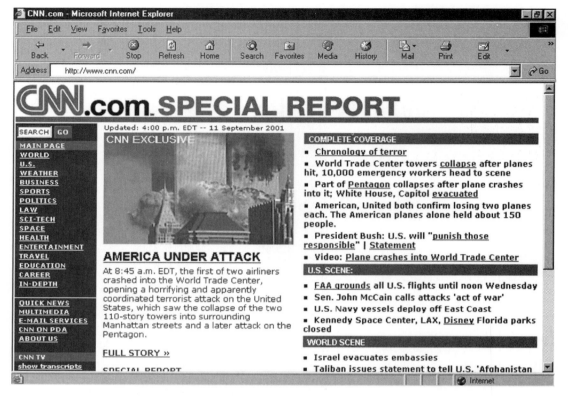

The terrorist attacks of September 11, 2001, were covered by every news medium, but Web outlets such as CNN.com offered a unique mix of photos, video, illustrations and in-depth articles.

SOURCE: CNN.com (accessed September 11, 2001). Used by permission.

Oddly enough, almost exactly one hundred years earlier, on September 7, 1901, another major tragedy in American history took place: President William McKinley was assassinated. The nation was shocked, yet Americans didn't find out about it immediately, or even quickly. There was no Internet, no News.com, no MSNBC Online or CNN Interactive. In fact, there was no CNN or even NBC. American households had neither television nor radio yet. As a result, news of the assassination took many days to spread across the nation via newspaper stories, wire service reports and word of mouth. In fact, the first time many Americans in small communities saw an automobile was when someone drove into their town to spread the news of McKinley's death.

What does this have to do with online news? In both 1901 and 2001 news organizations and individuals used all the technology available to spread the word. At that time, many decades before anyone dreamed of streaming video or even

TWENTIETH-CENTURY NEWS MEDIA TIMELINE

1880s–1890s: First use of photographs in newspapers; first widespread acceptance of professional reporters; trains first deliver newspapers daily

1900s: Marconi sends first radio signals across Atlantic Ocean; technical improvements in radio, telegraph and printing

1910s: Type composing machines invented to speed newspaper publication; radios get tuners and loudspeakers

1920s: First radio stations begin broadcasting entertainment and news; first news photos sent by wire and phone lines; introduction of talking motion pictures (and newsreels); birth of teletype machine

1930s: First regular radio network newscasts; early television experiments; Hindenburg crash broadcast recorded and replayed nationwide

1940s: First television networks (and television network newscasts); first electronic computers; community antenna television born (forerunner to cable TV)

1950s: Television takes over as most popular medium; first computerized election projections; earliest cable TV systems; first transistor radios; radios now outnumber newspapers printed daily; first use of videotape to cover news; microchip invented

1960s: Introduction of satellites; first half-hour nightly network news broadcasts; President Kennedy's assassination first event to focus nation's attention on TV news coverage; first use of color news footage; cable companies import distant signals; TV takes over as most popular news medium; first videotape cassettes

1970s: First microprocessors; introduction of VCRs; widespread adoption of cable TV; local and national news outlets use videotape and satellites regularly; earliest home computers

1980s: First all-news cable channels; major improvements in computer technology; introduction of laptop computers; videotext services born (and fail); first widespread use of computers in newsrooms; first home satellite dishes sold

1990s: Cable News Network dominates worldwide Gulf War coverage; first widespread use of Internet; birth and proliferation of commercial Internet news sites; many college newspapers create online versions; Internet reporter Matt Drudge breaks story of Clinton-Lewinsky scandal

2000s: First online news awards given in international competition; September 11, 2001, terrorist attacks heighten public interest in news and world events across all media; more and more citizens get news from Internet

SOURCE: The Media History Project (n.d.), *Discovering the News, Voices of a Nation,* http:www.mediahistory.umn.edu/index2.html (accessed December 2002).

e-mail, the use of wire services and automobiles as means to spread news was at the cutting edge of high technology. When Abraham Lincoln was killed in 1865—just 36 years before McKinley was shot—many Americans in the West didn't learn of it for weeks. In contrast, 44 years after McKinley was killed, most Americans learned of the 1945 death of Franklin Delano Roosevelt within hours of the event, courtesy of the national radio networks. Details may have been sketchy, but there was now no longer any need for motorists to act as town criers. Radio had stitched together a nationwide audience that could be informed of any news quickly and efficiently, making the best use of the technology then available.

By 1963, when John Kennedy was assassinated, millions of Americans found out about the shooting before Kennedy was even pronounced dead. Television spread the breaking news instantly although satellite technology was not yet advanced enough to allow for immediate live coverage from Dallas. In spite of these early limitations, television helped turn Kennedy's death and its aftermath into an all-encompassing four-day event. By the time Princess Diana died in a car crash in 1997, news technology had reached a new level. On both television and the Internet, the world saw live video of the crash site and received minute-by-minute updates on Diana's condition for hours before her death was announced. In both cases, hundreds of reporters spent thousands of column inches and hours of airtime (and, in the latter case, many megabytes of **bandwidth**) analyzing the deaths and their impact.

In 1901, when McKinley was killed, there were only a few hundred reporters in all of the United States. The occupation of professional news reporter had been in existence for only a decade or so and was generally limited to large newspapers in major cities. Yet the central objective of the journalist was exactly the same as it is today—to report news as quickly and accurately as possible. This intent hasn't changed, but technology has radically altered the standards by which we measure several aspects of news.

Most notably, the notion of the **timeliness** of news has been completely redefined. Technology has allowed reporters and news organizations to transmit information almost instantly, and audiences have become conditioned to expect immediate coverage of any breaking event. In 1901, publishing major international news stories within a few days of their occurrence was considered timely. Even in the days of radio and early television, information traveled far more slowly than it does today. For example, when England's Queen Elizabeth II was crowned in 1953, the American television networks raced to scoop one another by flying film of the ceremonies across the Atlantic and showing it to American audiences within 12 hours of the event. Today satellite transmission brings the event and a report of its occurrence on the news into our homes without any lag time.

The notion of **proximity** has also changed. With freeways and airlines shortening travel times, the notion of what is "local" has expanded. Depending on the circumstances and subject matter, these days most news within a state or a region of the country is considered local. The notion of **prominence** has changed as well due to the explosion of media outlets on cable and the Internet. With so many more content providers cranking out hours of programming and pages of coverage, there is far more opportunity for exposure, and thus many more people are considered "famous" today than earlier in the century.

In the 21st century, journalists have all the complexities of modern society to consider, yet they also have unprecedented resources. In the 20th century, the menu of tools available to reporters grew from pen, paper and typewriter to include the telephone, the camera, the tape recorder, video cameras and computers. Tools for gathering news have evolved beyond simple observation and interviewing to include government records, archives, computer databases and, most recently, the Internet. Combined with the unprecedented ability to transmit stories far and wide, individual journalists now have a far larger impact than ever before.

As technology has improved, however, expectations have risen. It is no longer sufficient to simply go to the scene of an event, jot down some notes and write a story. Audiences first came to expect photos with their news, then film or video footage and eventually live coverage. People want the immediacy that these features bring to a story; if one outlet doesn't have the type of coverage that best suits the story, they'll find another one that does.

For example, the 1993 attack and fire at the Branch Davidian compound in Waco, Texas, could have been covered in the traditional way, with photos and reports appearing in newspapers the next day. Yet the immediacy of seeing the compound burning live on television made people aware of the horrifying scope of the event, and footage of that fire provides one of the lasting images of the 1990s.

Television raised expectations among audiences, and the Internet has raised them still further. The multimedia environment of today has so many capabilities and is being utilized in so many innovative ways that traditional reporting is changing dramatically. Audiences simply demand more.

THE DEVELOPMENT OF ONLINE JOURNALISM

In the late 1990s and early 2000s, the Internet went from a specialized medium used mostly by university personnel and computer experts to a true mass medium. An ongoing Pew Research Center study (*Pew Internet and American Life Project,* 1995, 1998, and 2002; http://www.people-press.org/) found that only 14 percent of Americans had gone online by 1995. Just three years later, that number had risen to 36 percent, and by 2002 the number of Americans online increased to 62 percent. By the end of 2002, not only did the majority of Americans have Internet access, but 40 percent of them had been online for more than three years.

Even before the Web existed—when only computer-savvy government, military and university employees used the Internet—one of its most popular features was news. At that time, however, Internet news competed with non-Internet commercial online news sources. Archived news from assorted sources was made available without Internet access in the early 1980s. The Lexis-Nexis database service provided this material to libraries, and several large newspapers experimented with delivering news through non-Internet online text services throughout the 1980s and early 1990s. As commercial Internet service providers such as America Online, CompuServe and Prodigy emerged in the mid-1980s, they also provided news to subscribers. But it wasn't until 1994, when the Netscape **browser** gave the Internet a graphical interface, that online news became available to the majority of Internet users.

News sites quickly became among the most widely viewed sites on the Net— some were affiliated with print and broadcast news outlets and others were independent. For pre-existing news organizations, developing a Web site quickly became a high priority. According to the *American Journalism Review,* in 1994 only

STRENGTHS AND WEAKNESSES OF DIFFERENT NEWS MEDIA

MEDIUM	STRENGTHS	WEAKNESSES
Newspapers	Format allows for greatest breadth of information; allows for explanation of difficult concepts; can include photos; can cover many subjects in great depth; allows for unique writing and reporting styles	Publishes only once a day, with rare exceptions; can't use video or audio; can't cover events live; requires close concentration; deadlines often hamper efforts at thoughtful analysis
Newsmagazines	Offers deeper analysis of news than any other medium; excellent color photos; allows for unique writing and reporting styles; can cover a variety of subjects	Usually only publishes once a week and therefore often covers "old news"; can't use video or audio; can't cover events live
Radio	Convenience—most people have radios in their cars; doesn't require full attention; can update instantly; can provide live coverage of events; can use audio of events or interviews	Can't use pictures or video; lacks depth of print and visual components of television; reports often dropped in during entertainment programming
Television	Compelling—can show high-quality video of most events and interviews; can cover events and breaking news live; can update instantly; ubiquitous—TVs are everywhere	Often superficial—format limits depth of coverage; can't cover as many subjects as print or online media; reports often dropped in during entertainment programming
Online News	Can update instantly; can include photos, video and audio of events; can cover stories live; can go into greater depth than broadcast media	Inconvenient—must start up computer; video quality is poor; requires close concentration; download times inhibit quick access to information; sources sometimes questionable

20 newspapers in the entire world had Web sites. Less than five years later there were more than 5,000 newspaper Web sites.

In the beginning, online journalism differed little from print journalism. Many news Web sites, particularly those affiliated with print outlets, simply posted the text of some or all of the day's news stories online. Even TV stations with news pages often put the text of their reports on their Web pages. Some news outlets added photos, some didn't. But as computers, modems and network connections got faster, and as news editors began to realize the possibilities inherent in online journalism, these news sites began to evolve.

While the heart of online news remained text, editors discovered two main characteristics that distinguished online journalism from its print counterpart. Online media offered multimedia capabilities and the ability to update stories instantly. Some outlets began offering sound clips from interviews or press conferences, giving online audiences something in addition to the stories found in print editions. Others, particularly TV stations and networks, began to offer video clips of reports and news footage. Meanwhile, when news was breaking, even print news outlets could now post stories within hours or even minutes, giving them the chance to compete with broadcast outlets on quickly developing stories for the first time.

In spite of these capabilities, many news outlets still limit their online content to the text of each day's news stories and little else. Some in the industry who have jumped on the multimedia bandwagon chalk this up to an unwillingness to change, to being behind the times or to outright laziness. They scornfully refer to the practice as **shovelware**—essentially "shoveling" text from a print edition to an online edition with little regard for how additional Web content might enrich stories for readers. Editors who stick with basic text often respond that they have limited budgets or staffing and point out that of all the news outlets with Web sites only a few, such as the *Wall Street Journal*, have yet turned a profit with Web operations.

Regardless of one's point of view, it is clear that online news is a mass medium that is growing exponentially in the 21st century. In 1996 only 2 percent of Americans went online to get news at least three times a week (Pew Research Center, *Pew Internet and American Life Project,* 1995, 1998, and 2002; http://www.people-press.org/). By 1998 that number had risen to 13 percent, and by 2002 it was 25 percent. By October 2002 the Pew Center reported that 82 million Americans had gone online for news, up from 52 million just two years earlier. This is an impressive statistic, but more than half of that same group (59 percent) also watch TV news daily. The tremendous surge of Net news readership in just a few years' time suggests that it is on the cusp of dominance.

THE ONLINE NEWS AUDIENCE

In journalism writers and editors are concerned with three primary entities when preparing stories for publication or broadcast. These are the facts, the medium and the audience. Every news writing or editing course tells aspiring journalists how to put facts together into stories, and higher-level classes often deal with the particulars of crafting stories for different types of media. Yet there is comparatively little effort put into understanding the audience for each medium. For online journalists, this can be a fatal error because the online news audience has its own unique characteristics.

In the United States the content of commercial media is generally driven by a combination of the medium's own characteristics and the likes and dislikes of its audience. Whether it's an entertainment program, advertising message or news report, the audience generally makes its feelings known. Although news reporters and editors often maintain that they are more interested in adhering to their professional standards than in pandering to the lowest common denominator, they'd be fools to ignore the people who pay the bills.

With a local news organization, the demographics and preferences of the

|||||| **FROM THE FIELD**

ABC News

Sam Donaldson
Anchor, SamDonaldson@ABCNEWS.com
Co-anchor and reporter, *20/20*
Former Chief White House Correspondent, ABC News

Sam Donaldson would be the first to admit that he is not a full-time online journalist. He is primarily known as one of the leading broadcast journalists of his generation. But when given the opportunity to create the first regularly scheduled live video network news program on the **World Wide Web,** he jumped at the chance.

"A lot of people who are smarter than I am think it's the future," Donaldson says. "The company and I agreed on a new contract, and one of the options they gave me was to do a **webcast.**"

Donaldson's program debuted in September 1999. He was familiar with many news Web sites and knew what he could add to the mix. "I knew coming in that we would try to do a television program," he says. "I know how to do that. I've been doing that for three or four decades. But I also knew coming in that the screen size was about two inches by two inches within the Web page. So we weren't going to be ambitious and show a lot of pictures which no one could see."

The program's focus has been on business, politics and technology-related issues. "We want to bring information of a different character," Donaldson says. "Stuff that's from a different angle than what you might hear on the regular newscast, but more often stuff that Peter Jennings doesn't have time for. It's not the top of the news, but it's interesting to people who are computer literate, they're Web literate, they're upscale, they're interested in markets, they're interested in business, they're interested, yes, in politics, but cutting-edge politics."

He admits that he is still learning about online journalism, but like so many online journalists, he has been impressed by the interactivity of the medium. "I wish I had more time to respond," says Donaldson. "During the webcasts, I tell people, 'Type in your questions for guests,' and they do. But I can never get around to more than one or two of them during the program. And I tell people, 'If you want to say something to me, if you want to ask a question of me, send me an e-mail,' and they do. But it's really hard to deal with that volume of material. That's why we've had the 'Ask Sam' shows with no guests, so I can answer some of their questions."

audience are generally well known. Yet the bigger and more diverse an audience is, the harder it is to conclude what it likes or wants as a group. Given the disparate nature of the American television audience, it is hard to generalize much about the average TV viewer's tastes and preferences. For example, cop shows and situation comedies may both be popular, but that doesn't mean everyone likes both genres. In contrast, programmers for the Home and Garden Network or the Golf

Donaldson didn't consider going online a huge risk at this point in his career. "I'm very fortunate," he says. "I don't have to say, 'I'm giving up conventional broadcasting, and I'm going to plunge over the brink here and see if there's this big net that's rising called the Internet.' I'm doing both still—I'm continuing to do full-time work in conventional broadcasting while I'm getting my feet wet in the Internet."

Some might be surprised that a veteran newsman like Donaldson would get into computers, but he's been using them for years. "I bought my first computer in 1986, an IBM PC XT," he says, "which today couldn't run a single program you would buy, in order to write a book. And I don't see how authors ever wrote a book before the computer. It made it so easy to move paragraphs around, even from chapter to chapter, that it was a real joy. And from that experience I began to become more computer literate. Then three or four years ago, I began to explore the World Wide Web."

This doesn't mean he treats his webcasts simply as a curiosity. "I could start out and say, 'I don't care how many people "hit me" on this program,'" Donaldson says. "I think that's fine for a while, but if the smart people are right, if this becomes the battleground for advertising and all of that, no! I'm not going to be satisfied just to say, well, I've got six people who are really intelligent, and they're watching me, but I'm a commercial failure. I simply won't do that. I want to be successful editorially, but I also want to be successful commercially."

Donaldson's primary goal—online or off—is to engage the audience. "Early on [veteran newsman] Howard K. Smith told me, 'The most irresponsible thing in broadcasting is to be dull,'" says Donaldson. "And I agree with Howard. He wasn't saying 'be inaccurate' or 'be misleading' or 'be biased.' This is not Drudge, this is not Rush Limbaugh, what I'm doing. We apply the normal journalistic standards to it. But you can do that and still not be dull. That doesn't mean you do irresponsible things. That doesn't mean you only do 'today's rape.' It means that you try to do subjects and present them in a way that people who are sitting there find interesting. Why should you be sitting at your desk, having lunch at 12:30 Eastern time, with all these available broadcasts and cable channels? Why should you come regularly to watch me come to the computer?"

Donaldson believes beginning journalists need to learn core journalistic principles—accuracy, completeness, balance—before they worry about how Web pages work. "I think it's pretty easy to learn the technical skills of using the World Wide Web," he says. "If I can learn some of them, these young people, who are light-years ahead of me in their ability to absorb and learn, can learn them overnight. I'm saying in order to be successful there, you need the fundamentals of how to be a reporter. You can learn the skills. It's just like if you come into television, I can teach you in a short period of time how to use cameras and videotape and all of this. I can't know that you'll be successful. But you have to have those fundamentals."

Channel have an easier task because their content is so much more specialized. Researchers and programmers can more safely respond to the wants and needs of viewers of one of these channels than to the more general audience of NBC or CBS.

Given this standard, the worldwide Internet audience might seem impossibly heterogeneous. But in many ways, the current online news audience is more like that of a specialized cable channel than that of a broadcast network. Several factors contribute to this:

- Reading news online requires both a computer and Internet access. A majority of Americans now have access to computers at home, at work or in the community, but this still weights the online audience heavily in favor of those who have home computers. When compared with television, which is in more than 98 percent of U.S. households, this is a serious limiting factor.

- Online news requires closer concentration and interest than broadcast news because it is based on reading. The reader takes an active role in selecting stories and paging through them. This weights the audience in favor of those who read well as opposed to those who process information better visually or aurally. It also weights the audience in favor of those who are already highly interested in the news rather than those who learn about news more peripherally.

- Thanks to search engines and customizable news pages, online news viewers can choose to highlight stories on subjects they're interested in at the expense of other subjects. This eliminates a lot of incidental learning, which often comes from leafing through a newspaper or waiting for a particular news segment on TV. It also helps to create an audience of people who know a great deal about a few subjects and next to nothing about others.

Because of these characteristics, certain types of people have thus far tended to gravitate toward online news. Many surveys indicate that the online news audience is younger than the average news consumer and more likely to be male, well educated and affluent. A 2002 Pew Research Center survey (*Pew Internet and American Life Project*; http://www.people-press.org) found that more than one-third of college graduates (and 47 percent of college graduates under age 30) go online to get news at least once a week. The study also found that 34 percent of those surveyed who make more than $50,000 annually get news online at least once a week.

In addition to being affluent and well educated, the online news audience has a voracious appetite for information. Most research indicates that online news sites are a haven for "news junkies"—people who follow the news far more closely than the average American. Many surveys indicate that online news users follow the news in many media and go online to get more detailed information or different points of view. As a result, the online audience is known as a choosy and fickle one. Users have regularly indicated that they are more than willing to abandon one source for another if the new source provides information more quickly or in a more manageable format.

All this audience information presents online news outlets with a mixed blessing. The online audience is a very desirable one—youth and affluence are always favorite traits with advertisers. Yet with their tendency to jump ship, online readers are also a frustrating group. They tend to insist not only on high-quality reporting but also on a well-designed Web site with features that go far beyond the simple text of news stories. Online audiences expect both accuracy and speed, as well as in-depth information, audio and video clips and some form of live coverage for breaking news, and they want all of it wrapped up in an attractive, easily navigable package. In short, they are a very demanding group. As of December 2002, the Pew Research Center's *Pew Internet and American Life Project* (http://www.people-press.org/) reported that 69 percent of Americans expected to be able to find reliable, up-to-date news online; this was true for 85 percent of Internet users, compared with 43 percent of non-Internet users.

GIVING THEM WHAT THEY NEED

The online audience may seem like a tough bunch to please, but their basic concerns are the same as those of news audiences over the past 100 years. They want accurate, clearly written stories that get across lots of information quickly. One difficulty is in finding a balance between giving users what they want (the latest information in quickly digestible chunks) and what they need (news in its full context, understandable and useful, and relevant to their lives).

In *The Elements of Journalism: What Newspeople Should Know and the Public Should Expect* (New York: Crown, 2001), veteran journalists Bill Kovach and Tom Rosenstiel discuss this issue in some depth. They acknowledge that information is everywhere but argue that bits of information devoid of context are not news. For example, many cable news channels now have a continuous "crawl" of headlines across the bottom of the screen. These may be attention-getters, but they often raise as many questions as they answer. For example, if the crawl reads "SD Police Charge Jackson with Murder," the average viewer won't know (a) who "Jackson" is, (b) who he or she is charged with murdering, or (c) whether SD stands for San Diego or South Dakota. In a newspaper, the reader could simply look at the story below such a headline, but with no context, there's no real reason for a viewer to pursue the story further. This sort of thing is also common to the online news environment, where all a user might see on a home page is a handful of words devoid of context.

Against this backdrop, Kovach and Rosenstiel introduce the concept of **sense-making journalism,** not only providing information but the context needed for users to understand it:

> The new journalist is no longer deciding what the public should know. She is helping audiences make order out of it. This does not mean simply adding interpretation or analysis to news reporting. The first task of the new journalist/sense maker, rather, is to verify what information is reliable and then order it so people can grasp it efficiently. (p. 24)

Within this model, journalists become interpreters of information rather than simple conduits or processors of facts. The notion is only a slight variation on the skills taught in traditional journalism education—learn as much as you can about a subject, talk to the people involved, then pass along your accumulated wisdom to the audience.

This sounds simple, yet in many ways it clashes with the online environment.

Web content is notoriously transitive, and Web users are accustomed to hopping quickly from one site to another. How does a journalist get a detailed message across in this environment? Through a variety of discussions, interviews and exercises, this book tries to answer that question.

SUMMARY

Online journalism is unlike any news medium that preceded it. In many ways, it offers the best qualities of both broadcast and print news and some specific features of its own. It can possess the depth of information found in print journalism, the immediacy of television through immediate updates and live audio and video, plus the unique ability to take users to sites where they can read more about a topic if they wish. Unlike other media, its standards and formats are still relatively new and evolving. Online journalism is the most exciting new field in today's journalism industry.

RELATED WEB SITES

American Journalism Review
http://www.ajr.org

Pew Research Center
http://www.people-press.org

The Media History Project
http://mediahistory.umn.edu

CNN coverage of 9/11 terrorist attacks
http://www.cnn.com/SPECIALS/2002/america.remembers/sept11.section.html

CNN coverage of Princess Diana's death
http://cnn.com/resources/video.almanac/1993/index.html

ABC News
http://www.abcnews.com

EXERCISES

1. Find a story on a news Web site of your choice, then find a story on the same subject in a local or national print media outlet. In as much detail as possible, discuss the differences between the two treatments of the story across media. What choices did the respective editors make, and how did those choices lend themselves to the characteristics of the medium?

2. Use your home VCR to videotape a local or national television newscast. Choose one story and transcribe it. Then compare the text of that story to a print or online story covering the same subject. How does the text of the television story differ? What does it indicate about the nature of television coverage versus news based on written coverage?

3. Look in your university library's newspaper archive for a story from at least 50 years ago. What differences do you notice between this story and news coverage today? Look particularly at the use of language, graphical elements and story structure.

4. Choose a story from InfoTrac College Edition or from your local newspaper and discuss how you think it might be modified and improved for publication online. Be sure to note where you would include links or multimedia elements. Give some examples of the types of materials and linked sites that might be useful in telling the story well on the Internet.

2

||||||

The Job of the
Online Journalist

Many students are interested in getting into online journalism yet have little idea of what the job actually entails. This chapter uses interviews with online journalists to explore the similarities and differences between the duties of an online reporter and a print or broadcast journalist. At the center of the discussion is the notion of interactivity—the characteristic most online journalists believe makes their medium most distinctive.

"Do I interview computers?" One student applying to be a journalist at a new university online newspaper asked this question. Perhaps it was a joke (though it didn't seem to be), but it is indicative of how unclear most students are about the nature of the job of the online journalist. Students have some idea of what it means to be a reporter or an editor for a newspaper, but the notion of what an online journalist actually does for a living seems to escape them, and probably eludes many readers as well.

For this book, several online journalists have been interviewed, and all of them were interested in sharing their knowledge and experience with students. This chapter looks at the job of online journalism largely in the professionals' own words.

APPROACHING THE JOB

Most professionals agree on one thing—you can't go into online journalism thinking you are going to be strictly a writer or an editor, or have any other single, narrowly defined job. In this new medium, rules are still being defined and so are job duties.

"Flexibility is the first job skill that I look for," says Owen Youngman, who headed the launch of the *Chicago Tribune's* Web site in 1996 and led it for four years as Director of Interactive Media. "Just because I hire you to do one thing today doesn't mean you'll be doing that tomorrow. When I say flexibility, I mean the willingness to do lots of different kinds of tasks—maybe in the same day, maybe in the same week, certainly in the same career. Flexibility and the willingness to listen to customers are probably the two main differences between old-line and new-line reporters. If you need a lot of certainty, the Internet is not the place for you."

Many students in various fields learn the value of specialization—mastering one skill and focusing on that—in the course of their college lives, but online journalism is different. If you want to succeed, it helps to know how to do a lot of things. You need traditional reporting skills, but it also comes in handy to know HTML, layout, multimedia and a host of other things. That way, if your organization's needs change, you can easily adapt. From the point of view of your editors, they can plug you into any job.

"You need to think versatility," says Stan Austin, the Online Managing Editor of the *Kansas City Star.* "You need to know a little bit about a lot of things. A person who is a whiz-bang page designer but can't write a declarative sentence is really of no use to me in what I do every day. I could maybe get them a job in another part of the department, but people who are working with content have to be competent editors first."

The need for versatility is emphasized by the fact that the average college graduate who goes to work in a Web newsroom is often not hired as a reporter but as a **content producer.** This position often involves writing, but it also frequently entails copyediting, researching, headline writing, layout and many other duties. This might not immediately sound appealing to an aspiring writer, but it's what the economy and the marketplace of the 2000s dictates.

"We try to produce content that works on the Web," says Scott Woelfel, one of the co-founders and former Editor-in-Chief of CNN Interactive. "Our people take a variety of sources, from our TV content, wire services and elsewhere, and produce it for the Web in a way that works in that medium."

The tough economic conditions of the early 2000s made full-time online reporting jobs scarce. Only the largest outlets were hiring full-time Web-only reporters. However, as increasing numbers of consumers get **broadband** Internet connections and as more people turn to the Web for news, this is likely to change, and aspiring reporters need to be ready to produce original online material containing multimedia, links and many other online-specific elements.

The *Chicago Tribune* uses its ties to other newspapers and to radio
and TV outlets to enhance its online content.

SOURCE: ChicagoTribune.com (accessed September 2, 2003). Used courtesy of ChicagoTribune.com.

The *Washington Post*'s Web operation may provide a clue as to how online
news will operate in the future. "At the *Post*, there are something like 100 people
working in the newsroom for washingtonpost.com," says Retha Hill, who helped
launch the *Post*'s Web site and is now Vice President for Content Development at
BET.com. "That allows each producer to have, more or less, a beat—there are
two or three people who are just working on metro. There are 11 to 12 people
working on the online guide—the going-out guide and the style area. There are
four or five people just working on politics, there are a couple of people just working on national. So they could think about the beat—how do you take what's in
the newspaper that day, enrich the experience by bringing in hosts, guests, newsmakers to interact with users, building a poll, building an interactive time, something like that."

Content producers working on a beat may not always be reporting; they may work on layout, research, copyediting or whatever else is necessary to cover that given subject. Even if you are hired as a reporter, however, your duties and your concept of the job may be very different from what you would expect in a traditional media job. "As a regular reporter, basically you don't have to worry about creating a product," says Hill. "At a newspaper, you're reporting stories for whatever section of the paper you're working for. So that product is already created, whether it's the metro section or the national section or the arts and entertainment section, etc. So that's your relationship—you go out, you report a story, you bring it back, you write a story, it's edited, it goes into the newspaper. But online media is so new, as a content developer, you're concerned not only with the daily and weekly content you're creating, but also you're trying to create a new product. You don't know what will be a hit with users, so you're trying a lot of different things."

PRODUCING AND STRUCTURING CONTENT

Even with the different duties inherent in the job of content producer, most professionals agree that the core skills needed to function effectively are not all that different from traditional journalism. Gathering, assembling and writing up information for the Internet is generally just a variation on the same theme.

"The act of reporting doesn't differ at all," says Hill. "I think that if your assignment for that day is to report on an issue and get it online, and you're moving faster, you report it the same way. You call up the traditional sources and you bang out a story."

"Honestly, I don't feel there's a whole lot of difference between reporting for print or for online," says Ken Layne, former Washington, D.C. and International correspondent for United Press International and now a guest columnist for *Online Journalism Review*. "You need to get all the facts, or as many as you can get, and you need to know a little bit about what you write about. As far as interviewing people and getting material for a story, it's pretty much the same. The difference is in how you write it up, how you present it."

Others do see some differences between the actual task of reporting online and in print. "When you're writing for a newspaper, you have a desk and you make a lot of phone calls and that sort of thing, but you're also away from your desk a lot," says John Christensen, a former senior writer for CNN Interactive. "You're off talking to people, interviewing people. I used to do a lot of feature writing, so I would go off to a hotel or their home and interview them. For a long time, this has been much more of a desk job—you're making calls, looking at wire material, putting together packages. More recently, though, I've been working in our special projects section, which involves getting out more and doing some feature-type things, some original reporting, which I must say is very refreshing. But still, you're pretty desk-bound."

|||||| **FROM THE FIELD**

Owen Youngman
Director of Planning and Development, *Chicago Tribune*
Former Director of Interactive Media

Owen Youngman is a rare individual—a man with decades of experience in traditional news who is also a tremendously capable online editor.

"I've been at the *Tribune* for 28 years," Youngman says. "I was in charge of what we did on America Online when the editorial department took control of that in '93. It was pretty much text-driven, and we were one of the first newspapers to put our full text on the Web."

The *Tribune* experimented a great deal to find out what worked in this new medium. "We made mistakes," says Youngman, "but as the users voted with their feet, or their thumbs, we shifted resources away from things they weren't interested in seeing. Early on we devoted a lot of resources to doing stories on the Web that didn't appear in the paper in any form, and there was just no payoff. Instead we saw that people valued information that enhanced their use of the newspaper, or that was in categories of news that the newspaper typically did. We did a lot of breaking news, put a lot of emphasis on databases, and on things that change during the day."

Youngman was able to combine his journalism experience with a great deal of online expertise. "I've been a user of online services since 1982," he says, "and the newspaper used dial-up services of various kinds internally for a long time. But I started using the Web, probably in early '94, just as part of my overall responsibility for understanding interactive services. We also had people who were involved with the University of Illinois, so we were aware of the kind of work that was being done at the supercomputing lab while they were developing Web browsers."

Beyond the act of gathering information, reporters need to think of ways in which the strengths of the medium might enhance their stories. If reporters can keep the characteristics of Web pages in mind while preparing their stories, they can produce work that is utterly unique to the medium.

"If you're not doing any video or any audio, you're going to gather information in pretty much the same way," says Mindy McAdams, a former content developer for the *Washington Post*'s Digital Ink site, and now a Knight Chair Professor in the Department of Journalism at the University of Florida. "But because of the medium, because you have all this space and can go into more depth and tell stories in such different ways, you need a lot more perspective. In order to make a really interesting set of information that's layered and clustered, you actually need to have more context. You need to interview people in much more detail,

One of the great advantages the *Tribune* site has had from the beginning is its ties to the Tribune Company-owned WGN TV and radio stations. The site has long-standing agreements with the broadcast outlets to share video and audio. "We have access to that stuff right here on the fourth floor," says Youngman. "There are some things that have been digitized, more all the time, and we have real-time access to the audio and video servers that all the broadcast outlets use."

The *Tribune* remains one of the few outlets that regularly features online-only content, though Youngman says it hasn't yet reached the stage of numerous online-only beats for reporters. "We have some people in areas like sports and business and technology," he says, "but pretty much everybody is general-assignment because we do pick and choose which things to feature on any given day. We do have a Web site, Silicon Prairie, which is devoted to high-tech stuff, out of which we also produce a monthly magazine. So that staff does produce some stuff on a daily basis for them."

The *Tribune* has also experimented with having reporters carry digital cameras and recorders. "It depends on the assignment," says Youngman, "but we have some print reporters and photographers take out those kinds of things as well. Again, early on, we experimented with doing a lot of that and didn't really see that people who were doing it did it very well."

Youngman says that at the *Tribune* more than at most outlets editors of all types of media work together to accentuate the advantages of each medium. "The editors of the various media—radio, TV, print, Internet—confer on who might be best to cover a story at that given time," he says, "given what the deadlines are and the kind of story it is. Sometimes it'll be a print person, sometimes it'll be a radio or Internet person nominally, but it's all about gathering the news and getting it back and out to the viewers, the readers, the users."

According to Youngman, if you want to work in the big leagues of online journalism, you shouldn't have your heart set on one specific duty, or even a particular reporting beat. "If you're writing story after story on a topic," he says, "and the server logs show that no one is reading it, you may need to be redirected. Versatility is important, and it starts with having an open mind about what you're gonna do, how you're gonna do it. You've got to be willing to accept the verdict of the marketplace."

you need to follow up a lot more. Because the online medium allows so much more complexity, in a way the standards for coverage and completeness and context should be higher, because we're not bounded by those puny little news holes."

The size and scope of your news organization, and its commitment of resources to the Web, will often determine the number of ways you can supplement your coverage. "My job doesn't really differ much from traditional journalism except that we have at our disposal various interactive technologies and tools," says Brock Meeks, Chief Washington Correspondent for MSNBC, the multimedia powerhouse jointly owned by Microsoft and NBC. "So instead of just thinking like a print journalist—get the facts, get the quotes and wrap them into a story— I can also begin to think like a broadcaster or somebody on radio. I can get

REPURPOSING

The editor-in-chief of every online news outlet in the world would love to have a huge staff and unlimited resources. However, the fact is that most news Web sites are affiliated with traditional news outlets, and most of these outlets do not allot huge budgets to their online brethren. This means that, at some point, most outlets engage in a practice called **repurposing**—taking a print or broadcast medium's content and using it as the basis for the online product. This is decried by many in the news business, but it is the only way many smaller outlets can afford to produce an online product.

"We spend a lot of time reformatting stories from the print newspaper to go on the Web," says Stan Austin of the *Kansas City Star*. "That's true for probably 99.9 percent of Web sites in the country—they're repurposing. I can pretty much name on one hand the papers who are doing original Web content on a wide scale. The *Chicago Tribune*, the *New York Times*, the *Washington Post* and the *Wall Street Journal*. That's

pretty much it. Everybody else is kind of hit-and-miss."

"It's not glamorous," says John Christensen, a former senior writer for CNN Interactive. "In fact, when I first heard about it, it kind of sounded like a rewrite job, which is what they would call it in a newspaper." Yet Christensen discovered that at an outlet like CNN, which deals not only in text news but also in audio and video, there was a lot more to the job than simply reformatting written stories. "When we're doing a story, say, on a plane crash or whatever," he says, "we'll have an AP story, a Reuters story, we may have a wire CNN report, and then we'll also have a script, perhaps, from someone who's been on the site. We'll take all that material and combine it into one story. In a sense, it is rewrite. But it's very demanding, given the time constraints, the immediacy of the Internet, and the importance of having something up as quickly as you can. Taking all this material and blending something together—it's a tough, gritty job, frankly."

somebody on the phone and we can record an audio clip and pull that in, have my multimedia team edit some video that is shot either by NBC or MSNBC cable, and pull that into the story. And I also have a whole team of interactive producers, which can work up an interactive graphic to put into the story as well. So instead of just writing the straight-ahead journalism, now what I do is in pictures and in sound as well as words, to put together an entire package instead of just cranking out straight text."

Local and national outlets often differ in what they expect from journalists. Local journalists might find themselves rewriting print content for Web use, but those at larger outlets may be assigned much different tasks. "We have some people that just do rewrite, whether it's CNN material or wire material," says Woelfel. "That's often one of the most efficient ways to keep up with a breaking story. But we also have people that work 100 percent on original material. We have quite a bit in the way of in-depth journalistic content where people are reporters. So it's a mix. Often before the television script is finished, you have raw material that comes in from the field—sometimes it's just raw facts, sometimes it's sort of a semi-finished script, and that's what we access. In most cases, we don't wait for a finished television package to try to turn it into Web material."

The craft of writing isn't lost in the middle of this—it is just heavily influenced by the continual deadlines that are part of the process. As is true with traditional

BREAKING STORIES: THE CASE OF JOHN F. KENNEDY JR.

One of the online medium's acknowledged advantages over traditional media is in reporting breaking news. The combination of instant updating and the ability to produce an archive of material on the subject make it utterly unique among news media.

One of the biggest news stories of 1999 was the death of John F. Kennedy Jr., his wife and sister-in-law in the crash of his private plane in the early morning hours of July 17. The ways in which online outlets covered the event show some of the greatest strengths of the medium.

Jim Trageser of the *San Diego Union-Tribune* was first interviewed for this book just three days after the crash occurred, before the bodies had been recovered from the wreckage. He said that his paper's online site could provide readers with the kind of updates not available in print. "Here on the West Coast this morning," Trageser said, "the story in the print edition is that the Kennedy family is preparing a memorial service in New York, but overnight they located the plane with the bodies in it. So rather than going with the story the newspaper has this morning, we have a much fresher story. Readers visiting our site will find out that the bodies have been located, and my guess is that by this afternoon they'll pull them to the surface and we'll update that again."

Later, several online journalists reflected on how their outlets covered the story. "When we have big breaking news like that," said Brock Meeks of MSNBC.com, "we can actually stream the video broadcast that's coming in from our MSNBC cable partner. For example, when they were actively pulling parts of JFK Jr.'s plane up from the bottom of the sea, we were able to stream that on our site."

For Josh Quittner, then in charge of *Time* magazine's Web site, the event pointed out the huge differences between a newsmagazine and an online outlet. "The JFK Jr. story was a little bit unusual," he recalled, "because it was breaking at the last possible moment in *Time* magazine's production schedule. Normally you'd still have a few days to do what would normally be called a 'tick-tock,' where you'd write about what happened in this sweeping, magisterial way, so it just becomes a really great read. But they couldn't do that here—they had to rush around to put something together. On a Web site, you're almost like radio—every time there's a new development in the story, you're reporting it or trying to report it. But our approach was not to compete head-to-head with CNN and other sites that update all the time. Our main story on JFK was updated maybe three times, when we had something new to say, something new that was meaningful, as opposed to just writing it and writing it every time the story changed a little bit."

At CNN, Web boss Scott Woelfel discovered that the Web even had advantages over the global leader in TV news. "For one thing, in broadcast news you really can only handle one subject at a time," he said. "JFK Jr. is a good example. If you're covering the actual search for the plane, that's pretty much all you can show at the time. You can talk about other things, but the search footage is really the only new video you have. We had the case of hours and hours of ocean shots, where on the Web, we can cover the search, but we can also go off in 10 other directions and cover other things equally well."

Many news sites put together special sections on the event, letting readers peruse all sorts of archived stories. Quittner was immediately able to take advantage of *Time* magazine's vast resources. "We started grabbing from *Time* and *People* magazine, and any other resources we could find," he said. "And we put them in kind of a library, and grabbed any pictures we could and put them there. You create a 'supersite.' That's traditionally how breaking news stories are handled online. On the front page, we have the top story that pertains to it, with a prominent hypertext link to a supersite that has everything we've written about him so far, so that you can give a reader everything in the world they want to know about this guy in one place. It's a real terrific advantage that you have online that you don't have in any other medium—that is, you can archive things for the readers' use. So if you want to get really, really deep into John-John, and go everywhere from the footage of him saluting his dad's coffin to his marriage, you can do that, and we can give it to you. If you want to spend two hours digging through our archives, more power to you. It's there for you."

print reporting, deadlines dictate a great deal about the styles and characteristics of online writing.

"You're writing on deadline all the time," says veteran San Diego online journalist Jim Trageser. "In terms of the quality of the product you can give to the readers, it's the best of both worlds. In terms of the intensity of the work while you're doing it, it's probably the worst of both worlds. You want the immediacy of broadcast with all the details of the print newspaper. Yesterday, for example, the mayor had been indicted by the grand jury, and the district attorney in court was to tell the judge whether he wanted to proceed with the case or have it dismissed. So we were competing with the broadcast outlets to get it on the Web site immediately. At the same time, we also wanted to be able to present the depth of reporting that people expect from print. So you don't have the 24-hour news cycle that you have at a newspaper, where you know 'I have until 8 o'clock to write this.' You're always writing on deadline."

Reporters also must always keep in mind that their stories need to attract attention and keep the reader hooked. This is particularly true in a medium that caters to short attention spans. "You have to remember that you're writing for the reader," says Layne. "You're not writing this to get an award. Make it interesting—make somebody care about what you're talking about. My old city editor at the (Oceanside, CA) *Blade-Citizen*, Tim Mayer, gave me a great education in this. He said that you need to get all the facts, and learn all you can about a story first, but his big rule was always, 'Make it sing!' Make this story matter. Find the punchy part, find the weird part, whatever it is, stick it up top, get the reader into the story. That's particularly true online."

If you work for the online site of a print outlet, you also have to deal with reporters who are not primarily producing content for you. Getting their cooperation is vital. "Part of our mission has always been to educate the newsroom," says Austin. "I think the first step was to get them familiar with the Web and explain to them what we were doing and what the Web is. Then we tried to get them to understand how the Web can be a reporting asset. And as Web access began to be expanded across the newsroom, our job, in that respect, became easier."

To make the fullest use of the characteristics of the Web involves more than simply reprinting the text of stories, however. This point has too often been lost on editors with traditional backgrounds who don't understand the value inherent in providing unique content. In other cases, budget and staffing issues constrain organizations' abilities to innovate with their online sites.

"Originally, the idea was that they put the newspaper content online, and gave people searching functionality," says Hill, "so you could type in the word 'police' and get all the police stories for that day. That's one way you can approach it. But what I tried to do, as Metro and Style editor at washingtonpost.com, was to provide people a richer, deeper experience. Not only could they get additional information about crimes in their neighborhood, but they had a way to, every once in a while, interact with the decision makers who are making decisions about crime and justice in their community, to being able to do things like take polls. So you extend that metaphor—you sort of try a lot of different things to provide people information and a richer experience."

"It's all a matter of the information structure," says McAdams. "You need to think of it in terms of the possibilities that the readers might want to pursue, and what directions of pursuit would make sense. You can think of the flow of information like the flow inside a building. It's like this—you can walk into a hallway that has three or four or six doors. You need to have a reasonable expectation what to find behind those doors. You don't want to have to open all six doors and waste your time looking in there. In certain houses or buildings, you'll walk through a doorway, and you're faced with a wall, and you suddenly need to turn right or left, and it seems odd. Like, why did they put a wall right here in front of the doorway? So things need to be labeled, pathways need to be inviting and clear, and the structure needs to make sense, and that's what an editor's job is."

INTERACTIVITY

Virtually every online journalist agrees that over and above everything else **interactivity** is the feature that most clearly distinguishes the online medium from any other. Rather than simply publishing a news product and sitting back and waiting for tomorrow's deadline, online journalists seem to feel that their medium has a much more reciprocal relationship with its audience.

"The major difference between online journalism and traditional media, I believe, is interactivity," says Jon Katz, the former lead columnist for *HotWired* and a former producer for CBS News. "Online, I write and gather stories in an environment where more people than me are involved. There's a broad sense of feedback, and a willingness to take diverse opinion. There's the chance to write about technology in a sort of meaningful and nonthreatening way."

"Interactivity is great!" says Patricia Sullivan of the *Washington Post*, formerly of the *San Jose Mercury News*' Mercury Center Web site. "I've been writing for more than 20 years, and I worked for a small-town newspaper for a long time, where I got a lot of phone calls and got accosted in grocery store aisles and in the farmer's market downtown. So I was used to what I thought was a lot of reader interaction and response to what I wrote. It has multiplied exponentially since I've been on the Web. I get 5 to 10 comments every single day about every single column I write. And it's not because I'm such a fascinating columnist. It's because people recognize that the column is a Web column. They feel a need to say, 'You're off your rocker,' 'You're right,' 'You should have done this,' or 'You should have done that,' 'I like this,' or 'I don't like that.' And I learn a huge amount from these people."

Interactivity might seem best suited for a local outlet; it has always been vitally important for local reporters and editors to remain in tune with issues important to their communities. Yet for national outlets, interactivity offers quick feedback at a level previously unimagined on such a large scale.

Woelfel sees all sorts of benefits from interactivity. "We've got a great ability to find out how people are reacting to the way we cover information and news," he says, "and that can guide us while we're in the middle of producing things, which is very useful. At the same time, it's created its own new source of content, in that people want to talk to other people about the issues and stories that are of interest to them. We allow that to happen and facilitate that as well. So you really have a couple of different ways that it's changed how the consumer has become involved in the process."

Hill says interactivity adds whole new dimensions to news. "Let's say a prominent figure in Washington, D.C. is injured or killed," she says. "If I'm writing for the newspaper, I'm going to get all kinds of reaction from people, I'm going to write that story, and then the next day I'm probably going to step back and probably do a profile of that person. If we're doing it online, we'll get the story posted online, but then we might say, let's see if we can bring somebody on who's close to that person, to maybe interact with the users. Who would the readers like to talk to about the subject? We may give them a chance to ask questions of someone they've always wanted to talk to."

Other observers see benefits beyond these new features. Critics claim that in recent decades U.S. news organizations have gotten too caught up in their ability to set the agenda for discussion at the expense of examining fresh stories from different angles. Many have said that this has rendered them too isolated from the average reader and that this is why news audiences have shrunk during this time period.

In this vein, Katz maintains that traditional journalism suffers from its unwillingness to foster the two-way relationship that interactivity provides. "Interactivity really means sharing power," he says. "It means stepping down from the role as the primary agenda setter. It means letting your readers have some say in how you think about events, and giving them more voice than they now have. I don't really see any sign that journalism is moving in this direction, frankly. They think the public is stupid, they don't really care what people think, they don't really want to hear their opinions, and they don't want to listen to them. Online is completely different."

Austin agrees with this assessment. "The attitude on the print side is, 'Let me write my story, don't bother me, public,'" he says. "On the Web side, we want the feedback. We appreciate the immediacy of the feedback, even if it's negative. But most of what we get is very constructive—'You guys should really do this,' 'I use your site this way, therefore I'd like you to do this.' You get a lot of good ideas from that."

While Katz sounds harsh in his criticism of traditional media, he says it all boils down to appreciating the give and take on the Web. "I like hearing from people," he says. "I like getting e-mail from them, and I like hearing their opinions, and I think I benefit from their criticisms. And I think journalism suffers from its refusal to do any of these things."

THINKING OUTSIDE THE BOX

The picture that emerges from these discussions is that professionals in the online field believe the medium shares a lot with traditional journalism, yet it requires a new approach, new ways of thinking. The phrase "thinking outside the box" has long been used to denote looking beyond the traditional boundaries of any field, and it is commonly used in the field of online journalism. The notion is to abandon some of the limitations that other formats have traditionally imposed on journalism.

"It's really been difficult to get some people to open their minds up and not think in the print structure," says Austin. "Maybe this is less of an issue with younger people than with people of my generation, whose only experience has been the newspaper world. I would encourage people to start thinking first about how people are using the information, and let that be the base point for design, for reporting, for packaging. How are people going to use this information, and how do they want to receive it?"

"Doing journalism online opens all kinds of possibilities, way beyond audio and video, because we can do that in other media," says McAdams. "It opens these possibilities of not only customization, which everybody likes to talk about, which has dangers as well as benefits. But it has a lot of possibilities for additional context and understanding that people can gain from information that's well structured and detailed, that gives context to really important stuff in their lives—that stuff that affects the way they live their daily lives. You can present that in different ways online. You can present more of it. You can connect it to other similar things in ways that make more sense to the readers."

This sense of envisioning what readers might want—even if they don't know they want it yet—pervades the thinking of many people in the business. "You have to ask yourself, how much do you need to entertain—and I'm using that term broadly—the people who are coming online?" says Hill. "Do they want to interact with that product in a way that you can't interact with the print product? So, for example, do they want to be able to speak to or chat with the author of an article? Do they want to be able to interact or talk to the subject of an article? So you're thinking to yourself in terms of balance. How do you provide just the news for the people who only want the quick hit? How do you make it more interactive without doing it in sort of a silly way? How do you add value to the user's experience?"

SUMMARY

There is no single job description for the position "online journalist," which presents challenges for those seeking to enter the field, but these challenges are not insurmountable. At its heart, journalism is still journalism. Reporters have to gather information, check its validity and present it in an engaging and informative way. However, your first job might not be in straight reporting, and you need to be prepared for that. People within the field agree that if you bring strong basic skills to the table, along with a willingness to apply them in many different ways, you will likely succeed. In that pursuit, they also agree that it is vitally important to understand the strengths of the medium and to craft your work to make the best use of these strengths to maximize engaging and informing the user. Not everyone agrees on the best ways to do this—online journalism is so new that it is still evolving—but there is a sense that there is much more untapped potential in this medium. One way or the other, those working in this field all seem genuinely excited to be in on the process of online journalism's evolution.

RELATED WEB SITES

Chicago Tribune
http://chicagotribune.com/

Kansas City Star
http://www.kcstar.com/

Washington Post
http://www.washingtonpost.com/

BET
http://www.bet.com/

Time
http://www.time.com/

Online Journalism Review
http://ojr.usc.edu/

CNN Interactive
http://www.cnn.com/

MSNBC
http://www.msnbc.com/

San Diego Union-Tribune
http://www.uniontrib.com/

San Jose Mercury News
http://www.bayarea.com/

University of Florida Department of Journalism
http://www.jou.ufl.edu/jou/Default.htm

Jon Katz
http://www.freedomforum.org/technology/katzcolumns.asp

EXERCISES

1. Visit the AJR Newslink job search Web page (http://newslink.org/newjoblinkquicksearch.html) and click on "writer" or "editor." Choose three ads, print them out and analyze how the qualifications the ads ask for fit with jobs described by online journalists in this chapter.

2. Print a copy of the day's lead story on CNN Interactive, then videotape the same story on CNN's news broadcast or Headline News. Write a one to one and a half page report on the similarities and differences between the two stories.

3. Using InfoTrac College Edition and a major online news outlet (CNN.com, MSNBC.com or others), search the archives for stories on the 1997 trial of Timothy McVeigh for the bombing of the Federal Building in Oklahoma City. Did the Web coverage at this early stage offer content not found in the print coverage of the InfoTrac College Edition articles? If so, what was offered? If not, judging from the discussion in this chapter, what factors might have kept online journalists from using different kinds of content?

3

||||||

Generating and Focusing Story Ideas

In the traditional world of journalism, the range of a journalist's reportage is often limited by fairly strict definitions of beats, specialties and circulation areas. By radically redefining the nature of both the product and the audience, online journalism has forced reporters and editors to take a fresh look at the types of stories that will win readers and bring them back for more.

If every day were like January 22, 1998, reporters wouldn't have to worry about generating ideas for stories. On that day Americans first learned of taped conversations between White House intern Monica Lewinsky and her friend Linda Tripp, alleging an affair with President Clinton. It was also the day that Ted Kaczynski admitted to being the Unabomber, pleading guilty to avoid a possible death sentence. That same day, Pope John Paul II held the first Mass in his historic visit to Cuba, in which he condemned abortion as "an abominable crime." He chose this as his central topic because that same day was the 25th anniversary of *Roe v. Wade,* the Supreme Court's decision to legalize abortion. On top of all this, it was the Friday before Super Bowl XXXII.

On days like this, with big news stories seemingly falling out of the trees, all you have to do is cover the story (or perhaps its local or subject-specific angle). If the United States is attacked by terrorists or is going to war in the Middle East, coming up with story ideas is pretty simple. However, this situation is the exception rather than the rule. The times that prove what you're made of are slow news

On the day the Bill Clinton–Monica Lewinsky sex scandal broke, *The Detroit News'* paper edition (on the left) had to move several major stories on its front page. The *News'* online edition (on the right) also moved stories, but due to the different layout characteristics online, the same stories appeared in very different locations on the Web page.

SOURCE: *The Detroit News,* January 23, 1998; detnews.com (accessed January 23, 1998). Used by permission of *The Detroit News.*

days when there seems to be nothing going on and you have column inches, newscasts or Web pages to fill.

To combat this, reporters meet with their editors to devise and refine story ideas. This is often a simple process because reporters cover certain beats (geographic areas, institutions or other subjects). Within those subjects and those areas, news is often cyclical—the community's assorted goings-on tend to produce news stories at regular intervals. Local calendars, legislative and corporate schedules, weather-related cycles and other regularly scheduled events can provide reliable material for stories. Local reporters and editors tie into the customs and rhythms of the community they serve.

Well, what do you do when your community is the whole world? More specifically, what do you do when your potential readership—even your most loyal core of readers—is scattered throughout the country or around the globe and is impossibly diverse? How do you even begin to serve such an amorphous audience? From what perspective should you approach stories? These are some of the questions that will be addressed in this chapter.

KNOWING YOUR AUDIENCE

Selecting and developing stories depends completely on the audience for your news outlet, whether it's primarily local or global. As such, the best place for a new reporter to start is by getting to know his audience. For an online reporter, it's not as simple as attending a few local functions and meeting people. You need to know everything possible about the dynamics and characteristics of your readership—its ethnic, economic, ideological and social makeup, its politics and power brokers, its hot-button issues. It's not a "virtual community" per se—it's a group of real people with real lives who are drawn to your outlet for reasons that you should learn.

Reporters shouldn't assume that Web users or Web publications are all alike. "They have to look at the Internet as having a lot of different kinds of audiences," says veteran Web journalist J. D. Lasica. "It depends in a lot of ways less on what audience you're writing for than what online publication it's going to be appearing in. Salon has a certain kind of readership that's completely different from Wired, which is different from CNN.com. You basically have to look at the readership, the audience, the users and the demographics."

The ways to do this vary with the nature of your publication. If you're working for the online edition of a local publication, the traditional notion of going out into the local community and making connections has some merit because it's the area you're primarily serving. By getting in touch with this community, you'll do your job better in a variety of ways.

Yet even in this case, you must look beyond your immediate geographic area. A large portion of the online audience for local news is made up of people who have moved away from that area and use the site as a way to keep tabs on their hometown. Obviously, you must know that community to report on it, yet to keep the site a vibrant online entity, its stories must have their own unique qualities.

News organizations of every stripe do detailed research to find out who is reading, watching or listening, which can give a reporter some idea of the demographics and general opinions of the audience. Such research often includes assorted surveys and focus groups—small groups of readers or viewers who comment on the presentation and other aspects of news coverage. Most large news organizations employ an **ombudsman**—a liaison between the newsroom and the public—who solicits comments and complaints from readers and viewers in the community.

Even online editions of major news outlets must not assume that their online readers are the same as the readers of their print editions. Rich Jaroslovsky, managing editor of the *Wall Street Journal*'s online outlet WSJ.com, saw this firsthand as his site developed. "People were coming to us in order to get the contents of the print journal along with 24-hour-a-day updates and other things," Jaroslovsky says. "But they also had an insatiable desire for news and information about the Internet itself and new media and e-commerce and technology, and an insatiable amount of desire for information about online investing and using the medium to manage their money. So those sorts of things suggested to us that we needed in those areas to make a special editorial emphasis that goes beyond what the print journal does or what the newswires do. It is a different audience. It is a complementary audience, but it is not the same as print, and we try to meet those information needs."

Like WSJ.com, many online news outlets do not represent a specific geographic community, but they have one major advantage over print or broadcast media—the interactivity of the medium itself. Online news organizations can use this characteristic to obtain more in-depth information on what readers want. For learning about your readership and for finding story ideas, here are some of the most useful interactive features:

- **Feedback pages.** These pages invite readers to comment on news coverage and to suggest story ideas. They generally involve a form that readers fill out and submit, with spaces for e-mail address and other information, and a large area for them to type in comments, suggestions or complaints. These are sent directly to the news organization and are not posted for general viewing.

- **Message boards.** Unlike feedback pages, message boards let readers post their opinions for everyone to read. They also allow readers to respond to others' posted messages. These are similar in structure to discussion groups.

- **Chat rooms.** Similar to online chat rooms found all over the Web, news chat rooms let readers submit questions to reporters, editors or newsmakers at preset times, to be answered on the spot. Unlike some Web chat rooms, however, these are usually moderated due to many users asking questions of one respondent. These are most often found at larger news organizations.

- **Online polls.** While hardly scientific, these polls give readers a chance to express their opinions on the subject (or subjects) of the day. Clever editors ask questions designed both to interest readers and to generate story ideas. It should be noted, however, that such polls have their limitations. Their results are far from scientific and cannot be treated the same as polls done nationwide with random samples. Depending on how online polls are put together, they can sometimes be exploited by readers who vote multiple times.

- **E-mail lists.** By publishing e-mail addresses for editors and reporters, news organizations make it easier than ever before for readers to respond to stories. When an e-mail link with a reporter's address is at the end of a story, it's a simple matter for a reader to click on the link to send positive or negative comments. In addition, readers at some online news outlets can sign up for e-mail lists to receive stories of prescribed types (business or sports, for example) every day. This gives readers customized news and lets the news outlet know which types of stories are popular.

Each of these features gives online news reporters and editors plenty of opportunities to get to know their audience and to find out what the public thinks about their product. For reporters, these features often provide both general and specific story ideas. Most online journalists say that thanks to the ease of e-mail, readers are not shy about suggesting new story ideas, new areas and subjects to examine and whole new approaches to reporting.

SURFING FOR IDEAS

Looking within the community you serve, whether geographic or online, is the surest way to find a good story. It's not the only way, however. Some reporters are loath to admit to their editors that the pickings are slim, but working with an editor often uncovers new ideas or provides a fresh perspective on old ones. Editors do expect reporters to formulate their own story ideas or to stick to assignments, but the occasional story session can result in lots of ideas to keep a reporter busy. Developing good working relationships with your editors is a good idea in any kind of journalism, and you will discover that good editors are worth their weight in gold.

If you're still stuck, consider the medium you're working in—the Internet. If you know where to look, the Web is a truly spectacular source for story ideas. Here are some places to start:

- *Internet newsgroups.* Formerly referred to as Usenet newsgroups and now operated by the search site Google as Google Groups, newsgroups are older than the Web itself, dating back to the days of the text-based Internet. Newsgroups are forums for discussion that allow users anywhere in the world to post and reply to messages from other users. Groups are broken down by subject, and you can find online opinions on literally hundreds of topics. Look for titles beginning with the prefixes "alt," "rec," "comp" and the like, with suffixes narrowing discussions into more and more specific topics (such as "alt.politics" or "rec.sports").

- *Discussion groups and blogs.* Similar to newsgroups, discussion groups are most often found as a feature of commercial Web sites. They can take assorted forms, from message boards and forums to e-mail lists. **Blogs** (short for "Web logs") are less formal but often the site of heated discussion on all kinds of different topics. Again, these are good places to sample opinion on particular topics and perhaps to locate an underpublicized idea.

- *Search engines.* Sites such as Google, Yahoo, AltaVista and Lycos can be used to find Web pages by keyword. These **search engines** are particularly useful when you want to find new ideas within particular areas or to refine general ideas into specific stories. If you find many pages or articles dealing with different angles on a topic, you've got a story you can pursue within your own area. (Searches are discussed in depth in Chapter 4.)

- *Special-interest home pages.* Oftentimes search engines will lead you to pages devoted exclusively to specific topics, whether it is the Kennedy assassination, the Brady Bunch, the avocado or the Slinky. On one hand, there is no

HOT TOPICS FOR WEB NEWS

The Web news audience, while far from being monolithic, tends toward certain characteristics. Typically, it is a bit more white, male and affluent than the general public. The topics most popular online, however, change dramatically depending on current events and trends, which makes it impossible to present any definite list of hot Web topics. However, according to those in the business, certain general types of stories do tend to predominate and flourish online.

Just about anything related to the Internet or to technology is popular, but some subtypes deserve particular mention along with subjects only tangentially related. Here are a few of the most popular general story topics:

- *Privacy and freedom of information.* The free-wheeling culture that has developed on the Web is considered to be a bastion of both free information and privacy, and any threat to these freedoms is seen as a threat to this culture. Web users are often more passionate about these twin issues than any others, and heated debates can result from stories about them.

- *Government and corporate control of the mass media.* As corporations merge, fewer and fewer of them own larger percentages of the available media outlets, which causes huge debates on the Web. Similarly, when the government gets involved, tempers flare in many ideological directions. Stories about these subjects will draw readers and ignite debate.

- *The inadequacies of current U.S. politics.* The Web is the chosen news venue of thousands of people who consider themselves not only nonpartisan but neither liberal nor conservative. To many of them, being pigeonholed by ideological leanings or party is abhorrent. Any story dealing with stepping away from partisanship, going against the political grain or simply looking at politics from a different point of view will appeal to these readers.

- *Popular culture.* Most Web news readers are fairly young and have been raised in an environment dominated by popular culture. For them, popular culture is an essential part of their lives. Whether it's movies, music, television or Web content, they work it into their lives in ways that traditional news outlets and audiences often don't understand. Serious discussion of television and movie characters as role models and icons will attract Web readers and will spark lively debate.

- *Applications of new technology.* The typical Web news reader is not at all afraid of technology. These readers have a certain optimism about what technology can do beyond the Internet or the classroom. Looking at technological breakthroughs or new products as possible useful tools for the future resonates with them.

- *"Revenge of the nerds."* Sure, the notion that the friendless, socially inept, superintelligent geeks have come to rule the world is a cliché. Nonetheless, it remains popular online—not in the abstract but when applied to specific people in specific positions. Web readers like to read about formerly downtrodden people making it big in the high-tech world.

- *Comparisons between the Web and other media.* The Web is not the only outlet in these readers' media-saturated lives. Looking at the changing roles of all media, particularly when these changes are related to the Web's role, will likely prove popular.

- *Freedom and repression.* These big-picture issues are closely related to some of the previous points but are farther reaching. To a degree that would surprise many people with little or no online experience, Web news readers are genuinely passionate about these issues. Home pages dealing with specific instances of repression are found all over the Web—in many cases, such issues receive far more attention on the Web than in traditional media.

limit to the inconsequential topics that have their own Web pages. On the other hand, many worthwhile topics are better represented on the Web than in the traditional media. One way or the other, if you can find patterns of interest among Web users, you may have a story on your hands. (If nothing else, pages like these can produce a story on interesting or obscure Web pages, perhaps containing interviews with their authors.)

- *E-mail lists.* Mentioned previously as a way to get to know readers, you can also subscribe to subject-specific e-mail lists that you think might provide you with story ideas. However, don't limit your reading to these e-mail messages—you need to broaden your horizons, not narrow them.

- *Other news sites.* Particular topics often become hot-button issues regionally. Look at what is popular on other sites and see if these topics pertain to your community or might appeal to your audience. Sometimes a political or social change in a neighboring region or similar subject area can be the catalyst for something new involving your audience.

One word of caution should be noted in each of these cases. You can apply another site's ideas to your community or audience or use topics from that site to spur a look at a given topic within your area, but do not use another site's content without attribution. This is **plagiarism,** not influence, and it violates strict rules of journalism. When in doubt, give the source site credit within your story. If you have concerns about using information, don't be shy about contacting people at the news outlet in question and going through your story idea with them. It's always best to err on the side of caution in matters like these.

In searching for story ideas, you shouldn't limit yourself to the Web. You can certainly look at newspapers from surrounding geographic areas as well as magazines and anything else you can use as a possible news source. Also, don't discount books as sources for story ideas—often the premise for a popular book can be examined for relevance to your community. Nonfiction books often yield more usable story ideas than novels. But again, be careful to use these sources for inspiration, not for actual content.

If you're working for an online news outlet that doesn't serve a particular geographic area, you can also flip the process of looking beyond your community for story ideas on its head. Talk to people within your local community about what they think is important within the larger subject area you're working on. While you shouldn't look exclusively within your own location, there's nothing forbidding you from doing so.

UNIQUE APPROACHES
TO FAMILIAR TOPICS

Maybe what you're battling isn't the lack of stories but the sameness of them. The same old things are happening to the same old people. The same issues are being raised with little hope of anyone changing positions or shedding new light on the subject. Or perhaps there's national and international news of interest but nothing within your beat or specific area. In any case, you may find yourself covering the same topic in the same way for the umpteenth time.

Loss of enthusiasm for the news is a concern for any reporter, but it's sometimes a fact of life. The best journalists fight their way through these lulls by finding new sources for stories and also by coming up with different ways to look at familiar topics. Maybe the story isn't new, but your approach to it can be. Here are a few ways to breathe some life into otherwise mundane topics:

- *Find a local or subject-specific angle on national or international news.* This is the oldest trick in the book, but it works. The most straightforward way to do this is to look for local ties among those involved in a story. If you're not a local news outlet, however, you have to be more creative. How might a natural disaster, court case or corporate merger have an impact on your audience? These types of stories often have wide-ranging consequences that go far beyond obvious ties. The more closely and creatively you can link a big national or international story to your audience's interests, the better your story will work.

- *Follow-ups.* Remember the 10-year-old college student you reported on or read about last year? How's he doing at MIT at the ripe old age of 11? Readers love to have their memories jogged and get updates on the subjects of previous stories. These aren't always features—frequently, reporters look back at a hard-news story and analyze the consequences of the story, the policy implications or what the next move may be. The online medium is particularly well-suited to follow-ups because you can provide links to the original stories for those that want to read more about the subject.

- *Advance stories.* These are the polar opposite of follow-ups. Is something significant within your subject area scheduled to take place soon? What should readers expect to happen when it takes place? Who are the likely participants and what roles will they play? Such questions usually pique the interest of readers, whose interest in the coming event may draw them back to your site when the event finally occurs.

- *Trends.* Stories on emerging trends are always popular, and you can easily provide fresh angles on them even when they've already been covered. Is a particular trend unexpectedly popular among an unusual group? Has it taken off among very young or very old people? Are there different social or ethnic aspects to a trend? Is a local college or other institution actively bucking a trend? Even when a trend has seemingly faded, there's always the story of "Whatever happened to . . ."

- *Areas related to a topic.* Perhaps you've covered a given topic to what seems to be its logical conclusion. You've learned a great deal about it, but seemingly exhausted your resources. The next step is to look to areas related to it— what kind of impact does it have on previously unexplored areas or aspects of society? For example, if you think you've covered every angle of privacy and security issues on the Web, think about the myriad ways it might affect people who never use the Internet. How might it affect banking, insurance and other fields not traditionally associated with the Web? Most issues have an impact far beyond the obvious—see how far you can trace the influence of your topic.

- *Profiles of people who have been in the news.* All sorts of people make news by being part of a story or due to their association with an organization or an institution. Your readers may recognize their names, but that doesn't mean they know about them as people. People are often surprised at what assorted newsmakers do in their spare time, regardless of whether the newsmaker in question is a political figure, a corporate boss, a college professor or the guy who saved the drowning kids.

These approaches won't always win you a Pulitzer Prize, but they can stave off that sinking feeling when you're staring blankly at your computer screen. In journalism, online or off, the cardinal rule is: When in doubt, write *something*. Be creative and come up with an interesting angle instead of writing one carbon-copy story after another.

Ultimately, the most important thing you can do to avoid running out of material is to constantly stay alert for possible story ideas. Whether you're at home or at work, online or off, keep your ear to the ground for anything that might translate into a story. Keep a notebook or PDA handy to jot down any ideas that may come to you. Don't assume you'll remember them later, and don't assume you can always type them right into your computer. (What if you're away from your computer, or what if it's turned off and you get interrupted while it's booting up?)

Good reporters often keep files of notes, articles and other material to use for story ideas. Even if this creates an awkward situation or two—telling your dinner companion, "That's a great idea! Do you mind if I write it down?"—it's worth the trouble. Remember, information is your business. The more potentially useful information you have at your disposal, the better.

TURNING TRASH INTO TREASURE

Let's say the well has run completely dry. You have space to fill, and there's absolutely nothing of consequence happening today. You've exhausted every semiliterate e-mail message and press release you can find, you've interviewed everyone even remotely interesting, you've profiled everyone who deserves attention. You end up having to choose between covering your umpteenth mundane ribbon-cutting ceremony, a farmer who's growing a small patch of horseradish in his cornfield, or a man whose granddaughter says he's the world's fastest whistling whittler.

Online and off, one of the most important skills a reporter can have is the ability to extract something worth reading out of situations that seem to offer nothing interesting. With a little imagination, you can make a man painting a house into a memorable article. There are two keys to this that go hand in hand— angles and details. Your approach to telling the story (the angle) requires details to explain why this angle is appropriate and to enrich the story.

Often the best way to approach a seemingly weak subject is to take note of the very elements you believe make it weak.

- *It's boring.* According to whom? Is there a segment of society that finds it interesting? Turn the story into a look at these people, using the event as the tip of the iceberg. In this day and age, almost every interest has a handful

---

THE GEOMETRY OF A NEWS STORY: FINDING THE RIGHT ANGLE

It's one thing to come up with a story idea that you think is interesting; it's entirely another to pick the right angle (story approach) to make it work within the context of your publication. This is particularly true for online news, where both the audience and the format are often very different from traditional media.

Because writing styles and types of publications on the Web vary greatly, there's no one perfect way to approach a story online. Tailor your story's focus to suit your outlet and its characteristics. Here are a few different types of angles and some examples of when they work best:

- *The local angle.* Is there some local tie to the story? Obviously, this works best when you're working for a local outlet, not for something national or global. While people tend to think beyond local angles in online stories, this is still perfectly appropriate for a local site. Readers living away from their hometowns appreciate this sort of story.
- *The technology angle.* These days just about every story has some tie to technology, and this is always a popular approach to stories

online. Sometimes this angle is obvious, and other times you'll find a significant technological element of the story and concentrate on that.

- *The subject-specific angle.* If you work for a specialty publication—one centered around a particular subject—then this is usually the way to go. However, looking at a story through the lens of a subject that appeals to a significant segment of your audience is also quite common. This is especially true online, where publications are much more likely to try to use a different approach to widely covered stories.
- *The personality angle.* The personality profile is a type of story unto itself, and it is used in all types of journalism. It's particularly popular online, where the audience frequently enjoys reading about people involved in computer-related pursuits. These stories can range from the standard profiles of cybertycoons to looks at some of the technical wizards behind well-known projects.

---

of Web pages devoted to it, whether it's spider webs or licorice or moist-towelette collecting. Find out who created and maintains these pages, and get more information from them. If those interested in the subject actually belong to a particular group, get as many details as possible about the group and its members, and find out the history of this and related events. Change your approach to, "These people think this is interesting, and here's what they say about it."

- *Who cares?* Someone must care or you wouldn't be staring at a press release or an e-mail about it. Is there an individual who has been e-mailing everyone under the sun to try to get publicity for this event? Interview that person in depth, and look into why this individual became so involved with this particular event. Does that person have mentors or associates you can interview? Turn the angle into, "Who cares about this subject? This person does, and this is why."

- *It's obscure.* Maybe it's obscure to you and everyone you know, but there are probably whole pockets of society that are interested in the subject. Get on the Web and do some searches related to the subject. You'll probably discover it has more devotees than you'd imagined possible. Was there a period of time in which such an event, activity or behavior was common-place? Sometimes historical rituals are observed for dubious yet researchable reasons. Change the angle to, "This may seem obscure to you, but look how many people are interested in it, and look at its history."

- *It's pointless.* Perhaps the subject appears to be a waste of time, whether it's a seemingly useless ceremony, an event signifying nothing in particular, or a person or group engaging in apparently arcane or meaningless behavior. Remember that virtually everything has meaning for someone. People spend their time in all kinds of unusual ways and commemorate all sorts of things. Is there a story behind the story? Do some research to discover the background of this event or of the people involved.

- *It's ridiculous.* This is a pretty all-inclusive area. Maybe someone's dressing up like a superhero and picking up litter. Maybe someone's sending out e-mails proclaiming himself to be God. Maybe a corporation is engaging in an obvious publicity stunt. Is any of this really news? Probably not, but when you're stuck for a story, sometimes you find yourself covering this sort of thing. A good place to start is with the "this is unusual" angle. What about it is unusual? Perhaps the person involved seems a trifle odd at first but turns out to be a fairly normal person going to great lengths to simply make a point. This lends itself to the "quirky" angle—"By day, Joe Smith seems like anyone else, but . . ."

- *It's a cliché.* Journalists quickly become wary of stale, hackneyed stories—the umpteenth child prodigy, rags-to-riches, local boy makes good or "little old lady from Pasadena." For the reporter, the challenge is to get more details about the story to find out what sets it apart from other similar stories.

- *Your interviewee has nothing interesting to say.* Perhaps you're writing a profile of an individual. You've interviewed this person multiple times and he is simply not terribly quotable. (If you've only talked to the interviewee once, try coming up with some different ideas for questions and talk to the person again.) Just because the person in question is not a stellar interviewee doesn't mean that the story is not worth covering or that the person's story is not worth telling. Some people simply aren't comfortable talking about themselves. Has this person accomplished interesting things? Perhaps the organization this person is involved with has a history you can explore. Talk to others about this person—oftentimes friends have stories that the interviewee had forgotten or didn't feel comfortable telling.

- *It's just like another story we've already covered.* Maybe this story seems exactly the same as another one on first look, but you should dig a little deeper to find the differences. Are the same people involved? Is the same specific activity involved? Was one event created in response to the other? You can sometimes do a "Tale of the Tape" feature comparing two similar events and breaking down their similarities and differences. The online medium lends itself well to this type of feature.

- *It's the same thing every year.* Annual events provide reliable news stories, but if this year's event doesn't depart from previous years' in meaningful ways, they can be drearily predictable. Sometimes taking the "long and storied history" angle de-emphasizes the sameness of this year's event and allows you to look at the ways both the event and the people behind it have changed over the years. If this isn't appropriate, perhaps the "quaint ritual" approach will work, again emphasizing the personalities involved.

- *Nobody wants to read about this.* Sometimes stories deal with unpleasant or distasteful subjects, but it's your job to determine what the public can gain from them. Does this story contain a lesson people can learn? Does it involve dirty work that will lead to benefits or gain? Does it illustrate a larger truth? By simply making people examine the subject in a new light, you'll gain readers.

- *Nobody will understand this.* A particularly technical or complex subject is always tough, but you should find a way to interpret it for your readers. Do as much research as is necessary to make sure you understand what's involved, then state it in plain English for your readers as best you can. You can always double-check your simplified explanations with experts you've interviewed before publication.

In most cases, personalizing the story—acquainting readers with the people involved—helps you get away from its formulaic aspects. Even the most humdrum subject can become interesting when you put a human face on it. In all cases, creativity and curiosity are rewarded. In particular, as you ask more questions, you should constantly look for elements that will grab readers' attention and separate this story from others like it.

SUMMARY

Even the best and most experienced reporters can run short of story ideas. The best way to avoid this predicament is to remember the focus of your publication and the traits of its audience. Online journalists have extra tools at their disposal that can give them new advantages in finding topics that will engage readers. With just a smidgen of creativity, you can take even the most hackneyed or insignificant item and turn it into something that online audiences will enjoy.

RELATED WEB SITES

Google Groups
http://groups.google.com

EXERCISES

1. Locate three different Web sites that contain at least two of the interactive features mentioned in this chapter (feedback pages, message boards, and so forth). Examine the content of these features at each site and write a summary of what the content suggests about the audience for each site. Cite examples from the site (quotes or characteristics) that indicate its intended audience.

2. Using the Web as a resource, list five good current topics for online news stories. For each of these, discuss both the story's central topic and why it is particularly appropriate for an online publication.

3. Find three different current news stories on the Web, and write a local or subject-specific angle for each one. Write one or two paragraphs outlining the new angle for each story, and print the original stories to turn in along with this exercise.

4. Create a list of three popular trends, then write a brief summary of a story that might be written about each of them. Be sure to include possible interviewees, settings and the angle you want to take with each story.

 5. Using InfoTrac College Edition, the Web or any other resource, list the three most boring, pointless or obscure story subjects you can imagine. Provide as much detail as possible about the subject, and list the reasons you believe the subject is so boring or obscure. Once this exercise is graded, the stories will be redistributed, and someone else will have to choose one of your boring subjects and write an interesting story about it.

4

||||||

Web Resources
and Databases

It may sound overdramatic, but it's true: The Internet is the single most comprehensive information resource in human history. But if you're a reporter looking for specific information, where do you start? Even though you may use the Internet regularly, you may not be familiar with how it works or how an online journalist can get the most out of it. This chapter first briefly discusses the Web and its protocols, then familiarizes you with some of the most popular and useful places to begin searching for information, and shows you some techniques for getting the most out of the abundant resources online.

For many of today's college students, the World Wide Web is part of the landscape, just another technology like TV and video games. Yet both its history and its practical applications are worth understanding for anyone going into the field of online journalism. It may seem like it's been around forever, but the Web is a mere infant in evolutionary terms. For reporters, it's literally a godsend in their quest for information.

HELLO, MY NAME IS URL

Did some brilliant computer genius foresee that one day a global network could provide a wealth of news and information at the click of a mouse? In a word, "no." The Internet actually began more than 30 years ago as a U.S. Defense Department mechanism to guard against nuclear annihilation. It was originally designed to allow authorities to communicate via a computer network after a nuclear war. In the 1960s, the RAND Corporation worked with the U.S. government and the military to develop a decentralized network with multiple send-and-receive stations (called "nodes") across the country and eventually around the world. The first nodes of the new network (then called ARPANET) went online in 1969, and in the 1970s and 1980s it developed into an essential tool for the government, the military and universities to exchange information.

It wasn't until the 1990s, however, that the network began to resemble what we know today. Until well into the '90s, finding one's way around the Internet involved staring at screens full of text and knowing a lexicon of cryptic commands. There was no "point-and-click"; every user had to type in various strings of text to execute functions in a computer language called UNIX, which was (and is) the operating system used by most Internet servers. Most users simply learned the commands and worked within the existing system, but some believed there should be a way to make using the Internet easier. It wasn't until 1989 that Tim Berners-Lee, a computer scientist working at CERN, the European Laboratory for Particle Physics, proposed a system called the World Wide Web for transferring and viewing documents over the Internet. Berners-Lee and his collaborators developed a system based on hypertext, which uses raw text as formatting to create documents with embedded links to other documents. Berners-Lee defined many of the early elements of the Web: he wrote the first browser program and outlined the standards for **HTML** (hypertext markup language, the language upon which Web pages are built), HTTP (hypertext transfer protocol, which allows browsers to read Web pages) and **URLs** (uniform resource locators, also known as Web addresses).

Whether you've used the Web much or not, you're probably familiar with what a URL Web address looks like. Here is the address for the publisher of this book:

http://www.wadsworth.com/index.html

Addresses like these have become commonplace, yet few people understand what the different sections of a URL are for. A URL points you to one file on the Internet. You may be able to jump to other files from there, or the file may be the parent file for framed windows, but regardless, every URL points you to exactly one file. The URL not only points you to the file's location but also describes the file by its type so your browser knows how to handle it. URLs are structured like this:

file type://file server.domain type/filename.extension

Let's break this down. *File type* describes the file's protocol, which tells the browser what kind of file it is. The *http* at this point in most Web addresses stands for "hypertext transfer protocol," which tells the browser that the page at this address is a hypertext (HTML) document for the Web.

Beyond the two forward slashes (known as "directory dividers") is the file server. This is literally the computer where the file is located—"www.wadsworth. com" is the name given to the computer where this publisher's Web site resides. A server is a computer that delivers (or "serves") information to another computer. With the right software and connections to the Web, just about any computer can act as a server, though most Web servers are powerful machines that can handle a lot of traffic. The "www" at the beginning of the server name indicates that this is a World Wide Web server, but this has become so universal in Web addresses that browsers will generally fill it in if it's missing, and some sites no longer require it at the beginning of their URLs (for example, amazon.com and cnn.com).

The ".com" in this address specifies the domain type of this server. The domain type tells you the kind of institution that is running the site, which is important because different types of businesses and groups must conform to different rules on the Web. The .com domain type is far and away the most common—it's for commercial entities (companies)—but it's not the only type. Other domain types include .edu (for educational institutions), .net (for network), .org (for organizations) and .gov (for governmental institutions).

Finally, the filename.extension is the name of the file you're accessing. The extension is actually part of the filename, as with any file on your computer. The extension is noted separately here because it's another way of telling the browser what kind of file it's dealing with.

The html and htm file extensions are the most common, but on the Web you will also encounter all kinds of other file types, each with its own extension. Some of these files require a separate program, called a **plug-in,** to operate properly.

While we're on the subject, there are a few more things you should know about URLs. When you type in a URL without a filename, you may have noticed that you usually end up at a file called index.htm or index.html. These are the default filenames a browser looks for when no filename is specified in a URL.

Within a URL, the slash between the file server name and the filename indicates that the file is within a subdirectory on the server. Sometimes a URL will have an extra slash or two in it, like this:

http://www.wadsworth.com/sitemap/index.html

In this case, the index.html file is in the subdirectory called "sitemap." If a file is within several subdirectories, these will have to be specified within the URL.

Another thing to be aware of with URLs is that you have to be very precise when typing them in. Most Web servers run on the computer language called UNIX. It's a very powerful language, but it's also very case-sensitive. Most URLs are written strictly in lowercase letters to keep things relatively standard.

USING ONLINE INFORMATION RESOURCES

In traditional journalism, a really good reporter is often referred to as "someone who knows where all the bodies are buried." This may be true, but a more accurate description might be "someone who knows where all the facts are buried." Reporters must not only become familiar with people and institutions but must develop a certain facility for finding facts.

The Google search engine is a favorite of online journalists because of
its comprehensive database and its ease of use.

SOURCE: google.com (accessed September 3, 2003). Used by permission.

In studying to be an online journalist, the last thing you probably expected was
to be compared to a librarian. Nonetheless, good journalists and good librarians
have something in common. They both know where to find reliable information
on just about any subject, and they do it quickly. They both know the **resources**
that cover particular subjects, and the dimensions of those resources—their
strengths and weaknesses, the types of information they contain, how they organize that information, and other important characteristics. By using that knowledge, they get the most out of the material that is available.

In the online world, this may seem like an outdated concept. These days, anyone with a computer and a semideveloped brain can get online and do a quick
search and sort through a giant pile of pages on just about any subject. (This is an
absolutely staggering technological achievement that we now take for granted.)
Yet both the ease of use and the comprehensiveness of search engines can cause
serious pitfalls for journalists.

The Web is only a useful resource for a reporter if it saves more time than it wastes. Most of us have, at one time or another, started out looking for something on the Web and ended up spending lots of time looking at material on a seemingly unrelated subject. The way search engines and Web pages are designed encourages this. News articles in print are **linear** in nature—that is, they generally follow one subject by using narrative elements that guide the reader on a single logical path. But with the addition of links to outside information within pages and in their margins, most Web pages are **nonlinear**—they encourage you to drift away from the subject or line of reasoning on a page and learn more about different aspects of it.

Going off on tangents can be interesting, but a reporter on deadline must stay focused and must find the most relevant information as quickly as possible. This is why good search skills are indispensable for reporters using the Internet. They make the time you spend online far more productive, giving you more time to do other kinds of research and to write your story.

Nobody really knows how many pages there are on the Web, but most experts agree that the number passed 4 billion some time ago, with more pages being added around the world every minute of the day.

For Web users—reporters and everyone else—the ability to sort through this incomprehensibly vast amount of information is essential. This is why search engines are vitally important. We take them for granted these days, but the notion of a site that allows users to enter keywords and returns lists of pages containing those keywords was not something that just appeared out of thin air. It arose from the explosion of information on the Web and the concurrent need to be able to sort through it.

Search engines are usually made up of three elements:

- A program called a spider that scans the Web for pages, reads them and follows links on those pages to find all the pages on a site.

- A program that takes the spider's results and creates an index of the pages that have been read.

- The user interface, a program that takes keyword search queries, scans the index for those keywords and returns results to the user.

Some of the most popular sites on the entire Web are search engines such as Google, Lycos and AltaVista. Another popular site, Yahoo!, is a searchable directory that functions much like a search engine. Ask Jeeves is a site with a different approach—it encourages you to eschew standard search terminology and ask a question such as "How do I install a DVD burner?" In addition, metasearch sites such as Dogpile and MetaCrawler allow you to search multiple engines all at once. Sites like Yahoo! have evolved into general purpose start pages called "portals," which provide services beyond search functions. Other portals with search functions include Microsoft's MSN.com and America Online's AOL.com.

To be able to sort through such a staggering amount of data is both a necessary process and an incomplete one. You can't expect to hop onto your favorite

|||||| **FROM THE FIELD**

T. J. Sullivan
Staff Writer, *Ventura County Star*

These days many college students feel like they couldn't survive without the World Wide Web. T. J. Sullivan says he couldn't do his job without it.

"I can't imagine now doing reporting without it, but I did," says Sullivan, a staff writer for the *Ventura County Star,* a Los Angeles area daily. "I've been a reporter long enough that we didn't have Internet access at many of the papers where I've worked, and it didn't exist when I started. But now it's become as important a tool as the telephone."

For reporters like Sullivan, the Web makes a huge variety of tasks easier and more efficient and creates possibilities that didn't exist before. He offers an example of how he would use the Web to investigate someone accused of wrongdoing.

"The first thing I'll do is a simple Google search," Sullivan says. "I'll just put in their name to see what comes up. This can get you started, give you some ideas of where things might be. Then it becomes a little more advanced. If you're lucky, you pull up some news stories that some other publication did about this person that can give you some tips as to where to look for more information about them. But as we learn more about what they do and what their business is, then we can find other databases to tap for information about them. For instance, the state of California has several databases online, depending on the departments or agencies that you're looking at. You can enter the name of the business or the person and pull up records of businesses that they've registered with the state. You can do the same in other states too. This is a great tool, especially when you're reporting on someone who's been doing business, because you're able to find out about companies that in the past would have been very difficult to find."

By letting one resource lead to another, Sullivan can gather a huge amount of information for a story. He can also get important materials from far-flung locales without having to drive for hours or get on a plane to search for them by hand. "I tracked down a document I needed

search site and have it look through absolutely everything out there. The most comprehensive search engines are lucky to index about half of the pages in existence. Even the most popular engine, Google, does not claim to completely index every corner of the Web.

Once you've learned some of the techniques discussed later in this chapter, spend some time experimenting with different search sites to see which ones you like the best. That way, when you're on deadline, you won't have to waste time deciding on your favorites.

to a courthouse in Utah," Sullivan recalls. "Before the Web, I'd have had to fly there and go to the courthouse in person to look for the document. But now I was able to get the document number off the Internet using their court search engine, and then call up a copying service that was in the courthouse. They ran up to the clerk's office, pulled the file, copied it for me, billed us $25 and faxed me the report in an hour. Just amazing."

Sullivan says that more and more agencies and institutions are finding that it saves them time to put important materials online, which in turn helps reporters. "I was helping another reporter do some research," Sullivan recalls. "He calls me up and says, 'Hey, we need to get a copy of a press release that came out of this federal office in D.C. five years ago.' Now, to do that before there was an Internet would take untold days, because you would have to call a public relations person and try to explain to them what you want, and of course they'd want a precise date. If you didn't have that, then they'd want as much identifying information as you had about the press release. It would take a remarkable amount of perseverance on your part to get it, because it would be a great deal of work for them to go back in their files to find it, then fax it to you. But you can find it in a matter of minutes on the Net by going to that federal agency's Web site. They all catalog their press releases now. Nothing comes out of these departments that isn't put on the Web—it saves them time. They don't have to hassle now with reporters and other organizations calling them for these press releases."

Sullivan cautions, however, that reporters can't just rely on the Internet—they have to get out of the office and personally interact with the people involved in their stories. "They need to force themselves to leave the computer and go look at what they're writing about," Sullivan says. "You can look at the agenda for a city council meeting online, and you can get the bios and backgrounds and campaign contributions of all the politicians. But if you don't actually interact with the people that are impacted by that decision or by that story, then your stories are going to be hollow. They need to have the soul of the people that are affected by them."

Sullivan says that personal interaction is as important in reporting as gathering facts. "You need to get out of the office and interact. That's why we're reporters. We're gifted as writers, and hopefully we're also gifted as observers. You can't observe on the Internet. We need to talk to people, we need to see things and describe them. Otherwise, all we're doing is processing electronic information, and what good are we?"

DATABASES AND OTHER RESOURCES

It is true that online reporters get a majority of their information from computers. However, depending on what type of publication you work for, you may have to break down and use some old-fashioned print resources to get information. Just because you're in the high-tech online world doesn't mean you should turn up your nose at this. If you're working for a local outlet, you may well be called upon to look through local public records of various kinds, whether they are city contracts, land deeds, maps or any one of a hundred other types of physical records.

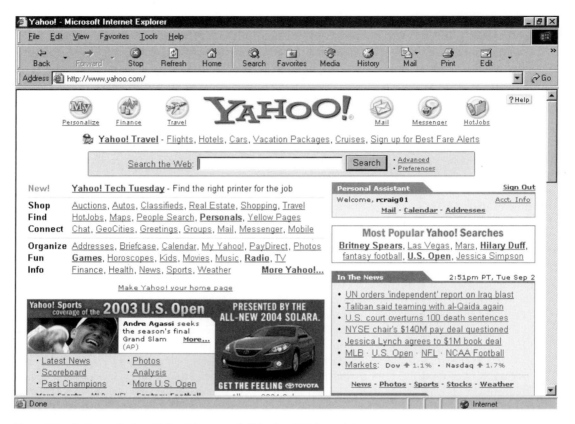

One of the first search sites, Yahoo! is now a full-fledged Web portal
that serves journalists and the general public alike.

Local public and university libraries can also provide a great deal of help with reference materials. University libraries in particular can provide lots of important information from regions beyond your local area.

If you work for the online site of a newspaper, you'll likely have an additional valuable resource at your disposal. Almost every newspaper keeps previous editions for at least a year, as well as keeping an archive containing clippings sorted by subject and often microfiched versions of previous years' editions. Some outlets refer to the stacks of prior editions as the "morgue" and the other resources as the "library"; others lump the two together under one title or the other. Even if you're not working for a print outlet, your organization should have some sort of archives that you can check for previous stories about a given topic. This can be very handy in examining how the dynamics of a topic have changed over time and can let a new reporter know if a story has already been heavily covered. In the online world, knowing what your outlet has already published about a topic is

A BRIEF HISTORY OF SEARCH ENGINES

Before the World Wide Web even existed, people wanted to be able to find things on the Internet. This was not easy to do despite the fact that the network had only a tiny percentage of the users it has today. The problem was that the files were spread around the network and around the world in no real order. This led programmers to try to come up with a way to index files so that people could find them.

Generally considered the earliest ancestor to today's search engines, Archie was created in 1990 by students at McGill University in Canada. This was a searchable database of sites that was created by a program that periodically searched all known sites for keywords. (The name Archie was a colloquial shortening of the word "archives.") This site primarily searched for files at sites that used FTP (file transfer protocol) to transfer documents between computers. Soon other search facilities emerged for other kinds of sites, adopting names that took their cue from Archie—two of these were called Veronica and Jughead, after characters in the "Archie" comic books.

When the Web emerged in the early 1990s, programmers rapidly determined the importance of search functions and began creating their own search sites. The World Wide Web Wanderer created a database that tracked the growth of the Web, while ALIWEB (short for "Archie-Like Indexing of the Web") invited webmasters to post their own index information. Programmers developed "spiders," programs that methodically scour the Web for pages and their contents. Some of these looked just at page headers; others scanned all the text on each page. The first of the full-text engines was WebCrawler, which originated at the University of Washington and debuted in early 1994.

The best-known early Web search site also went online in early 1994, although it was technically a searchable directory and not a true "search engine." Two Stanford University doctoral students, Jerry Yang and David Filo, had created their own large lists of categorized links to Web pages of all kinds. They put these lists online and called their site Yahoo!, ostensibly because they considered themselves to be a pair of "yahoos." While Yahoo! was originally just an organized hierarchical directory of links, it soon incorporated search functionality and began some automated gathering of data.

Universities produced several successful Web search engines. Excite, originally called "Architext," was also started at Stanford and actually predates Yahoo! by a few months. Lycos began at Carnegie-Mellon University in mid-1994. Soon, however, the corporate world got into the act. Infoseek Corporation launched its search engine in mid-1994, Digital Equipment Corporation debuted AltaVista at the end of 1995, and Inktomi Corporation launched HotBot in mid-1996.

The current most popular search site is Google, also started at Stanford University. Computer science graduate student founders Larry Page and Sergey Brin originally designed a search tool called BackRub, which analyzed the "back links" pointing to a given Web site. This developed into Google, founded in 1998 and now possessing the capability of searching more than 4 billion Web documents. (If you'd like to learn more about the history of search engines, check out The WebDeveloper.com Guide to Search Engines site listed at the end of this chapter.)

essential—not only to avoid repetition but also to allow for links from your story to previous stories on the topic. Most news outlets also keep an assortment of other reference materials on hand, such as city directories and state manuals, which provide all kinds of useful cross-referenced local and regional information.

As this reliance on traditional print sources attests, not everything is yet available on the Internet. That doesn't mean, however, that it's not available on computers. Indeed, long before the Web existed, computer-assisted reporting was a hot topic. Since the late 1970s and early 1980s, many important and useful

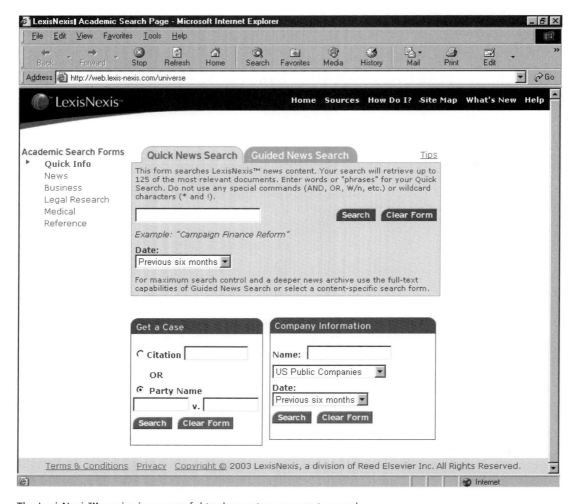

The LexisNexis™ service is a powerful tool reporters can use to search hundreds of newspapers and periodicals.

SOURCE: lexisnexis.com (accessed September 25, 2003). Used by permission.

databases have been available to reporters via computer. Some of these have since moved onto the Internet, but several remain available only to subscribing institutions or individuals.

For students as well as reporters, the most familiar of these are probably the commercial database services. These services have a tremendous amount of private information not freely available on the Internet—all sorts of searchable, cross-referenced news articles, legal documents and other items—and they charge subscription fees for access. There have been several of these over the years, but two of them are most commonly used by reporters. LexisNexis™, which began as a legal information service and grew to include news and business information, is available at many libraries and on the Web through subscriptions. Dialog, also available at many libraries, has great scientific and medical holdings as well as all sorts of government and business information. Through mergers in recent years, Dialog has gained access to some of the largest European databases as well. Each of these (as well as other commercial databases) has relatively easy search commands for reporters and students to learn, which makes it possible to sort through an immense amount of material to find what you need.

Reporters can also get their hands on vital information through government databases, though sometimes the methods required to search them are more challenging than with commercial database services. Depending on the agency and the records in question, facts and figures may be kept well organized in a modern spreadsheet or other database program, or they may be haphazardly arranged using some outdated program on an obsolete computer. For decades, many government agencies kept records on data tapes rather than hard disk, and in some cases such records have not been transferred to more up-to-date formats. Reporters wishing to gain access to long-term information have to learn to work with such formats, in some cases even installing tape drives in their office computers.

These days, thankfully, most government databases are on more up-to-date formats, and many are more readily accessible than you might think. While government offices are the obvious place to look for them, many databases are available at university libraries for research purposes. Sometimes these are kept on CD-ROM, used for its easy compatibility and inexpensive format. Large university libraries frequently subscribe to government and academic databases and receive updates regularly via CD-ROM. In many instances, government information is kept in common spreadsheet or database format, so reporters who know how to use programs such as these can get a wide variety of information that can be sorted by category.

Regardless of where you go to get your information, you'll need to be careful about how you use it. Government information is often considered fair game for publication, since it generally concerns public programs paid for with public money, but there are sometimes laws and provisions you should know about. Commercial databases usually state clearly how you may use their data, but others may not. You need to be wary of copyrights and other usage restrictions—if there's any doubt about publication rights, be sure to obtain permission.

Beyond permissions, however, a familiar question arises when dealing with databases: Why should I believe this information? More specifically, is there a reason for skepticism about figures in these databases? Neither private firms nor government agencies are above cooking the books from time to time, and this includes all sorts of statistical information in databases. You may not know why figures may have been altered, but that doesn't mean they haven't been. If a particular set of numbers or a block of data seems suspicious, do additional research to corroborate the facts.

In general, reporters and editors use searches for one of four functions, which often correspond to different stages of writing a story:

1. *To come up with a new subject for a story.* When you're starting from scratch and fishing around for topics for a new story, a search may be helpful.

2. *To find information on a newly chosen subject.* Once you've chosen a new topic, you may not know much about it and need to find out more before you can start interviewing and writing.

3. *To find supporting information on an established subject.* You may already be working on a story on a given topic and want to learn more to help you make decisions about the direction of the story.

4. *To check facts.* You may do a certain amount of this as you go along, but you'll want to give most stories a final round of fact checking before submitting them.

Each of these uses requires a different searching approach for a reporter. The first requires a very general approach—"What about this?"—which can be very time consuming and should be avoided near deadline. This situation often lends itself to using a search site that is as much a directory as a full-text searching tool. If you have a hierarchical directory of subjects to choose from, you're more likely to follow a productive direction in gathering your information rather than simply taking shots in the dark by typing in random keywords.

The second function can also take some time, depending on how much you already know about the chosen subject. Most often, the more you know about the topic and the directions your story might take, the more specific your search can be and the less time you'll waste sifting through unrelated results. You should be able to get even more specific with the third function—at that point, focus on tying up loose ends, answering lingering questions and otherwise making the story complete. Don't try to reconceptualize the story at this point—if necessary, this can be done with a follow-up later.

The fact-checking function is at once the most necessary and the most frustrating of these four uses. Do not rely solely on Web searches to verify information—use all media available to you. In addition, as with any information, you'll need to consider the validity of the source—there are plenty of pages with dubious information out there. Verify facts with as many solid sources as possible. Even a company's own home page may contain information that is, if not blatantly inaccurate, at least outdated. When it comes to checking facts, you want both quality and quantity of sources.

The key for reporters is to identify the function for searches before beginning the process. If you're not clear about exactly what you aim to find, you can easily get sidetracked and waste time on tangential subjects. Paradoxically, this is where one of the best traits of a reporter—curiosity—can become troublesome. If you catch yourself going off the subject and into an unrelated area that you'd like to return to later, jot down the URLs in question or bookmark them, then get back to your original task. You can't aimlessly Web-surf all night when you have a story to write.

For online journalists, there is actually a fifth possible use for searches—to locate articles that can be linked to your page to give your readers further information about the topic of your story. This is discussed in detail in Chapter 9. If you're interested in linking an article you've found on the Web to a page that will appear on your site, notify the page's author or copyright holder. This is not required by law, but it is a good idea (see Chapter 14).

KEYWORD SEARCHES

What is the best approach to keyword searching when you're working with a deadline looming fairly soon? To get the most out of Web search engines, you need to refine your search abilities. This section tells you how. If you're not on deadline and are looking for a completely new subject, stay away from keyword searches and look at **Web directories** such as Yahoo! instead.

Being specific is the most important thing to keep in mind when searching for material. This is true even before you search. Before searching, think about exactly what you want to find, and write it down or save it on your word processor. Specifically stating your search goal is a good way to avoid lengthy and unproductive tangents—only stray from this goal if you believe a new direction will be vital to making your story better.

The actual syntax (word and symbol patterns) involved in searching is pretty simple. While search syntax differs slightly from site to site, the vast majority of it is consistent, so these tips should work on most popular search sites. But always double-check a search site's instructions for how to formulate searches. A good general rule is to type in all search queries in lowercase letters as some systems handle uppercase letters differently than others.

A single example is used throughout this discussion to illustrate ways to search for particular topics. If you're at your computer and it's online, you can follow along using a search site of your choice. Let's say you're looking for information for a story on the breakup of the Soviet Union in 1991. An ordinary Web surfer might find a search site and simply type in the following:

```
breakup of soviet union
```

If you do this, you're going to get a whole lot more information than you'll ever be able to read. For example, this exact search done on the AltaVista search site produced 1,012,959 hits. Obviously, this is far too many results to contemplate much less sort through or read in any depth. If you approach a search in this way, you're sending the wrong message to the search program. In fact, you're asking the search program to locate every document in its database that contains *any of these words*. It's no wonder you received so many results.

It would be one thing if all one million-plus pages were full of pertinent information, but that's not the case. A nonspecific search like this almost always points you to a vast multitude of pages that are useless to you. In this case, among the results were hundreds of pages of seemingly endless addresses of business pages, personal home pages, newsgroup and chat conversations, and all manner of disconnected material, little of which would be useful to you.

Good search syntax can help you immensely. The first piece of syntax to learn is to use the plus symbol (+) for words that must appear. This tells the search program to find only pages that contain all the words with pluses in front of them, not just any one of the words. (Some sites such as Google use "all the words" as a default setting, but others do not; using this syntax will produce the results you want on most search engines.) Since two of the words in your query—"breakup" and "union"—appear in contexts far outside what you're looking for, it makes sense to assure that all three words are found within the pages you're trying to locate. With this in mind, type the following search request:

```
+breakup +soviet +union
```

By using this simple piece of syntax, an AltaVista search eliminated more than 96 percent of the pages it returned in the first search—most of which, it's safe to assume, were fairly useless for our sample topic. Unfortunately, in this example, having started with such a large number, eliminating 96 percent of the hits still leaves 39,602 pages to shuffle through. This is still far too many pages to help you, and too many of them still have little to do with our topic.

Here is where a second piece of syntax can help. Since the Soviet Union is a two-word phrase, it makes sense to search for it as a phrase. In general, you should use quotation marks around phrases. This tells the search program to look specifically for a set of words in a particular order. This works for phrases of any length, though very long phrases are likely to return few or no results unless they're widely used. In our example, the logical next step would be to type this:

```
+breakup +"soviet union"
```

Note that the plus sign remains in front of the phrase in quotes to make sure that the search program knows this is a required phrase.

Using this phrase search syntax eliminated about seven-eighths of the 39,000 hits from the previous search, again dropping many pages that might have provided little useful information. Still, in this example, you're left with 4,982 results. This is a much more manageable number than the tens of thousands you had a minute ago, but it's still far too many for a reporter anywhere near deadline to peruse.

At this point, you might think that while you'll never read 4,982 pages, at least you've narrowed them down to where the first few dozen results could get you the information you need. In some cases, this is true. Search sites generally display results according to "relevance"—a calculation of how prominent your search term is within the page. Frequently, however, when you start looking at the pages listed in the results of a search at this stage, you'll discover there are still many pages of dubious value.

For example, in our Soviet Union search, at this point several of the first few dozen hits pointed to a single site featuring excerpts from the work of the renowned Soviet novelist and poet Vladimir Nabokov. While he's certainly a prominent figure in Soviet literary history, he died in 1977 and had nothing to do with the breakup of the country in 1991. Thus, even though these were among the first results returned, they're basically useless.

There are two reasons a search might return results like this. First, the excerpts on the site might have contained all the query words. However, in this instance, this was not true. Instead, this document was returned among the top-ranked results because of something written into its HTML code.

Among the items scanned by search engine programs are pieces of HTML code known as META tags. These tags usually contain information about a document and the program it was created with and do not have any effect on what shows on the screen. Until fairly recently, most search engine spiders lacked the capability to search the full text of Web pages; instead, they only scanned items between a document's HEAD tags. To help make this process work smoothly, HTML authors were encouraged to put keywords relating to a document's content within the META tags.

While this may have been well-intentioned in the beginning, many enterprising Web page designers discovered that they could make their pages show up regularly on search result pages by packing their META tags with anything even remotely related to the subject of the page. Some authors have abused this, listing literally hundreds of unrelated or barely related keywords in the hopes of getting more unsuspecting people to visit their pages.

The Nabokov pages found in our search, while not the most extreme of examples, boasted META tags containing 101 keywords. Within this group was the phrase "breakup of Soviet Union," which is why it showed up in our search. This type of thing can cause all sorts of problems for a reporter in a hurry.

How do you get around this? Sometimes the best way is to take a look at the results you've gotten and see if the remaining unnecessary pages have anything in common that you can exclude from the search. To do this, use the minus (–) sign to exclude terms. If you're pretty sure you won't need anything about Nabokov to write this story, you can get rid of these pages by typing in the following:

```
+breakup +"Soviet Union" -nabokov
```

This is one way to narrow down the results, and in some cases it works very well. Unfortunately, for our sample search this action only knocked out about 150 more pages. This is a move in the right direction, but it's still not specific enough for your story needs. While the minus sign didn't help much here, it can be quite important. For example, a search for information on former president John F. Kennedy garnered more than 100,000 hits; by adding "–jr." to the search to eliminate pages about JFK Jr., this figure was cut by almost one-third.

A different approach involves adding more specific terms to the search, based on your knowledge of the subject and the focus of your story. For instance, knowing that the Soviet Union broke up in 1991, you can add that to your search to narrow it down some more:

```
+breakup +"Soviet Union" +1991
```

This eliminates another one-third of the hits and leaves us with 3,095 pages. Now you're beginning to get somewhere—most of the results finally look fairly promising. Still, this remains a large number for a reporter to sort through. Specificity and focus become vital at this stage, and previous knowledge also can help.

Perhaps you're primarily interested in the coup attempt that took place in August 1991 when the KGB attempted to oust Mikhail Gorbachev from power. This might result in the following search:

```
+breakup +"Soviet Union" +1991 +coup
```

Suddenly you're "down" to 476 pages—a daunting afternoon's reading assignment, but at least you're now looking at something shorter than *War and Peace*. More important, you now have listings of very specific pages closely related to your core subject matter. Now you can wade in and begin to read pages, keeping your original assignment in mind and looking specifically for information that relates to that assignment.

Clearly, the more specific you can be about what you're looking for, the more manageable the results will be. Not every hit will link you to a wealth of information, but the specificity of your searches increases the chance that the pages you find will be closely related to what you're looking for.

The two key ingredients are getting to know the syntax used at your favorite search site and thinking in concrete, specific terms about how to optimize your searches based on that syntax and the facts of your assignment. In general, the more searching you do, the better you get at thinking of well-targeted search queries. By learning to think in specific terms about what you're looking for, you can take full advantage of the information available to you on the Internet, and do so quickly and efficiently.

OTHER TYPES OF SEARCHES

Using keywords is the most common way to search the Web, but it's not the only way. A different approach is taken with Q&A searches, sometimes called "natural language" or "plain-English" searches. Rather than using the search syntax detailed previously, in Q&A searches you simply type in a question using normal language. For example, if you're looking for information on the Unabomber, you might type this simple question:

```
Who was the Unabomber?
```

Several search sites now offer Q&A searching, but the best known of these is Ask Jeeves, named after a famous literary butler. These types of searches have their drawbacks—they seldom return a large volume of results, and they don't allow for the precision of keyword searches. However, they are very popular with novice users and require no specialized search skills. These types of searches are not generally recommended for journalists on deadline, but they can be useful as a starting point if you don't know much about the subject you're about to cover. For instance, if you're doing a profile on a professor of metaphysics and you're unsure of what metaphysics is, a Q&A search on "What is metaphysics?" might produce a useful and manageable list of results for you.

In general, however, journalists want to answer specific questions rather than

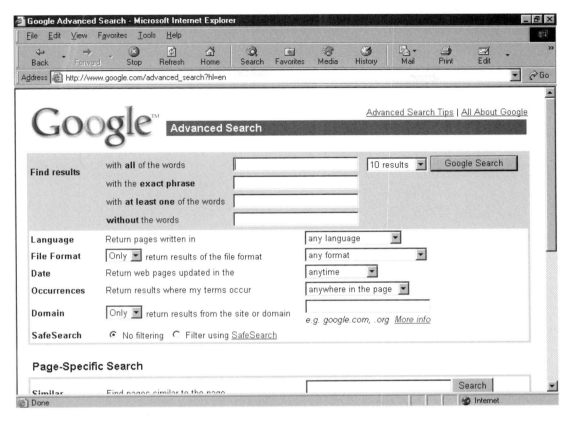

Google's advanced search page allows more specificity and detail in use of keywords than its general search page as well as allowing you to search particular domains, languages and dates.

SOURCE: google.com (accessed September 3, 2003). Used by permission.

general ones. To do this, use a boolean search, which is available in the advanced search areas of many search engines. The term *boolean* refers to the relationship between one word and another, using connecting words such as AND, OR and NOT. These connecting words are called "operators." Boolean searches allow you to combine and exclude words and phrases in a useful and intuitive manner using these operators. Operators are usually capitalized to set them apart from other text. Also, please note that on some sites you need to go to an "advanced search" page to use boolean commands.

One example of a boolean search might be to look for information on certain Andrew Lloyd Webber musical productions. If you're specifically interested in earlier productions in which he collaborated with lyricist Tim Rice, you might type in the following:

```
"andrew lloyd webber" AND "tim rice"
```

This will bring you only results that list both names. You can use boolean operators to further narrow this search. Let's say you're primarily interested in the Broadway musicals of Webber and Rice, but you discover that many of the results from your search focus on the 1996 movie *Evita,* starring Madonna, which was based on the earlier stage play. An easy way to get around this would be the following search:

```
"andrew lloyd webber" AND "tim rice" NOT madonna
```

In this case, excluding Madonna knocked out more than 25 percent of the original hits and left a lot of useful information. Some search sites require the term AND NOT instead of NOT—check the site you choose to make sure you're using the correct syntax.

Suppose, however, you decide to focus on Rice instead of Webber, and you know that Rice has collaborated with composer Alan Menken. To get information on Rice's collaboration with either Menken or Webber, try the following:

```
"tim rice" AND ("andrew lloyd webber"
OR "alan menken")
```

This returns more hits than an AND search with either collaborator. If you'd used AND with both collaborators, you'd have ended up with only pages listing Rice with both men. The parentheses around the OR query tells the search program that one or the other name must be included on each page.

Finally, if your topic is so obscure that your favorite search engine is finding few if any references to it, you might try your search on a site called a *metasearch* or *meta engine.* Instead of searching their own databases, these sites send your queries to multiple engines all at once and return lists compiled from hits on all these sites. Metasearch sites include Dogpile, Savvy Search, Metacrawler and others; in addition, some conventional search sites are introducing metasearch functions to their menus of services.

If you're writing a story about efforts to save from extinction an endangered but little-known bird called the California Gnatcatcher, you might find a metasearch very helpful. For example, you confidently enter "california gnatcatcher" as a search term at your favorite site, but it returns exactly two pages about the bird and neither is particularly helpful. By accessing a meta engine and typing the same query, you suddenly have 38 results to choose from. For the sake of speed, it's not usually a good idea to enter general topics at a meta engine—you'll end up with a truly massive list of hits. However, if a topic isn't producing results at a regular search site, this is a very helpful alternative.

SUMMARY

By learning the ins and outs of searching on the Web, you can quickly and easily find information that would have taken many hours of research just a few years ago. While you still need to engage in standard reporting, using Web searches can add a lot to your stories. They can yield additional context and background for your stories, provide links for your readers to follow for more information, and make you a better-informed and more well-rounded reporter.

RELATED WEB SITES

Bruce Sterling's "A Brief History of the Internet"
gopher://gopher.well.sf.ca.us:70/00/Publications/authors/Sterling/fsf/
internet.fsf

European Laboratory for Particle Physics
http://public.web.cern.ch/Public/

CERN's history of the Web
http://public.web.cern.ch/Public/ACHIEVEMENTS/web.html

Browser information and history
http://www.microsoft.com/windows/ie
http://home.netscape.com

Web glossary
http://www.whatis.com/

Google
http://www.google.com

Yahoo!
http://www.yahoo.com

AltaVista
http://www.altavista.com

Excite
http://www.excite.com

HotBot
http://hotbot.lycos.com

Infoseek
http://infoseek.go.com

Lycos
http://www.lycos.com

Ask Jeeves:
http://www.ask.com

Dogpile
http://www.dogpile.com

Savvy Search
http://www.savvysearch.com

MetaCrawler
http://www.metacrawler.com

Descriptions/definitions of search engines
http://www.whatis.com/searchen.htm

Search engine reviews
http://www.searchenginewatch.com

The WebDeveloper.com Guide to Search Engines
http://gsd.mit.edu/~history/search/engine/history.html

EXERCISES

1. Locate your school's home Web page using your browser. For that one page, list each of the following attributes:

   - File type (protocol)

   - Server name

   - Domain type

   - File name

   - File extension

   Then find one other page within your school's site (a department home page, any other organization's page, a faculty member's page) and list each of the above attributes **plus** the subdirectory where the page resides (if applicable).

2. Suppose you're writing a story on why certain birds are vanishing in your area, and you want to find information on cardinals. Visit one of the search sites listed in this chapter, and search for the term "cardinals." Then narrow your search to exclude various athletic teams named the Cardinals. Then narrow it further to remove references to cardinals within the Catholic Church. Describe your initial results, the procedures you used to narrow the search, and the results you found as you narrowed your search.

3. Using any two of the search sites listed in this chapter plus InfoTrac College Edition, search for the term "webcast." Then write a summary of the differences between the results found on each site—not just the number of page hits returned but also the way they're presented. Discuss some of the general characteristics of the first few results of each search and what those results may reflect about the way each search site organizes its information.

5

||||||

Sources and Interviewing

Many aspects of reporting have changed dramatically with improvements in technology, but the acts of gathering sources and interviewing may have changed the least. Journalists still have to locate knowledgeable people, ask them important questions and report answers accurately. Yet technology offers the promise of new approaches and the reality of easier contact with potential interviewees. This chapter covers the cultivation of sources, preparing for the interview, notetaking and the use of new technologies to make interviews possible, expedite them and report them in new ways.

As you enter the world of online journalism, you may have a somewhat idealistic notion of how reporters find **sources** and interview them in such a high-tech profession. Surely it must be full of writers questioning world leaders via streaming video and arranging virtual press conferences. Imagine staring into your screen and giving a foreign dictator the evil eye while asking him tough questions, or exchanging a quick e-mail with the pope for comments about the latest Supreme Court ruling on abortion. No phone calls to schedule interview times, no sitting around waiting for some official to emerge from his office or a court proceeding, no begging for a minute of someone's time. Technology has relieved us of such menial tasks, right?

Many online sites, such as Journalism.org, have resources that online journalists can use to hone their interviewing skills.

SOURCE: journalism.org (accessed September 25, 2003). Used by permission.

Sorry to break the bad news to you, but for most online journalists, the act of interviewing doesn't have much to do with this futuristic vision. More often than not, it involves many of the same elements as interviewing for any type of news outlet. There are, however, some important things that a smart online journalist can do with technology to shorten the process of locating and contacting sources, as well as arranging the interview, doing research and performing the interview itself. In addition, the characteristics of online news dictate a different approach to reporting the interview. So while the fundamentals of interviewing—preparation, insightful questioning and accurate reporting—haven't changed, some of the tools at your disposal in online journalism have great potential for giving your interviews completely new dimensions.

Having said this, the most important tool in these pursuits is still an inquisitive and well-prepared mind. This central fact crops up again and again throughout the chapter.

SOURCES ARE PEOPLE TOO

When people think of reporters these days, they often conjure up a fairly unflattering image. People tend to imagine a disheveled, swarthy man, working at some big-city daily paper, sealed off from society in an antiseptic newsroom, making countless pugnacious phone calls and poring over his bulging Rolodex. They don't likely envision a perfectly normal person going out into the community and making contacts. Yet, at one level or another, this is what reporters do to cultivate relationships with sources.

For a reporter, keeping in regular contact with people within the community (online or otherwise) is a vital part of formulating ideas and getting information. This is true whether the people in question are official representatives of various institutions and organizations or simply reliable individuals working in various important places in the area you serve. These contacts enable you to cover a beat of any sort. Rather than relying on the knowledge and experience of one person (you), instead you rely on the experiences of many people from different walks of life. Collectively, they are at the roots of your own web of information—you can't remain isolated and be a good reporter.

It might seem that online reporters—especially ones who don't work for local outlets—would be more isolated than print or broadcast reporters. After all, local reporters are often recognizable figures who can be identified and engaged in conversation on the street and in the grocery store. Most online reporters, however, say that in a way they may be even less isolated than local reporters. Most print and broadcast reporters live in the geographical areas they cover, but local print and broadcast media do not allow for the interactivity of the online world.

By virtue of the e-mail links that frequently appear at the end of online news stories, online reporters are more immediately accessible than any other kind of reporter. Though viewers or readers of print and broadcast media may send letters or make phone calls to reporters, each is an arduous process compared with firing off a quick e-mail in the immediate wake of reading a story. This is why reporters who have worked in other media consistently say that their online work receives much more feedback.

Some reporters and editors are put off by the interactivity of the online world—some privately say it reeks of "giving people what they want, not what they need." However, just as many say that the interactivity of the medium not only keeps reporters on their toes but also provides all kinds of new sources for news. Instead of relying solely on going out and finding people with information, reporters have discovered that the medium's interactivity has encouraged people to come to them when they think they have something useful to share.

Regardless of how you come into contact with sources, you should know that all sources are not created equal. Some sources are in position to know all kinds of information, others may know a lot about a very specific area, and still others may simply pretend to know a lot. Sometimes the information you're given is accurate; at other times the truth is shaded for various reasons, and on some occasions the information is completely false. When dealing with an unfamiliar source, ask yourself these questions about the credibility of both the information and the source.

- *Why should I believe this information?* This is the most important question you can ask yourself when talking to a source, particularly one you've never worked with before. Is this person sharing the information because he truly believes it should be known, or is there something else at work? If you detect ulterior motives, you'll need to spend more time confirming the information with other sources. If you smell a rat and can't confirm a piece of information, *don't publish it.*

- *Who is this person?* This sounds like a silly question, but in the online age it's very important. You may get e-mails from people within major companies or institutions who want to give you information but don't want to tell you their names or positions. (This is different from keeping a source's name out of a story.) You should insist on getting as much information about the source as possible—name, position with the company or institution, how long they've worked there and so on. If appropriate, stress that you may be able to use their information without quoting them by name. If your source refuses to give you this personal information, even with a promise of anonymity, you need to look for other sources.

- *Is this person in a position to know this information?* A guy who works in the White House cafeteria can hardly be expected to know deep dark secrets about U.S. policy. However, a member of the secretarial staff at a major corporation may well know all kinds of things about what its board may do next. Sometimes well-positioned staff members have better information than highly paid executives and officials.

- *Does this person have an ax to grind?* This is a particular type of ulterior motive. If someone is trying to promote a particular agenda within their company or institution, he is quite likely to slant the information he gives you. This can include trying to make a given person look bad, trying to get good press for a possible course of action or helping a crony get good press.

- *Is this person using me for personal gain?* If you publish a story based on the information from a source, does that person stand to make a lot of money or move up within the company or institution? Reporters often become unwitting pawns in power struggles in companies and agencies. If you get the feeling you're being used to further a source's career, you need to confront the situation and question the information you're getting.

In the haste to get a big story and have it published quickly, sometimes these questions are overlooked, but they shouldn't be. Remember, your objective is to fairly represent the news, not to get a temporary scoop based on one-sided information.

Good sources can include everyone from high-ranking officials to spokespersons to desk clerks, as long as they share true and useful information. In the traditional media, for years even investigative reporters have gotten most of their information from **official sources**—press secretaries, PR people, officials speaking for the record and so forth. This information is supplemented by material from

unofficial sources, which can include anyone whose job description doesn't include speaking with the media. Depending on the type of story involved, reporters may also consult experts on the subject who have no real connection to this particular story but are acknowledged specialists within the field.

All of these types of sources are used by online reporters as well, but the Internet has expanded the boundaries for sources considerably. While the Web is often used to search databases, it can also lead a reporter to new people who may help develop a story. For example, rather than just interviewing U.S. government and military officials about an attack against a foreign country, the Web makes it easy to locate and interview people within that country or in neighboring countries to get their opinions. The Web also allows those affected by policies to seek you out to tell their stories. Proceed with care, however—people with Web pages often have their own agendas as well.

Regardless of whether you have sought out a source or the source has come to you, you should follow the same basic rules in dealing with these sources as you would in any other type of publication. You should always strive to be accurate, honest and fair, and avoid entering into any agreements with sources that you or your publication might regret later. Accuracy and honesty are particularly important in the online age because sources and readers can look to many other outlets for information. Following these rules will help you establish a strong professional relationship with sources and also help protect you from being exploited or manipulated.

Sources have an additional purpose beyond sharing important facts with you. Sources can also lead you to other people who might have relevant information. This is called **source networking.** One question you should ask in nearly every interview is, "Who else do you know who might know something about this?" For each suggested source, find out how you can reach them and whether you should call them yourself or have the first source call on your behalf. If necessary, you can use the first source's name to establish your credibility with the second source (for example, "Jim Smith told me to give you a call."). As you ask each source for names of people who might have information, your number of potential interviewees quickly adds up. This is how a reporter can start with one or two sources and end up with a dozen or more.

One word of warning, however; this technique has its limits. When covering controversial issues, make sure you are informed about the different sides of the story. This is true even if you're writing for one of the many Web publications that take sides on various issues. You may argue in favor of one side, but if you are not informed of opposing positions, you're doing harm rather than good. You owe it to your audience not to be ill informed.

INTERVIEW PREPARATION

Preparing for the interview begins with preparing for the story. As noted in the preceding chapters, you need to do some research before diving in and writing a story. Learn as much as you can about the topic of your story using the sources

|||||| **FROM THE FIELD**

Mindy McAdams
Knight Chair Professor, Department of Journalism,
University of Florida
Former Web Strategist, American Press Institute
Former Content Developer, *Digital Ink* (*Washington Post*)

Mindy McAdams has a vision. She imagines online news sites that are so inviting and well organized that readers are immediately drawn in and engrossed by the information there. "I'm in there, and I'm clicking and I'm reading and I'm viewing," she says, "and I'm gathering information without having to search intently with a lot of keywords. I'm traveling through a space that's well constructed. And that hasn't happened to me yet."

McAdams has been following online journalism longer than most. She began looking at news online on CompuServe in the mid-1980s, and she was interested enough to complete a master's thesis on the subject at Columbia University in 1985. However, she's still looking for her dream news site.

"What's missing is something that I acknowledge is very hard to do, and very time consuming. I'm looking for a really interesting set of information that's layered and clustered in such a way that it's effortless to navigate. It's the kind of complex structure where I can go into a set of information and lose track of how much time has passed, because I am just so into it."

McAdams says that one of the most important skills in building the structure she describes is solid, detailed interviewing. "When you're online and you have a bottomless news hole and you have these different ways of telling stories," she says, "you actually need to do more work, because you're no longer bounded by that tiny little 15-inch hole your editor gave you. You need to actually interview people instead of just getting a quote. And you need to actually listen to them so you can ask them intelligent follow-up questions. And before you know it, you're getting all kinds of depth and insight that you never ever had before."

One problem she sees with this is that it requires journalists to abandon some of their most familiar routines. "We have a really bad habit in regular journalism of just going out to get quotes," McAdams says. "Sometimes it's like you're doing your last three or four interviews just to get that quote. And you don't really care what they say, as long as you get a good quote out of them, because they're the name and the position that you want and you need a quote

and resources mentioned in Chapter 4. Find out about the past, present and future of the topic as best you can—you should be well informed about both the facts and any trends that might lead to future developments.

You need a clear focus when you start to write a story, and you should develop that focus while doing background research for the story. When dealing with a specific incident or event, the focus is often quite clear. Other times it's less obvious, such as when profiling a company or a person. In any case, as you focus your from them. Everybody knows we do it—even the best journalists do it. It's no big secret, and there's nothing unethical about it. But it's kind of utilitarian, and it doesn't lead to the kind of depth you should have online."

McAdams unexpectedly got her first chance to work in online news while working as a copy editor at the *Washington Post.* "At that time I'd finished this degree and finished this thesis and all I had in mind was online newspapers," she says. "So when they started one, in October '93, and put the notice up on the bulletin board, I was banging down the door. It's like, 'I *have* to work on this.' And of course I was already inside the organization, so that was pretty easy."

This particular foray into online publishing, however, wasn't on the Web. The product, *Digital Ink,* was being designed for a proprietary dial-up platform called AT&T Interchange. When Netscape was introduced in early 1994, however, McAdams and her colleagues suddenly saw the future, and it wasn't Interchange. "Every single person on the staff, not management, but everybody who worked on the actual product, was blown away by Netscape," McAdams says. "We were all suddenly using Netscape all the time and surfing the brand-new early graphical Web, but management had already spent a lot of money on something else, and so they were kind of committed. So you ended up with a whole lot of people who knew this wasn't the future working on it anyway. It was a funny kind of situation."

By the time the *Post* got on the Web, McAdams had left for the American Press Institute. Then, in 1999, the University of Florida offered her a Knight Chair professor position. She jumped at the chance. "These Knight chairs are really amazing academic positions," says McAdams. "You get to really do something different—you don't take over established courses. You get to really create something, and this one was focusing on journalism technologies, which I defined as online journalism. And it was like, 'Great! I get to make a whole new program in online journalism. This is wonderful!'"

These days McAdams is imparting her vision of Web news—and the structure behind it—to the next generation of online journalists. "It's a matter of clustering groups of information, pieces of information, that are connected to other pieces," she says. "Structure is always difficult for them to learn, even in a plain old 12-inch written story. But this is like a higher level of structure design. And even though they've been immersed in it their whole lives, from video games and flipping channels on the TV and everything else, just because you're used to consuming it doesn't mean you know how to create it. You can't just put your hands in and do it—you have to think a lot about what goes with what."

story, you'll undoubtedly begin to come up with questions about the topic that need to be answered. Start jotting down these questions (or saving them on your computer) and you've also taken the first step toward doing interviews.

A simple way of deciding who to interview is to ask yourself this question: Who is in a position to have information about this topic? Sometimes this is pretty straightforward—if a story deals with specific individuals, you try to interview them, the people closest to them or the people who represent them legally or otherwise. In most cases, though, you're going to want to dig a little deeper. You should become familiar with the spokespersons for organizations connected to the topic, experts on the topic and other people in positions to know the answers to your questions. A little well-targeted Web searching (supplemented by a few phone calls) can usually make this process fairly comprehensive. By doing your homework on the topic, you should have a good idea of the people who can help to give you the best and most relevant information.

As you learn about the topic, you should also note the different sides of the issue. If you're going to write balanced, nonopinionated stories, you need to know the dynamics of debate on the subject long before you start writing. This can guide the questions you form along the way—how does one side respond to another's policies, statements or allegations? This can also point you in the direction of a second wave of interviewees—those who oppose your primary sources or who approach the issue from a different point of view. By being curious, you'll come up with questions that lead you to potential interviewees, which in turn will lead to more questions and more interviews. An inquisitive reporter often has more questions (and more interviewees) than can realistically fit into a story.

When you do a good job of research, the process feeds upon itself. As you learn more about the topic, jot down additional questions about various aspects of it. As you do this, you can start deciding who can best answer these questions. Once you've started a list of potential interviewees, learn as much as possible about each one, thus leading to more questions based on their respective backgrounds and positions in the topic area. These may, in turn, lead you to other sources with contrary opinions. As you learn about these secondary sources, this will lead to even more questions. For a truly sharp reporter, the process only ends when the story is turned in.

One of the great advantages of being a journalist today is that the Web generally makes it easy for a smart reporter to get background information on potential interviewees. Almost every major institution these days has a Web site containing some information about its most important people. Sometimes these are just quick synopses of a person's duties, other times they'll include detailed biographical and occupational data. Even when there isn't any convenient background information, you'll often find facts about them elsewhere, from personal home pages to previous employers' Web sites to news articles about them. Movers and shakers almost always leave footprints.

Preparation is important for any interviewer, but particularly so for students. Even students who are veterans of the school paper can find themselves intimidated when doing off-campus interviews with public officials or other important people. This is particularly true when interviewing a well-known local or national public figure—there is a tendency to become nervous or star-struck at the expense of conducting a useful interview. The best way to fight this is through rigorous preparation. The better you know the subject matter, and the more thoroughly you know what you want to find out from this person, the less likely it is that you'll be rattled or intimidated in an interview. Officials and other figures might assume you're not well informed because you're "just a kid," but there's no reason you can't be just as well prepared as a professional reporter. This is the best way to earn respect from interviewees (and editors).

SETTING UP THE INTERVIEW

The logistics of contacting someone and arranging an interview have always been a problem. It's one thing to identify people you'd like to interview and quite another to actually reach them and speak with them. Some people are simply busy, others are absent-minded and others just don't want to face a reporter. In the online age, however, you have several new tools on your side that can help you hook up with some of these hard-to-reach people.

Your first choice should be to contact them personally by telephone (or face to face, if possible) to set up the interview. You may be an online journalist, but with many of the people you'll interview, the personal touch still works better. It establishes a rapport between you and the interviewee that doesn't usually exist via e-mail, and it can help set the stage for a productive conversation. This doesn't sound high-tech in the least, yet the Web can provide lots of help here. It's true that every newsroom has phone directories and every reporter has a "little black book," but when dealing with unfamiliar sources or people outside your immediate area, the Web can become your electronic superdirectory. You can find business phone numbers on virtually every company's home page and home phone numbers from a wide variety of sites. Even if these sites yield nothing, a clever Web search can often unearth numbers from sources you'd never have imagined. If you know your potential interviewee's name, employer and area code, you've got a fighting chance.

Of course, some people guard their phone numbers more successfully than others. Some simply don't return phone calls. Others use the Web far more than they use the telephone. For these types of people, you may well want to set up interviews via e-mail. (Depending on your news organization's tolerance for long-distance phone calls, you may do this quite a bit.) While you lose a measure of warmth in using e-mail to arrange interviews, there's nothing inherently wrong with choosing to do so. Indeed, almost all of the interviews that appear in this book were arranged via e-mail. Be forewarned, however, that while some people will respond immediately to e-mail, many will not, and you'll have to follow up with a phone call anyway.

To an online journalist, e-mail may seem like the obvious way to go. Online journalists frequently cover high-tech topics, and potential interviewees within those subjects almost always use e-mail regularly and publish their addresses. Even outside the realm of high-tech, many companies list staff e-mail addresses on their Web sites. Beyond that, there are plenty of online sites that index e-mail addresses. It would seem like the easiest thing in the world to jump on the Web and find anyone's address.

Guess what? E-mail addresses can be just as difficult to find as phone numbers,

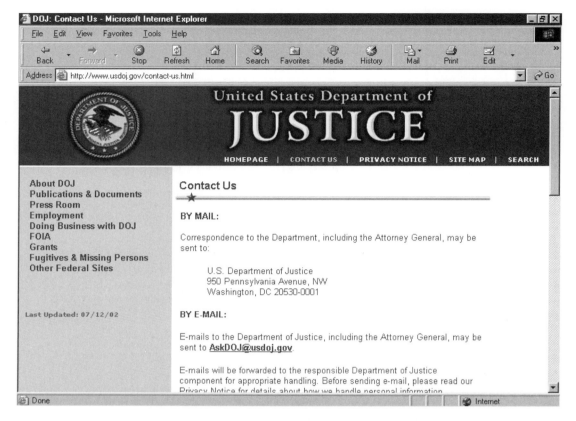

These days reporters can get lots of contact information about potential interviewees from organizations' official Web sites. Most, like the U.S. Department of Justice site, offer contact information for spokespersons and special areas with material for journalists.

SOURCE: usdoj.gov (accessed September 25, 2003).

and sometimes more so. While home phone numbers or direct office extensions can be tough to get, you can almost always get a central office phone number for a potential interviewee's company and leave a message. This may be unsatisfying, but it can get the job done. E-mail doesn't usually work that way—it's almost always directed to one specific person, and sometimes that person doesn't want everyone on the Web to know his address. This is particularly true of prominent people who fear being bombarded with an avalanche of messages from far and wide.

Furthermore, not all of society has quite caught up with this aspect of the information age. Few if any phone directories include e-mail addresses, and while some city, county, state and federal employee directories contain e-mails, most still don't. The Web contains hundreds of sites claiming to be able to locate any e-mail address, but people change addresses all the time, and as a result these sites fight an uphill battle. Even the ones that update their databases regularly will sometimes provide outdated addresses.

So what do you do if someone you'd like to interview isn't answering the phone and has successfully concealed his e-mail address? You have to engage in a little clever Web searching. This involves using the person's name and finding the domain name of the company or organization. This is a rather farfetched example, but let's say your state has just increased its tax on alcoholic beverages, and you want a reaction quote from the regional chapter of Beer Drinkers of America. The regional chair of the organization is a man named Joe Sixpack. You can't find a home or office phone number for him anywhere, but you did find the organization's home page at www.beerguzzle.org. It doesn't contain a list of e-mail addresses, but by learning the group's domain name, you now have the information you need to try to find Sixpack's e-mail address. Go to your favorite search engine and type in the following:

```
+"joe sixpack" +"beerguzzle.org"
```

Be sure to try this query both on the Web and on newsgroups, if necessary—your search engine will most likely offer the option of searching one or both of these areas. More often than not, this type of search will lead you to the address you're looking for. In some cases, it will turn out to be something that makes sense—like sixpack@beerguzzle.org—but just as often it will seem somewhat random, for example, jsix523@beerguzzle.org. Don't simply try to guess an e-mail address. You may be sending to a nonexistent address, which can cause your message to "bounce." This might not sound so bad, but sometimes your e-mail server will retry this process several times over a period of a few days before you're notified, which wastes quite a bit of your time. Additionally, you could end up sending your message to the wrong person, with uncertain consequences. (After all, who knows how many Sixpacks there are at beerguzzle.org?)

Once you've finally found a way to get in touch with your intended interviewee, you have to convince this person to talk to you. This is sometimes harder than it sounds, especially if you're dealing with someone who has been "burned" by critical coverage in the past. Toward this end, you can use a special advantage of online journalism. If you have a number of stories archived on your news outlet's Web site, select a few examples that show you as a fair-minded reporter and include the URLs of those stories in your message to the prospective interview subject. This gives you an opportunity to establish yourself as an individual separate from the rest of the crowd.

If it's at all possible, try to set up a face-to-face interview. Interviews almost always work better in person because it lets you see the person's facial expressions, gestures and mannerisms, which adds richness to the interview. It can also allow you to see where the interviewee works or lives, which can add even more depth. If an in-person interview isn't a viable option, a phone interview is a good second choice. If you're forced to arrange times and dates with a secretary or an assistant, be sure to stress that the conversation will be for the purposes of an interview, and tell them the subject of the interview. This avoids any misunderstandings. Although you may choose to arrange interviews using e-mail, you should only

INTERVIEWING VIA E-MAIL: A LAST RESORT

Being involved in an industry that revolves around computers and the Internet, online journalists use e-mail all the time. What might surprise you is that many of them do not actually perform interviews via e-mail. Many reporters consider e-mail an indispensable means for carrying on their jobs but a poor interviewing tool. Here are a few of their reasons:

- *You're stuck with a set list of questions.* Most reporters come into an interview with certain general topics in mind but not necessarily a hard-and-fast question list. The notion of having to sit down and write out a group of questions and submit them rubs reporters the wrong way for lots of reasons. It robs the conversation of any spontaneity, which is often the quality that gives interviewers the most detail.
- *There's no way to break the ice.* Even if you come up with good questions, there's no way to connect with the interviewee to establish a comfort level before the interview begins. This is often one of the best ways to get people to open up in an interview, but there's no effective way to replicate it through e-mail.
- *You give up control of the interview.* When interviewing someone in person or on the phone, you're the one asking the questions, deciding what the next ones will be, asking follow-ups and generally deciding the rhythm and direction of the interview. If someone avoids a question or gives a vague or unclear answer, you can ask them to clarify or be more specific. With e-mail, interviewees can answer questions entirely on their own terms. They can decide to re-order the questions to their liking, possibly changing the entire context of what is said. They can choose to be purposefully vague, give gobbledygook answers or simply ignore certain questions. Your only recourse is a follow-up e-mail, which may or may not result in a timely reply and may contain responses just as nebulous as the first one.
- *You're not absolutely certain who's responding.* Maybe it seems obvious that whoever is responding is who they say they are, but how do you know? It's not unheard of for busy people to have a secretary tend to e-mail. There's also the odd possibility that someone sat down at someone else's unattended computer and shot off a response to your questions. You're never as secure as when you see a face or hear a voice.
- *It makes quotes sound strange.* Even if an interviewee is answering your questions candidly and in detail, the responses will probably sound absurdly stiff and formal. Most people don't write the way they talk—often people who are articulate and engaging in conversation will sound very different in e-mail. They might sound like they're writing a term paper, or they might sound barely literate. Either way, you lose the warmth that comes with a person-to-person conversation.
- *You'll misquote them.* This can't be right, can it? You'd think that this would be a strength of e-mail—the interviewee's own words are right there in front of you. However, you'll be amazed at the atrocious grammar and spelling you'll find in e-mails from supposedly intelligent people (see Chapter 10). In the process of cleaning up a story for publication, spelling, capitalization and punctuation are often altered to make quotes grammatically correct. Sometimes copy editors also change misused words. If this sort of thing happens, interviewees have proof that you've changed their words—albeit only to make them look semiliterate—and they can raise a stink or even sue.
- *It's not very interactive.* This is richly ironic, but it's also the bottom line. While e-mail might allow for interactivity between writers and the audience, it's not the same as speaking personally with an interviewee. A good interviewer will listen to answers and respond to them with follow-up questions that likely were not imagined before the interview. The interview might take productive, yet completely unforeseen turns along the way as the reporter and interviewee respond to each other. This aspect of interviewing is vitally important, and it's completely lost in e-mail.

It should be noted that e-mail can be used productively for a couple of very precise tasks. If you need a specific fact or two (a birth date or hometown, for example) or to confirm given pieces of information or to ask one or two follow-up questions about specific items covered in a previous interview, e-mail can be useful. Otherwise, you should always aim for a personal conversation.

interview people via e-mail as a last resort, when they're unavailable through any other means or when you only need to ask one or two last-minute questions.

In some situations, e-mail interviews are a necessity because there are serious obstacles to doing in-person or phone interviews. When you can't reach someone any other way, e-mail is better than nothing. Interviewing someone halfway around the world eliminates face-to-face interviews as a practical matter, some organizations won't pay for lengthy long-distance phone interviews, and some reporters can't or won't perform an interview at 4 a.m. for a source's convenience. Also, in recent wars (Afghanistan in 2002, Iraq in 2003, for example) reporters have found it possible to interview both soldiers and civilians along the battle lines using e-mail when other means might not have been available. When e-mail is the only reasonable option, reporters should be conscious of possible cultural differences as well as understand the rules of e-mail conduct (see Online Standards in Chapter 14).

In the time immediately before you conduct an interview, there are several things you should do to prepare and make the most of the interview situation. Some of these should be done for any interview, while others depend on the method of the interview (in person, over the phone and so forth).

For any interview, go over the general notes you've prepared for the story itself, as well as any questions you've come up with along the way. If you've written out a bunch of general questions for interviewees, review your notes about this particular person and work up a set of specific items you'll ask about in this interview. This isn't necessarily a list of all the questions you want to ask—it's more of a guide to the most important topics, a list of things you shouldn't forget to ask about. Keep this list on hand during the interview and refer to it periodically. Even if you've informally put together a list beforehand, whether on paper or on your computer, it's a good idea to write it out by hand shortly before the interview. The physical act of writing it down helps fix the topics clearly in your mind.

Most online journalists use tape recorders or other means to record their interviews. Often these recordings will be used for online sound clips later. This doesn't mean you shouldn't take notes—in fact, taking notes is a good way to stay focused during the interview, and transcribing from notes goes much faster than from tape. These days, however, it's a good idea to record interviews even though you take notes or know you won't use sound clips from this interview. If there's ever a legal question about an interview you've done, a recording of the actual conversation can protect you and your news organization. In addition, if your notes are unclear or become lost, the tape is there as a backup.

Online reporters also need to think about multimedia elements—sound, video and other features—to take advantage of the capabilities of the medium. If you're going to use sound or video from this interview on a Web site, don't forget to make appropriate arrangements and test any equipment before the interview. (Some of the most common types of multimedia are discussed in Chapter 12.)

If you're doing a face-to-face interview at a workplace, a smart thing to do is to arrive early. This is especially true if you're going to record video for the interview as this will likely take a little time to set up. Regardless, take a little time before the interview to observe your surroundings. Anything you can learn about this business or agency will likely come in handy later, either during the interview or while writing the story. You may want to chat with a secretary or an assistant about how the place operates—sometimes these people become valuable sources.

THE CONVERSATION

Contrary to what you may have been told, stupid questions do exist. However, they're almost always the result either of a lack of preparation or of an intimidated reporter. If you go into an interview well prepared, there's no reason to be afraid. Well-informed people generally ask good questions, so you shouldn't worry. The key thing to remember is that once you know the subject, you're using that knowledge on behalf of your readers by applying it in your questions. If an interviewee scoffs at a question or two, let him scoff. You're just doing your job.

Whether in person or over the telephone (or through whatever electronic means you may eventually use), start by thanking interviewees for the chance to talk to them. This immediately conveys a little respect, and it's a brief and effective icebreaker. Since you're likely recording this interview for archival, audio or video uses, you should note right away that you are doing so, and note the purposes for which the recording will be used. If you're recording a phone conversation, you're legally required to notify the other party. In other circumstances it's also a good idea because it puts everything out in the open and establishes your integrity. This is particularly important for online journalists because many interview subjects will be a bit uncomfortable with the notion of their quotes being distributed on the Internet. People are often still spooked by this. The more you can let them know about how the interview will be used, the more comfortable they will be and the more freely they will speak.

If it's going to be a lengthy interview—15 minutes or longer—it's also a good idea to state up front the subjects you plan to cover. This isn't the same thing as revealing your questions—just say that the main subjects you'd like to discuss are these three or four things. People who are being interviewed like the idea of having some sense of what's coming, and even if you ask a critical question within one of the named areas later, they'll feel less threatened by it and likely will respond less defensively.

These actions seem designed with nothing but the interviewee's comfort in mind. However, by laying out all of this information before you actually begin asking questions, you're subtly taking control of the interview before it even starts. This is vitally important because interviews are like performances in many ways—every one has its own rhythms, moods and momentum. As the one asking the questions, you want to stay in charge of the process, and this is a very cordial and nonthreatening way to do it.

At this point, start recording or taking notes. If you need any quick facts—official job titles, length of time in this position and with the company, spelling of the name—ask about them first to get them out of the way. Asking them later may interrupt the flow of the conversation. Once these details are taken care of, you can begin the main substance of the interview. Remember to keep your list of the main topics to be covered handy.

The most vital element of good interviewing is *listening to what the interviewee is saying.* Maybe this is obvious beyond belief, but new reporters often get so tied up in the questions they're about to ask that they forget to pay close attention to the interviewee as he answers the current question. If you know the subject well, many of your best questions will come in response to an interviewee's answers. If you think of a great question while someone's in the middle of a response, and you're afraid you'll forget it, quickly jot a single word of the question in the margin of your notes. This is usually enough to recall the question later.

By paying full attention to the responses, you achieve many things beyond just getting the information you're asking about. You'll get ideas for new questions and also get a general impression of the interviewee. Does this person sound sincere? Does this person sound like he is trying to avoid a question or hide something? If the interview is face to face, is the interviewee looking you in the eye? Do his office, clothing or mannerisms convey something unique about this person? Or are there any nonverbal cues (squirming, avoiding eye contact, or other body language) that indicate there might be trouble here?

Above all, as the interview progresses, stay focused and follow your instincts. If you've prepared well and are paying attention to the responses, you'll have a good sense of the best question to ask next. You may not conduct the interview exactly like a colleague, but no two interviews (or interviewers) are alike. If a response makes you want to pursue a line of questioning not on your list, go for it. You can always get back to the list later, and oftentimes you'll discover a whole new approach to a story based on this new subject. If you think you may have wandered into unforeseen productive territory, don't be afraid to deviate from your original plan. Sometimes it will prove to be the mother lode of new and interesting information.

At the end of the interview, always be sure to ask the interviewee if there is anything else he would like to add. This sounds a note of fairness and helps tie up loose ends. When you're done, thank the interviewee again and see if there's a number you can call with any last-minute follow-up questions. This can be very important when you sit down to write the story.

TRANSCRIPTION, ACCURACY AND COMPLETENESS

As noted previously, the smart thing to do when interviewing for online stories is to record them but also to take notes. One way or the other, you'll want to start the process of transcription—typing the text of the interview into your computer—as soon as possible after the interview is over. The conversation has just taken place and is fresh in your mind, and you should remember most of what was said.

When you do this soon after the interview, you can usually work from written notes and transcribe the interview fairly quickly. If you find a spot in the

GOOD AND BAD QUESTIONS

Making a list of all-purpose good and bad questions is impossible. However, certain *types* of questions tend to work much better than others in certain situations for assorted reasons. Here are some examples where one type of questioning works and another doesn't:

GOOD QUESTION TYPES

Open-ended questions. This is a question that doesn't suggest the dimensions along which the question should be answered. As an example, you might ask the young president of a computer company, "When you were a kid, what did you imagine yourself doing in your mid-30s?" This is open-ended because you're not asking if he wanted to have a particular job or live in a particular faraway place. The interviewee can approach it from any of hundreds of angles. Questions like these yield very rich, personal answers and are often used early in interviews to set the tone and put the interviewee in a positive, thoughtful mood.

Neutral questions. If you don't really have an inkling of the answer, ask a question in a neutral, straightforward manner. If you ask the computer company CEO, "What prompted your interest in computers?", you aren't suggesting any particular ulterior motive or hidden agenda. This technique is also effective when posing more controversial questions. Simply asking, "Why did your company decide to lay off 100 workers?" is likely to produce a straightforward answer. Interviewees often expect a pugnacious approach to such issues and frequently give defensive answers to bullying questions. Forthrightness on your part will likely lead to straight answers. If it doesn't, you may need to get more specific and more critical.

BAD QUESTION TYPES

Yes/no questions. If you ask the same person, "Did you always want to be a computer baron?", he can simply say "No" and your question is answered. There's no challenge inherent within the question to make the interviewee think beyond the reflexive response. Obviously, there are cases where you'll need to ask yes/no questions, but they're usually limited to quick fact checking or other specific purposes late in an interview. When trying to get someone to open up, they should be avoided.

Leading questions. Many people seem to think that a smart reporter is someone who steers interviewees into saying things they don't mean or will regret, but this just isn't true. Framing questions in a one-sided way seldom gets you any closer to the truth. For instance, if you confront the computer baron with the question, "Why are you putting 100 people out of work when you're a multimillionaire?", he likely will object to the question itself and never answer it. Phrasing a question in this way carries the implicit assumption that you know the answer already.

interview where you're somewhat unclear on what was said, you can check the tape. If you remained focused on the interview while conducting it, you'll be amazed at the accuracy of the results. You might mistake a "the" for an "a" or transpose a word or two, but you'll almost certainly convey the substance of the interview using the interviewee's own phrases.

Why not simply use the tape in the name of letter-perfect accuracy? The answer is speed. If you're on deadline, the story must be written quickly, so the transcription must be done quickly. Transcribing from notes is a fairly steady process — you move through the notes and reconstruct what was said. Using the tape is a much slower and more laborious technique full of starts and stops. Most reporters can't type as fast as people talk, or at least with any degree of accuracy, so the process involves typing a sentence or two while the tape plays, then spooling it back

GOOD AND BAD QUESTIONS, *continued*

GOOD QUESTION TYPES

Specific questions. Start with general questions and then follow up with more specific ones in response to the interviewee's answers. You might ask, "What elements of the computer business appealed to you?" This suggests the dimensions of the answer—elements of the computer business—and follows logically from the question about his interest in computers. This is also where a more critical line of questioning might follow, as in, "In what ways has laying off 100 workers improved the company?" This question is more specific (and more critical) than its predecessor. Yet by following a line of reasoning from the previous question, it's a logical response rather than a leading question and will likely be treated as such by the interviewee. By making a critical question seem like the next logical step in the interview, you'll often avoid defensive responses and get better answers.

Wrap-up questions. Usually asked at the end of an interview, these questions provide an opportunity for the interviewee to add anything that may not have come up. By simply asking, "Do you have anything else you'd like to add?" or "Have I forgotten anything?", you'll sometimes get an entirely new and productive subject going. You can also use wrap-ups to summarize topics ("Let me make sure I understand this . . .") or to clarify something, as in "When you mentioned employees working in assembly, did you mean they assemble circuit boards, monitors or what?" Questions like these can help tie up loose ends and avoid call-backs when you're writing the story.

BAD QUESTION TYPES

Double-barreled questions. Rather than focusing the discussion, double-barreled questions confuse the issue. For example, consider the question, "Did firing these workers help you line your pockets and keep the stockholders off your back?" Aside from the fact that it's a yes/no question, it also asks two different things. The interviewee may be put off by the question or may well choose not to answer one part. Questions like these are better asked separately as two questions.

---

several seconds, then typing another sentence or two. At best, this means you'll have to hit the "rewind" button three or four times per minute, which slows the process considerably. At worst, you'll obsess over getting every nuance of every sentence correct, and take 90 minutes to transcribe a 15-minute interview. The difference in the results of using notes versus tape is generally negligible, so you should get used to taking notes and working from them. Besides, what if you happen upon a big story without your tape recorder on hand?

This might sound like accuracy should take a back seat to speed. In fact, this is not true. If you have any concerns about the accuracy of your notes or recollections, check the tape. If you don't have a tape and you're concerned about accuracy, don't be afraid to call the interviewee and review the subject in question. This is commonly done not only to verify quotes and other information but to ask any follow-up questions that have since occurred to you or weren't adequately answered earlier.

Transcription has become more important than ever in the online age because of another distinctive trait of the medium. These days many Web sites publish the full text of interviews because, unlike print outlets, they have no real space limitations. It's not uncommon for major interviews to be published in their entirety in "Q&A" format, not only because of space and user interest but also for protection in the event an interviewee claims to be misquoted.

Once you've finished transcribing, it generally helps to scan through the text and note sections you'll likely use. For some reporters, this involves breaking the text into sections with headings. Others simply highlight or boldface quotes they think will work. One way or another, you should note which sections you want to use because stories often involve multiple interviews and you might waste a lot of time later trying to find a particular section of an earlier interview. If you haven't already started outlining the story in which these quotes will appear, it's a good idea to do so while working with the text of the interview. This way you can plug references to particular sections right into your outline, or possibly copy and paste entire quotes into it.

While transcribing, note any unconfirmed facts in the conversation. Your final fact checking will come when you actually write the story, but this is a good time to note anything that looks suspicious. If the interviewee quotes someone else as making a particular statement, or cites facts and figures, or otherwise might not have direct knowledge of a subject for whatever reason, make a note to check it out.

This is also the point at which you should decide on choices for possible audio or video from the interview. While the conversation is still fresh, look through the text and see if you can pick out sections that might work online. Once you've identified these, you'll likely need to consult with your site's editor to agree on details of how this material might fit into the story package. Different sites handle these matters in different ways, but this is the stage at which you should address the multimedia question.

The key thing to remember about interviews and transcriptions is to keep them as organized as possible. Within your computer files, keep a separate directory or folder specifically for interview transcripts, and possibly a separate one for audio or video clips you've used. At the top of every interview transcript, include the name of the interviewee, the date and time of the interview, and whether it was done in person, over the phone or in any other way. Many reporters use special file-naming schemes for transcripts. If you interviewed county assessor Jack Sprat on October 15, you might call the transcript file "sprat1015.txt" or something similar. The main thing is to make it easy to find any interview later in case you need it for any reason.

SUMMARY

Students and young journalists are often nervous about interviewing. They fear looking silly in front of an important person or asking dumb questions. However, with adequate preparation, there's no reason a student can't ask good, well-informed questions just like anyone else. Lots of little techniques can help you get the most out of the interview, but the most important aspect is knowing what you're talking about.

RELATED WEB SITES

Washington Post
http://www.washingtonpost.com
University of Florida Department of Journalism
http://www.jou.ufl.edu

EXERCISES

1. Pair off with a classmate and interview each other with the aim of writing a profile. Learn as much as you can about your classmate in terms of background, interests, activities and goals. Use the techniques discussed in this chapter to make the story interesting. Since it's a classmate, you might take a less formal approach than with a public figure, discussing some of the scariest or silliest things you've done in your lives. Write a story of two double-spaced pages and turn in your interview notes along with it.

2. Make arrangements to interview the dean of your department or another school official. Learn about some of the issues facing this official by reading your school paper or talking with professors or staff who might be informed on current issues. Talk to the official's support staff to set aside time for the interview (no more than 10 or 15 minutes). Interview the official, then transcribe the interview and turn in a copy of the transcript along with a description of the work you did to prepare for and arrange the interview.

3. Search the Web and find the e-mail addresses of three important people in your community: city officials, corporate figures, media members or others. This may take some time and effort, but you need to end up with a list of three. Then send each one a message explaining that for a journalism course you're trying to find out how frequently public figures use e-mail and how often it's used by them to set up appointments, meetings, interviews and other scheduled events. Give them a week to respond, then choose one respondent (you may not hear back from all three) and arrange and conduct a brief interview about his use of e-mail and the Web in conducting job duties and keeping in touch with the world beyond those duties. Write a story on the subject and turn it in along with all your notes.

4. Your instructor will make a list of controversial issues and assign you to prepare to interview a particular individual on one side of the issue. Do some

research on the issue on InfoTrac College Edition or elsewhere to find out the arguments on both sides. Then make a list of 10 to 15 questions you would ask this person about the topic, addressing both his side of the issue and the opposing side. Try to be as specific as possible with your questions. When finished, turn in the lists of questions and any printed material gathered during your research.

||||||

PART II

Writing for Online Journalists

Now that you have learned how to gather information, Part 2 will help you learn to write effectively for the online market. This entails learning both traditional writing techniques and new approaches to journalistic writing.

6 Online Writing Styles

Before getting into the nuts and bolts of writing online, this chapter looks at some of the different styles of writing that have emerged on the Web. In particular, the irreverent style employed at many early online magazines is examined along with a discussion of how this style has developed in the ensuing years. You will also learn how to balance this style with the traditional writing skills needed for straight-ahead reporting.

7 Hooking and Keeping Readers

How do you grab a reader in an age when it's so easy to zoom from one page to the next? That's the central focus of this chapter, which looks at both traditional and new techniques and at types of leads and story structures. This chapter also stresses the importance of organizing facts in ways beneficial to online readers.

8 Revving Up Your Writing

Writing flat and uninteresting prose is unacceptable in traditional journalism, and it's absolute death in a medium where people can go somewhere else with the click of a mouse. This chapter focuses on the elements of storytelling that work best on the Web and on the ways in which traditional writing skills can be fine-tuned to produce better results online.

9 The Last Minute(s)

In a medium where stories are updated immediately and constantly, there is an entirely different notion of deadlines from those at traditional media outlets. This chapter looks at how these qualities make the job of an online journalist much different from that of a traditional journalist. It also points out both the attractions and the pitfalls of these characteristics.

6

||||||

Online Writing Styles

Not everyone online writes in the same way, but most writing for online outlets takes advantage of some of the characteristics that set the medium apart from others. This chapter looks at those characteristics and at different styles and techniques of writing that have emerged from them. In particular, it examines a new style adopted by many Web news outlets—a more irreverent, confrontational and freewheeling way of writing sometimes called "Way New Journalism." An in-depth report From the Field provides the point of view of one reporter who has employed both traditional and "Way New" styles.

When federal judge Thomas Penfield Jackson ruled in November 1999 that Microsoft Corporation held a monopoly in computer operating systems, it was front-page news worldwide. News outlets of every stripe analyzed the possible fallout of the ruling, but as might be expected, it was an even hotter topic in online news. Both traditional and online news outlets covered the ruling in depth, but the difference in the tone and style of coverage between old and new media was readily apparent.

For example, here is the beginning of the lead story from the *New York Times'* newspaper coverage of the ruling:

WASHINGTON— The judge in the government's antitrust trial against the Micro-soft Corporation issued a broad denunciation of the software giant Friday evening as the first part of his verdict in the landmark case.

> *The judge, Thomas Penfield Jackson of Federal District Court, said the company had used its monopoly power to stifle innovation, reduce competition and hurt consumers.*
>
> *"Most harmful of all is the message that Microsoft's actions have conveyed to every enterprise with the potential to innovate in the computer industry," Judge Jackson wrote in his 207-page findings of fact.*

This is standard, straightforward, no-nonsense reporting. Depending on your point of view, it might be solid and informative or stuffy and uninteresting. Compare this to the coverage of *Feed* magazine, a Web-only news publication:

> *MICROSOFT LOST. The Redmond software giant spent the weekend trotting out sports metaphors about "early innings" and "12 round fights" trying to spin Judge Thomas Penfield Jackson's finding of fact, but it's hard to spin a sentence like "The ultimate result is that some innovations that would truly benefit consumers never occur for the sole reason that they do not coincide with Microsoft's self-interest."*
>
> *Judge Jackson's finding of fact does not settle the case—there will be more, much more, before it is finished—but the most important battle is already over. Microsoft may not have lost its court case (nor its many potential appeals if it does), but after Friday's finding of fact, Microsoft has lost its aura of inevitability.*

Clearly, this coverage also contains useful information, but it has a somewhat less formal, more commentary-driven feel. Obviously, *Feed* isn't the *New York Times,* and it doesn't claim to be. But while lots of local news outlets still simply put their print content online, many online-only journals take this more freewheeling, less "just the facts" approach.

In fact, even the online sites of some traditional news outlets have begun to adopt a less formal style. For instance, *TIME Daily,* the daily online outlet of *TIME* magazine, covered the same story in perhaps an even more irreverent style. Here's how its story began under the headline, "OK, But Will He Make Microsoft Have Babies?":

> *Like so much else in the Microsoft antitrust case, Judge Thomas Penfield Jackson's findings of fact both stated what many suspected and left crucial details until later.*
>
> *The findings: Microsoft is indeed a monopoly, possessing a stranglehold over the PC desktop. It has abused the power, and that abuse has harmed consumers. The findings so closely paralleled the government line that you might have thought they were actually written by lead DOJ attorney Joel Klein. But that just shows Judge Jackson was paying attention, says TIME's Chris Taylor: "He's shown in this ruling a real grasp of the technology, and that he really understands the government's case."*
>
> *But we're not out of court just yet: While all this seems to clearly spell out a-n-t-i-t-r-u-s-t, a decision as to what to do about it is still a few months off.*

Why would *TIME,* the venerable old newsweekly, represent itself online with such a saucy piece of writing about such a serious trial? And why would this irreverent style emerge in online journalism and not elsewhere? These are the questions addressed in this chapter.

WHY A DIFFERENT STYLE ONLINE?

The online medium differs in a number of important ways from other news media, and these differences have a lot to do with the development of the style of writing unique to online news. However, the medium's history is just as important as its distinguishing characteristics.

For most people, the earliest form of online communication was e-mail. People have been using e-mail since the 1970s, though its popularity didn't really accelerate until the 1990s. Now you can send encoded files, images and formatted text through e-mail, but the majority of its use is simply to send text messages back and forth. Being limited to straight text presented problems for users since it was difficult to get across any nuances in what you were saying. This gave rise to assorted devices used to stress certain points—to show that you *really* meant something, or that you REALLY meant something. Later, when chat rooms and other discussion areas became popular in the 1980s, stating things in an over-the-top manner became part of the accepted way of communicating online.

As recently as the early 1990s, online journalism was very different than it is today. In fact, one might argue that it actually consisted of two different types of news. The first was the so-called professional product, produced by assorted news organizations and available through online services. The content of these was generally the text of some of the day's news stories, perhaps with a few modest graphics. The second type of news was produced by a much less organized array of individuals and distributed via e-mail over the text-based Internet and through earlier precursors to the Web.

Newspapers first attempted to bring their content into readers' homes electronically in the early 1980s. Since most homes did not yet have computers, some of the earliest versions of this were done with a user's TV set. A system called Videotex delivered news content to subscribing households through phone lines and into the television. A control unit allowed users to sit in their chairs and scroll through text on the screen. Many major newspapers and publishers, including the *New York Times* and Time, Inc., jumped on board and spent millions of dollars developing the technology. However, it never really caught on with consumers, mainly because it was expensive, cumbersome and slow, and only delivered news excerpts rather than full coverage.

As computers gained wider usage, news organizations went online to broaden their horizons. Many started their own bulletin board services; later, some entered agreements with online services such as America Online, CompuServe and Prodigy to distribute their content. In each case, however, a combination of underdeveloped technology and the great expense involved in creating it caused these efforts to fail. It is only in the past few years that print news outlets have gotten on the Internet, designed more sophisticated sites and attracted significant readership.

At the same time that all this was happening, a new notion of news was emerging online—one that fused online chat with the informative function of news. Beginning in the mid-1980s, online discussion groups and communities gave rise to the notion of spreading news among an online group rather than waiting for

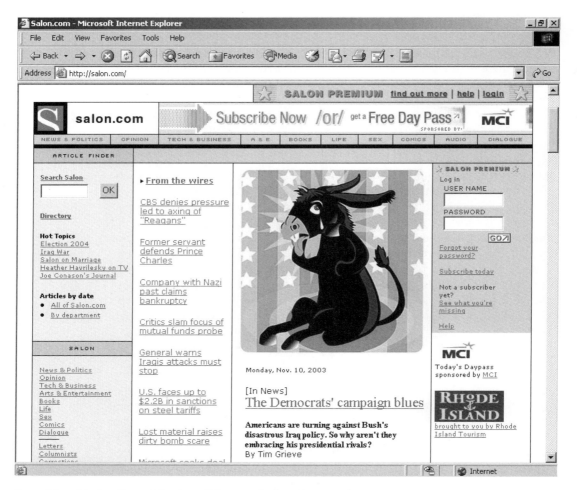

One of the oldest online publications, Salon.com looks at issues and provides viewpoints from commentators using a wide variety of styles.

SOURCE: salon.com (accessed November 10, 2003). Used by permission.

information to come down from on high. Often big events would be debated on-line among small groups of interested individuals. The dialogue in these discussions was much less formal and rigid than traditional news, and much more irreverent, humorous and opinionated. The level of discussion was largely intelligent, but participants couldn't take themselves too seriously.

The most oft-cited hotbed for this sort of activity was the WELL (the Whole Earth 'Lectronic Link), which began in the spring of 1985. A 1995 article in *Wired* called it "a salon of creative, thoughtful, and articulate participants who are interested in one another's stories in a self-absorbed, cabalistic way." The WELL gained a reputation over the years as something of an online Algonquin Round Table, drawing onlookers as well as contributors. Many people who went on to become major influences in online news frequently participated in WELL discussions in the '80s and early '90s, which influenced their later work.

Within these discussions, the traditional media were often the object of scorn, not just because of their perceived stodginess but because of their seeming lack of ability to connect with large segments of the population. This split between old and new media was reinforced when some of these people began writing on the Web—online writers took great glee in departing from traditional writing styles and thumbing their noses at the old guard. This helped set the tone for discussion within online journals and related publications.

Online magazines—often simply referred to as "zines"—such as *Feed, Slate* and *Salon* began to mock traditional journalists while still adhering to traditional reporting values. Brock Meeks' *CyberWire Dispatch* broke stories online before many traditional publications and won several journalism awards. And *Wired* magazine, launched in early 1993, was the first major print publication to tap into this online culture, presenting writings from WELL veterans and others with the confrontational tone that had become common in online journalism.

CHARACTERISTICS OF ONLINE NEWS

In addition to the online culture that helped create a new writing style, the actual physical traits of the medium helped determine the ways that news would work best online. Anyone who has spent hours staring at a computer screen knows that reading information on that screen is very different from reading a newspaper or magazine or watching TV news. Like any other medium, online news has its strengths and weaknesses, and all of them influence the way users actually read and perceive the news. This, in turn, means that these qualities should influence the way you write for the medium.

Online news is hampered by several traits of its physical delivery system, the computer. In some ways, the computer fails to offer the best aspects of either newspapers or TV news. Here are a few notable weaknesses:

- The sheer size of a newspaper—the fact that you can unfold it over an entire desktop—provides an easily scanned array of stories for the reader. You can hunt around for a story with a headline, subject or photo that looks appealing, all within a well-structured, easily understood format. By contrast, a computer screen is much more limited in size and cannot offer the sheer quantity of information found on a newspaper page.

- TV news offers a constant flow of appealing video images, both live and on tape, whereas online news can offer only limited video of much lesser quality.

- Research has shown that computer users tend to become uncomfortable when reading lengthy blocks of text online. Novice users have also been shown to become lost when navigating through news sites, making them frustrated and unlikely to visit a site again.

- On top of everything else, the computer screen contains small text on a backlit screen, so it essentially combines the main sources of eye strain of both TV and newspapers.

Time Inc.

||||||| **FROM THE FIELD**

Josh Quittner
Editor, *Business 2.0* magazine
Former Technology columnist, *Time* magazine
Former News Director, Time Inc. New Media

Josh Quittner didn't set out to define a whole new journalistic para-digm. He was just writing a story.

"I got here (*Time*) at the end of 1994," he says. "I had been a print journalist working at newspapers up to that point. I had done a certain amount of work for *Wired* magazine. Around the time I got here, I was asked to write an es-say for HotWired, *Wired*'s online site. They said, 'Why don't you write an essay for us telling us how the medium will change journalism?' So I wrote something that I called, archly, 'The Birth of Way-New Journalism,' which was sort of an homage to Tom Wolfe's seminal essay on 'The Birth of the New Journalism.' And it was done all in hypertext and was a huge amount of fun."

Quittner was familiar with the in-your-face writing style that had already developed on the pre-Web Internet. "Anyone who spends time anywhere online tends to pick up that style of writing," he says, "simply because it works. Being 'over-expressive,' I guess—stating un-equivocally how you feel by using CAPS and over-the-top expressions—works in an all ASCII environment like a BBS or chat room."

He was familiar with the style from his visits to the WELL. "It was the first thing I did when I got a job as info-tech reporter at *Newsday* in 1990," Quittner says. "I was not, how-ever, a big poster. I enjoyed lurking and getting story ideas from that place since in those days, all the interesting people hung out there. The whole *Wired* crowd was on the WELL—they had a conference there, and I believe reporters were encouraged to fuel discussion. It was kind of like a virtual saloon—a place where journalists hung out."

The style was much more opinion driven than standard journalistic coverage, which took some getting used to. "It's absolutely the opposite, in some respects, of everything I learned at newspapers," says Quittner. "Newspapers, first of all, aren't opinionated—you try to take yourself out of the story as much as possible. You try to stick to the facts, the verifiable facts, and don't interpret any more than is necessary for coherence. This was a very different method. And part of the problem when you try to do this is just finding the right people. You need wicked smart people, who not only can analyze things and are subject matter experts, but who aren't afraid to have opinions."

Of course, the medium has at least as many strengths as weaknesses. Here is a quick recap of some of the strengths of online news:

- You can use links to offer users a chance to read more about a subject.
- You can update stories instantly and regularly.
- The lack of space limitations allows great depth in reporting.

Quittner's freelance work for *Wired* got the attention of the folks at *Time*. "They were increasing their tech coverage, and they hired me to write about **cyberspace,**" he says. "I got myself so excited about the prospects of the online world, that even after I got to *Time,* I kept thinking about all the possibilities of the new medium that was just in its infancy. So after about nine months of working as a staff writer at *Time* magazine, I was getting very restless because it seemed like a huge amount of stuff was happening online, and I didn't want to miss it."

He considered leaving *Time* to create a special site for *HotWired*. "I thought the smartest thing that one could probably do at that point with limited resources," Quittner says, "was do a daily tech site covering technical news, news of the digital frontier. And of course that played right to their strengths and that was exactly what they were looking at as well. I called this thing 'The Netly News.' They wanted me to do it for them, and I was set to go. But Walter Isaacson, who was then the editor of New Media at *Time* and was the person who recruited me here in the first place, got wind of it and said, 'Why are you going to do it for them? Why don't you just do it for us?'"

Quittner stayed and began working on his experimental site, along with Noah Robischon, then a student in a class Quittner taught at Columbia University. In November 1995, the site went online, but it was hardly a high-profile addition to the Time Warner media galaxy.

"It was really just me and Noah," says Quittner, "but people thought that we were at a big place and therefore had huge amounts of resources, and so some people tended to be resentful of us. People thought that since we were working at Time Warner, we had 150 people at our disposal, when in fact it was a shoestring operation."

In spite of this, Quittner remembers Netly News very fondly. "Noah and I took turns writing a daily story," he says. "It was hugely fun. There were a huge amount of things we could report on—developments in the early days of the Web, as things were going online. Sometimes we wrote about Web sites. We spent a lot of time still writing about Usenet culture. Another student of mine named Chris Stamper virtually lived in Usenet, and used to get wild wonderful stories out of Usenet newsgroups. It was just so much fun to cover. And every time you would write about some new community, you'd get swamped with mail from that community, and get really nice dialogues. It was lovely. It was what I remembered journalism was like when I started working as a police reporter at the *Albuquerque Journal* back in the 1980s."

Quittner is now at the top of *Time*'s new media ladder and believes that the fullest use of the "Way New" style, incorporating interesting presentation and structural aspects as well as snappy writing, is still to come.

"Really, the kind of stuff I have in mind won't happen until we all have broadband connections," Quittner says. "It's too frustrating for a reader/user to get experimental news feeds via modem connections, which is why plain, old fashioned utility news, like CNN and Yahoo's news pages, is so popular."

- You can add audio, video and other online-specific content to stories.
- You can keep online archives of stories.

With these factors in mind, it might seem simple enough to produce a publication that maximizes the strengths and limits the weaknesses of the medium. It's not that simple, however, because different people use the medium in different ways.

For example, the average reader of *Wired News* online probably has little in common with the average reader of the *Kansas City Star* online. Each of these readers comes to the site for a different reason and expects different content, both in terms of stories and in features of the site. Writers and editors online must not only know how to best utilize the strengths of the medium but also must know their audience and how best to serve it.

The online reporter considers many factors when putting a story together. First of all, unlike print or TV, stories have no set news hole or time within a newscast to fill. This offers the promise of being able to tell the story fully, with no compromises based on trying to shoehorn it into a given spot. This sounds like a reporter's dream—no more arguing with editors over the importance of cutting one paragraph over another when they both need to be there.

The reality, however, is a little different. More often than not, in the online world editors still assign a rough length to stories. TV news stories are measured in minutes and seconds, and print stories are measured in column inches, but online stories are often assigned in terms of number of words. This can vary depending on the type of outlet—a reporter working for the online side of a print outlet may still get assignments in inches in case the story also runs in the print version. Some editors will grant the latitude of writing a story to an appropriate length according to a reporter's own news judgment, but this is generally confined to trusted veteran reporters. Editors often fear the "bottomless pit" syndrome, where a reporter gets carried away and writes at far too great a length to be read comfortably online.

The notion of what a reader finds comfortable to read online is an area where styles differ dramatically from one site to another. The average news story is too long to fit on one screen, at least at any readable type size. Because of this, many sites break up lengthy stories into several Web pages, so a reader doesn't have to read from one long page that must be scrolled through. Stories organized in this way usually contain links at the bottom indicating how many pages the story runs, with links reading "Page 2 of 4" or "Page 2 3 4" with each number serving as a link to that page of the story. Other sites simply place one story on one page, regardless of length. (See Chapter 13 for more on these strategies.)

In addition, reporters can't spend too much time crafting stories into works of literature because deadlines are very different in the online world. One of the great advantages of online news is the ability to update instantly, and particularly with breaking news, editors want their reporters to get stories done as quickly as possible so that the latest information can be posted immediately. This creates more of a **rolling deadline**—the notion that unless otherwise specified you need to write everything as soon as possible.

Just about every online news site uses **links** on story pages. These can appear within stories themselves, where the name of a company can be clicked on to travel to its site, or listed separately at the end of the story or in the margins. While they're writing, reporters need to be conscious of this factor and incorporate it into their writing. Some writers specifically aim to take advantage of this and use links as either footnotes for their work or suggestions as to where a reader should go to find information on a given topic.

Online reporters must also think of other online-only elements that might help their stories. How can a given story be enhanced through audio, video, background information, perhaps interactive charts or maps, searchable databases, maybe even discussion forums, quick public opinion polls and the like? Many people in the online journalism business would argue that anything that adds a nonlinear or interactive element to a story adds a new layer of storytelling. For example, interactive news polls and quizzes convey quick bites of information in a nonlinear fashion and sometimes provide links to more detailed information on the answer pages. Nonlinear photo essays and galleries, with detailed captions and links, can also provide an entirely new means of storytelling. Galleries with this rich content have become very popular in recent years, particularly in the wake of the September 11, 2001 terrorist attacks.

"WAY NEW JOURNALISM"

Quittner's 1995 article titled "The Birth of Way New Journalism" inspired a wave of literary journalism (and has been required reading for most college journalists ever since). In it Quittner discussed the traditional notion of how journalists survived—by working for large media companies that made lots of money from their ownership of the means of production and distribution of media content. The Web, he argued, removed the costs involved in these processes, allowing anyone the freedom to publish without these economic constraints:

> *Right now writers need Big Media because Big Media owns the means of distribution. But as soon as a standard for exchanging trivial sums of money is adopted on the Net, it will turn the tables on that equation, and Big Media will need writers. It becomes cheap to be a mass-market publisher, right? So if the financial terms of the relationship are unsatisfying, writers can publish their own Web sites, presumably taking readers with them. The news gatherers/storytellers with marketable points of view can dictate the terms for publishing their spin on the world.*
>
> *But the change I'm talking about has nothing to do with making money. Indeed, the change I'm talking about is much bigger than money. I'm talking about a sea change in journalism itself, in the way we do the work of reporting and presenting information. The change that's coming will be more significant than anything we've seen since the birth of New Journalism; it may be even more revolutionary than that.*

Quittner's article argued that while Wolfe helped redefine the traditional notion of reportage, the array of tools available for online journalists should redefine the acts of writing, presenting and reading news even more. "Imagine what those new journalists could have done with video and sound, with hypertext links and limitless bandwidth," Quittner wrote. He envisioned "a journalism that uses the best devices of the novel—and the movie! and the radio! and the CD-ROM! and networked communications!—to tell stories."

Many online writers had already begun to take advantage of these tools when Quittner's piece was written, and more followed in its wake. Independent news and commentary sites sprung up daily on the Web, and as in the world of

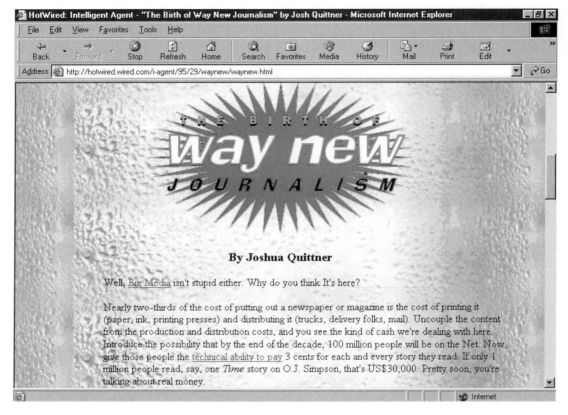

Josh Quittner's "The Birth of Way New Journalism" was an early call to online writers and editors to establish their own unique style.

SOURCE: hotwired.wired.com (accessed August 22, 1999). Used by permission.

traditional media, those who were able to produce relevant content consistently over time often found readership. Many online publications—*Salon, Feed, Smoking Gun, Suck,* and lots of others—persevered for years with little financial benefit, yet built solid bases of readers, which eventually paid off as advertisers began to embrace the Web.

The style that emerged had less to do with traditional, straight-ahead storytelling than with grabbing readers and shaking them to attention. Often the style had more in common with opinion columns than with standard front-page reporting—it would be witty, irreverent and challenge the reader rather than simply stating facts. Writers weren't shy about expressing their opinions, but the best writers still backed up those opinions with solid reporting and well-documented facts. The result was a more direct, less formal style that appealed to many thousands of online readers all over the world.

Ken Layne has done a little bit of everything in journalism. He's been a beat

Tabloid.net entertained readers with an irreverent style yet also informed them with some excellent reporting.

SOURCE: tabloid.net (accessed January 14, 1998). Used by permission.

reporter for local newspapers, edited a magazine, worked for a wire service, and served as a foreign correspondent in cities such as Prague, Budapest, and Slovakia. He's worked in print, broadcast and online. By the accounts of journalists who know him and his work, he's a respected and principled reporter.

When he's written for mainstream media, Layne has acquitted himself admirably, particularly for his knowledge of foreign affairs. Here's an example of a lead he wrote for a typical story in 1999 while working for United Press International:

> *WASHINGTON, April 26— The world's richest countries must give financial help to Balkan nations suffering economically from the war in Yugoslavia, leaders of the G-7 announced today.*
>
> *U.S. Treasury Secretary Robert Rubin, speaking after a daylong G-7 summit, named the Balkan crisis as one of the pressing financial problems in a global economy in its second year of sluggish performance.*

|||||| **FROM THE FIELD**

Ken Layne
Co-founder, *Tabloid*
Writer, *Online Journalism Review*

"We patterned *Tabloid* after the old metro tabloid newspapers that be-gan falling off the face of the Earth after TV," says Ken Layne. It fea-tured brassy headlines and stories that looked at serious issues from an irreverent perspective—aiming custard pies when appropriate, hold-ing feet to the fire when necessary, but always backing it up with solid facts. This provided an alternative to the mainstream media, which Layne believed had grown stupefyingly dull.

"The idea was, you are writing this for the reader," says Layne. "You're not writing this to get an award. You're not writing this to show how much you know about the county water system, or this developer or this issue, or to bring in a reader from a certain ethnic or socio-economic group. You're writing this for the general reader, so write it well! Make it sing, make it sound good. You don't need to distort anything, but you certainly don't need to hide the thing that makes it news."

Though *Tabloid* ceased daily publication in mid-1999, Layne continues to write in a simi-lar vein for the *Online Journalism Review* and other publications. He believes passionately in this writing style and sees it as a return to a more interesting form of journalism. "If you talked about online journalism being a little more confrontational and direct and personal as com-pared to newspapers," Layne says, "go pull up Jimmy Breslin's column in *Newsday* and throw it up against some seemingly outrageous thing I've written, and there's really no difference in tone. We used to have newspaper columnists who did this kind of writing every day—Mike Royko, Herb Caen, people like that. The corporations that own mainstream media outlets don't like these people. And as they've retired or died, they haven't been replaced. A lot of former newspaper people like myself have found that by going online, we can still practice the kind of newspapering that got us into this originally."

In spite of this, Layne believes there's very little difference in his actual approach to stories—in the act of gathering information—whether covering them for traditional or online media. He cites his years covering Washington, D.C. for United Press International as an example. "If I was covering a Federal Reserve press conference," he says, "or a congressional press con-ference or a Senate hearing on cyber-terrorism or whatever, I didn't put myself into a differ-ent mode or anything. You show up to cover something and you basically use the tools that

When writing for the Web, however, Layne often employs a dramatically dif-ferent writing style. Here's the beginning of a 1998 column Layne wrote in re-sponse to Linda Tripp's famous declaration, "I am you."

God knows I've heard some weird things during my 14 years in newsrooms, but Wednesday's speech by ubersnitch Linda Tripp may just be the most absurd, obscene jabbering yet to reach my ears.

you have—your eyes, and your ears, and what stands out and what you remember, and what sort of research you've done."

Layne says that the only real difference in approach comes when actually writing the story. "When you get to the keyboard, you write depending on what's needed," he says. "For straight news stuff, you just kind of act as a fly on the wall. You don't hammer people over the head with any absurdities—if there are any to report, you make them a little more subtle. You also take out the 'I' in standard journalism—you sort of remove yourself from the story. This is for straight news coverage—you let a little more of yourself into a column, and you let a lot of yourself into a first-person column. For *Tabloid,* we'd let a lot of ourselves in."

Layne chose a story covered by *Tabloid* in 1998 to provide an example of how he might write a story differently for different outlets. "Say I was covering the Asian financial crisis of a couple of years ago for a wire service," he says. "I would probably cover it from the market perspective, and I would probably get some quotes. If I felt it was a disaster happening, I would make sure to get that into the story. But rather than have Ken Layne saying, 'This looks like a disaster,' you go around and find some people who will say that. You're not writing Ken Layne's opinion of it, you're trying to get the market's opinion of it. Then I would find some people with different views, opposing views, who say, 'Nah, we're doing great.' You have to make sure the story has some balance.

"If I was writing for the *Economist* or the *Far Eastern Economic Review,* or something that mixes a little more irony and personality into its news—which I think is terrific—then you would be a little more telling. You might make some little jabs at people who were cracking under the pressure. You might find a neat little thing that was happening that serves as an analogy that would bring the reader in."

Covering the story for *Tabloid,* however, required a more absurd—though completely factual—take on the events. "We went to Thailand," Layne says, "where the Prime Minister's wife was doing this voodoo ceremony, cutting off chicken heads to save her husband's government and the entire economic system of the country. We wrote that story and ran it under the headline 'Black Magic Woman.' There were probably a lot of people who read that story who had never read a story about the economy of Thailand before, who didn't know that the Baht was the currency or anything else, and who got a kick out of it and learned a bunch."

From these examples, one might assume that Layne believes young reporters should simply start looking for weird stories and writing them up. This isn't the case, however. "If you are going to report news," says Layne, "you need to know the basics. You quote people accurately, you get your facts straight—we all screw up, but make a diligent effort to get your facts straight. Spend a couple of weeks reading E. B. White and the *AP Stylebook,* and the *Chicago Manual.* Learn how to write, and learn how to accurately say what you're trying to say."

You're me, Linda? Not a chance, sweetheart.
First of all, I look a helluva lot better in a dress than you do. Beyond that, I'm not a creepy voyeur who has spent the last decade trying to dig up dirt on the president.

Clearly, this is vastly different—it minces no words in expressing Layne's opinions. The latter column was written for *Tabloid,* an online publication co-founded by Layne, which was published daily for two years on the Web. The site provided readers with solid, fact-based reporting, yet its writing style was typical of the "Way New" approach—its articles were unabashedly opinionated, written in a no-holds-barred, in-your-face tone that was alternately shocking, thought-provoking, outrageous and hilarious.

Many traditional media outlets worldwide praised *Tabloid* for its honesty and informative reporting, unlike some similar sites such as the oft-scorned *Drudge Report*. The roster of publications that praised *Tabloid* is impressive and diverse, including *Time, USA Today, Editor and Publisher,* the *Los Angeles Times,* the *Christian Science Monitor,* and news outlets as far-flung as London, Tel Aviv and Sydney.

Not every online news site encourages this style, however, and many online editions of traditional news outlets have yet to jump on the "Way New" bandwagon. Young journalists entering the field should recognize this and act accordingly—while you can always push for change at your outlet, you shouldn't count on it. You should also note that although the style is everywhere, it's not always implemented well. There are many thousands of sites that are simply used as the sounding board for an individual's opinion, with no real concern for accuracy or verification of information. The best online writers, however, uphold journalistic standards regardless of their writing styles.

SUMMARY

Most online news still bears a strong resemblance to traditional print news, with a few bells and whistles sprinkled in to add a little spice. However, it seems clear that online news has begun to develop a voice and a style of its own, based largely on its characteristics as a medium. As with anything new, there are critics of the style and abuses of it, particularly because it's easy to go to ridiculous extremes with anything that allows unfettered creativity. Any fool can cop an attitude, but the best writing in the "Way New" style often contains solid, factual reporting behind the humor and irreverence. As the online medium grows and becomes more of a mainstream source for news, it's likely that we'll see a convergence of professionalism and wit, resulting in a great deal of innovative, fresh material.

RELATED WEB SITES

"The Birth of Way New Journalism," by Josh Quittner
http://hotwired.lycos.com/i-agent/95/29/waynew/waynew.html

The Epic Saga of The WELL, by Katie Hafner
http://www.wired.com/wired/archive/5.05/ff_well.html

Online Journalism Review
http://ojr.usc.edu

Microsoft
http://www.microsoft.com

EXERCISES

1. Search the Web for news sites that use the "Way New" style. Some of the more popular sites of this type have been mentioned in this chapter, but you can search for others. Find a story written in this style, then locate a story on the same subject in print or "traditional" online media and write a one-page essay on the differences between the two. Does the "Way New" piece feature solid, factual reporting or not? Are there other important differences?

2. Choose a story you find interesting from the print edition of your local newspaper. Photocopy the story (or cut it out of the paper), then list three or more ways you would change the story to make it work better online. If you want to rewrite a paragraph, that's fine, but also think about suggestions for photos, multimedia, links or anything else common to the medium. Turn in your suggestions along with your copy of the original article.

3. Your instructor will select a current news topic. First, write the first two paragraphs of a story about the topic in traditional inverted-pyramid style; when you've finished, write the beginning of another story about the same topic in the "Way New" style. Remember that the style doesn't just rely on humor or attitude but also on taking a completely different angle on a story. Why is this story unusual, and how can you make light of that aspect of the story? Is there some way you can take a completely different approach that might appeal to Web audiences?

7

|||||||

Hooking and
Keeping Readers

Grabbing readers with an interesting and informative lead has always been important, but never more so than in the online age. This chapter looks at both traditional and new techniques and types of leads, and then at how the nature of online journalism forces writers to be versatile and inventive in their leads. The chapter also discusses the importance of headlines and link text in online journalism.

Getting noticed online is not easy. Simply convincing a reader to look your direction instead of at the thousands upon thousands of other choices is a difficult enough task. Online writers must not only grab readers' attention with a compelling lead but also make them stay put through subsequent screens' worth of details. Online readers are notoriously fickle, but as with any audience, good writing keeps them interested enough to follow a story to its conclusion.

SO WHAT?

"So what?" is the main question you must ask yourself when writing any lead, whether for online or traditional media. A news reader can easily opt to ignore anything that doesn't look interesting, and this is especially true on the Web. Web readers aren't shy about abandoning any page that bores them or is otherwise unappealing.

Fox News has attracted television viewers with bold graphics. Its on-line outlet carries on this style.

As in traditional news media, the **lead** (the first paragraph) and the nut graph (the second paragraph, which fills in important details beyond those in the lead) must quickly convey aspects of the story that are both informative and compelling. What facts about the story are most interesting, useful or unusual? What would grab a reader's attention—particularly that of someone in your publication's target audience?

The traditional hard-news approach to writing leads is to boil everything down to the elements that are most often central to the story—the who, what, when and where of the story, often in that order. Leads that summarize these elements are called **summary leads.** The result of summarizing a story's central elements is a good hard-news lead—one that gets across the most relevant hard-news information quickly and efficiently. It's a good place to start in online writing.

This technique of writing stories, where facts are arranged in descending order from most to least important, is called the **inverted pyramid,** and it is a good

THE SIX BASIC QUESTIONS REVISITED

If you've taken a journalism class, you're familiar with the **six basic questions** of journalism—the five Ws and one H. They're familiar to many students, and they're practically programmed into the genetic code of professional journalists. But what do they mean in the online world? When your potential audience is the entire planet, and the subject matter can include almost anything, these simple questions suddenly become more complicated.

WHO?

Traditionally, the "who" has been easy to establish. This is the person at the center of the story—the victim, the suspect, the public official, the protagonist. However, it's often more complicated than this online. First, the "who" of a story can easily be a company or other corporate entity—much Web news deals with high-tech companies and their machinations. Also many loosely formed groups make news online, from hackers to crackers to virus attackers. On top of this, the anonymity afforded by the Web creates some strange examples of "who." For instance, an individual known only as phrink@webblast.com might be the subject of your next story. You wouldn't know gender, age, hometown or any

of a dozen other facts that a reporter can normally take for granted.

WHAT?

Again, "what" is traditionally not hard to figure out—what happened? But for a variety of reasons, "events" that occur online are sometimes difficult to describe quickly. Some of the biggest stories in the online world are about events that *didn't* happen—such as any number of computer virus scares, unfounded rumors and the infamous Y2K bug. At other times, a story is simply tough to fathom without detailed explanation. For example, let's say that you've learned that the largest local Internet service provider in your area has purged all its traces of information from e-mail sent by Microsoft Outlook users over a recent six-month period because it fears that, given recent disclosures about Outlook security holes, it might be the target of an attack similar to one it believes may have exposed Outlook users' message data at a rival ISP. This sounds incredibly arcane, but the Web is full of stories like these, and it's no picnic writing leads for them.

WHEN?

From a local point of view, "when" is a no-brainer—tell the reader the day and time that

---

way to organize information. You're forced to think about what really matters and to figure out how the story could be told most effectively. Sort through your interview material and other information and make an outline of the story before you begin writing. This doesn't need to be anything particularly formal—just a general overview of the elements you want to bring up throughout the story. For example, if you're writing a story about a fire, you might organize it as follows:

Lead—two people seriously injured when westside home burned down this morning

Secondary information—time of blaze, address of home, names of residents

Interview with neighbor (eyewitness)

Quote from fire personnel about origin and possible causes

Damage estimates

Any other supporting information or interviews

THE SIX BASIC QUESTIONS REVISITED, *continued*

something happened. National broadcast outlets often use the U.S. Eastern time zone as the default for reporting events, but you can't assume that your stories will be read only in the United States when you're on the Web. You might think you should report the time something happened in the zone where it occurred, but even that doesn't always work. If a movie premiere is held in several cities worldwide on the same day, and a special webcast simultaneously links several of the movie's stars from the different premiere sites, when do you say it took place? It might be evening at one site, afternoon at another, or even a day earlier or later somewhere else, yet all occur at the same moment.

WHERE?

"Where" might be the most difficult part of an online story to pin down. The average local story happens at a particular geographic location, but all kinds of online news happens out in cyberneverland. At least in the movie premiere example, you can identify a finite number of premiere locations. If you're writing about a worrisome trend toward organizing antigovernment militias on Google discussion groups, where does it take place? Is your dateline alt.conspiracy.

activism.militia? Worse still, what if it's organized via e-mail and you can't even cite one central source?

WHY AND HOW?

"Why" and "how" are lumped together because they seem to cause the most problems for daily news outlets. Newspapers are notorious for being good at the first four questions because they involve empirical details that can be gathered quickly on deadline. The last two, however, require a little more perspective, which newspapers don't always provide amid the daily rush for the next breaking story. "How" can sometimes be answered on the spot, if the actual sequence of events that occurred can be determined. Often, however, this is not established until after an investigation. "Why" is often not answered in any detail at all, except in major cases that are revisited during trials. While the abstract nature of these questions is troublesome for traditional media, it lends itself well to the online medium due to its ease of updating. Whether through follow-up stories, discussion groups or chat questions, online media offer the promise of addressing these questions in a volume and depth unseen in other media.

Organizing your information this way requires you to decide on the elements that are most important to the story. This is essential to writing the lead as well as the body of the story. It also allows for an early look at how sections might be broken up when the story is posted on the Web.

In this example, you quickly answer the main questions about what happened, which is what you do in a straight news lead. The inverted pyramid makes you think about the relative importance of your information. Your most important information is right up front, to inform and engage readers.

This works well for many kinds of stories, but not all of them. Suppose you're assigned to write a lighter feature story—in this case, an **advance story** on the Bass Ackwards Expo, a fair to be held this coming Saturday by the local chapter of the National Association of Left-Handers. If you organized the story using the inverted pyramid technique, your outline might look like this:

Lead—National Association of Left-Handers to hold expo Saturday at Union Hall downtown

Secondary information—hours, admission prices, activities at event

> Quotes from participants
>
> History of organization, nationally and locally
>
> Quotes on why organization was needed
>
> Any other supporting information or interviews

But since you're writing a feature story and not a straight news story, you might prefer a **feature lead**—something that highlights the unusual or interesting nature of the event, then follows with the facts. Such a lead might result from the following organization:

> Lead—guy with funny comment about being left-handed
>
> Secondary—National Association of Left-Handers holds expo Saturday at Union Hall downtown
>
> Information on hours, admission prices, activities at event
>
> Quotes from participants
>
> History of organization, nationally and locally
>
> Quotes on why it was necessary
>
> Wrap-ups on nature of being left-handed

The difference in story organization might not seem that great in the abstract, but it will dramatically influence the way you write your lead and the entire tone of the story that follows. Here's a likely straight-news, inverted-pyramid lead for this event:

> The local chapter of the National Association of Left-Handers will hold its annual Bass Ackwards Expo on Saturday at Union Hall downtown.
>
> The event will feature activities such as left-handed bowling, miniature golf and ring toss, as well as a marketplace of left-handed products. Visitors may also dance to the music of the Portsiders.

This gets across a lot of information about the event, but it doesn't capture its inherent absurdity. Indeed, "So what?" might be a relevant question after reading this lead.

With a feature lead you can create the beginnings of a more compelling story such as this:

> Dick Mitchell looks at the world from a slightly different perspective.
>
> "Being left-handed is a little like sitting in the passenger seat of your car all the time," says Mitchell, president of the local chapter of the National Association of Left-Handers. "You feel like reaching over and taking the controls, but somebody's put them on the wrong side."

You would then follow this with the information contained in the straight-news lead. While the feature lead doesn't convey as much material immediately, it puts a human face on the story, and it sets up the story to focus on the unusual nature of the event.

ELEMENTS OF NEWSWORTHINESS

What makes an event newsworthy? We generally know an interesting story when we see one, but what elements make us take notice? Journalism teachers have been working on this for decades, and the following list has emerged. Different instructors may substitute one or two elements, but these elements are generally the most common.

TIMELINESS

Timeliness emphasizes that an event just happened or is about to happen. Breaking news is almost always interesting—if something just happened or is about to happen, people will want to know about it right away. This is especially true online, where the ability to break news immediately and update it regularly are among the medium's most valuable assets.

PROXIMITY

Proximity refers to something that occurred or will occur in your media outlet's immediate area. This is obvious for local outlets, but for online publications without set circulation areas, this is an element that may be missing. For proximity to be a factor, there must be some geographic consistency among your target audience.

PROMINENCE

Prominence involves well-known people or institutions. Online or off, people are interested in celebrities and big companies or organizations. The bigger the name, the larger the audience and the more they will pay attention.

IMPACT

An event that will affect many people has impact. This can include anything from natural disasters to shortages to government shutdowns. Again, as more and more people are affected in greater and greater ways, the bigger the story will be. Online, this can include computer viruses, security flaws, legal issues and many other topics.

CURRENCY

Currency has nothing to do with money—it's the degree to which an event is a current hot topic. If an event relates to a current fad or area of interest, it will have greater news value than if it's related to last year's craze. In a medium where users tend to be young and follow trends, this is of vital importance.

CONFLICT

Anything that reports on battles between individuals, groups or institutions will have news value. This has been true from the Athenians versus the Spartans clear up to the recording industry versus Napster and its successors. Any clash of titans, whether people or companies, attracts interest, as does a conflict between a corporate giant and "the little guy."

ODDITY

Oddity is the home of the unusual, the bizarre or the extraordinary. Anything from an infant math whiz to a dog caring for kittens to a couple getting married while skydiving can qualify. Many feature stories look at something quirky, offbeat or peculiar. These are also very popular online—entire sites devoted to urban legends, strange deaths and other bizarre topics have become very successful.

The important thing to ask here is, "Why is this story newsworthy?" It isn't because of traditional hard-news elements, such as timeliness, proximity, prominence or impact. It's newsworthy because it's unusual—people might not have realized that a national organization for left-handed people even existed. The story has an offbeat appeal that lends itself to less traditional storytelling. Such stories are particularly popular on the Web, where whole sites exist solely to point out unusual news stories.

When writing a lead, think of the inverted pyramid as a useful tool for *story organization* rather than as an unbending structure. Ultimately, its main use is to help you know how to counter "So what?" with an effective answer.

But, first, readers have to click their way to your story.

HEADLINES AND LINK TEXT

On most news Web sites, your story fights a greater battle for the reader's attention than in a newspaper. Reading a newspaper basically requires readers to page through sections to see what looks interesting to them. Indeed, a newspaper page's wide-open layout invites a reader to look around, to scan the page for stimulating stories. Even magazines, which have index pages much like Web site home pages, can be paged through easily from start to finish.

By contrast, almost no one pages through each story on a news Web site. Most news sites offer a central index page, followed by subject pages. Both of these can serve as jumping-off points for readers. What this all means is that before readers can even get to your brilliantly crafted lead, your headline must attract them to it. This places as much emphasis on the headline as on the lead—an unaccustomed arrangement for writers trained in print journalism.

Online and print journalists need to make suggestions for headlines even though an editor ultimately decides what headline is published. Get in the habit of writing one or two good headlines on your stories. This helps the editor and gives you some influence in attracting readers to your story.

Be aware of the space limitations and characteristics of your Web site or publication. For example, CNN Interactive tends to run short headers on its index page to link to articles, whereas *USA Today* runs a header and a full sentence describing each story.

A CNN story about arms-reduction talks might have link text like this:

Geneva arms conference ends in deadlock

USA Today, on the other hand, might use the following header on its index page:

Arms talks end in failure
Administration officials vow to resume talks next year after disappointing sessions.

CNN has opted to provide a larger menu of stories on its index page. By using shorter **link text,** CNN can put links to 50 or more stories on its front page, whereas *USA Today* can show links to perhaps 20. *USA Today* has chosen to go with fewer story links on its front page, instead it refers readers to separate subject index pages corresponding with the print edition's News, Sports, Life and Money sections, as well as its Weather page. Neither *USA Today* nor CNN is inherently right or wrong in its approach—each outlet has made choices based on its core audience and its editorial strengths.

A typical CNN.com story features a large black headline, a boldfaced
lead paragraph and assorted other visual elements to entice the
reader.

SOURCE: CNN.com (accessed August 31, 2003). Used by permission.

Similarly, MSNBC places greater emphasis on headlines and leads on its story
pages than many of its competitors. While many major Web outlets still use simple bold black text for headlines and standard text for body type, MSNBC has
opted for a more distinctive format. MSNBC's headlines are in color, followed by
photo and/or video links. The first paragraph appears in large type and is followed
by an advertisement, then the body of the story appears with photos and links
throughout the text.

Because a reader of MSNBC will likely only see the headline and perhaps one
sentence in the first screen of a story page, the headline and lead are more important than at other sites. Fox News, for example, uses more standard heads and text,
enabling the reader to immediately see the first couple of paragraphs of most
stories.

MSNBC's story pages are unique because of the use of red headlines, video links and large art near the top of the story. The lead of the story barely makes it onto the first screen of information.

SOURCE: msnbc.com (accessed October 25, 2003). Used by permission.

Within the parameters for your site, be prepared to supply one or two well-considered suggested heads and subheads for your stories. In all likelihood, you won't have the final say in what headline appears on the story—that's the editor's job. However, by putting a little thought into a suggested headline (or link text), you can give your editor some help and probably exert a certain amount of influence over the header that will eventually appear.

A SQUARE LEAD IN A ROUND WEB

Over and above writing perfect headlines or link text, however, you have to write a lead that works online and takes into consideration the importance of your publication's formats, aims and audience. Since online news outlets have such different looks, it becomes vitally important to acquaint yourself with your publication's standards and formats and the variations that are used. How much of your lead will the average reader see? What elements of the story *must* appear in that space, and what storytelling elements will work best in those conditions? Whenever your site is redesigned, which happens fairly regularly online, adapt your writing to fit these new formats. The key, as with so many other aspects of journalism, is to be adaptable and versatile. Analyze what matters most in your story, and adapt that knowledge to the medium and the format, whatever it might be.

Regardless of the parameters of your site, one constant is the need to write tightly—to communicate a lot of information quickly in your lead. This is true of any sort of lead—hard news, features and others. You can write a clever lead, but it had better also be brief and informative. Writers for *The New Yorker* or *Rolling Stone* might be able to begin their stories with 200-word expository paragraphs, but online journalists don't have that luxury. Your audience is full of busy people who are reading the news to find out what's going on, not for literature. You need to stop readers from moving on before you can impress them with your writing skills.

Here's a feature lead that might be considered very entertaining and appropriate for a print publication:

CLANG! CREAK! Tink, tink, tink, tink. TING!
In days of yore, the sounds of a blacksmith's shop were among the most distinctive noises found in towns and villages across America. The sounds of a village smithy pounding, bending, twisting (and occasionally dropping) metal were commonplace in 18th- and 19th-century America.
Today, however, with a commercial hardware store every mile or two, the sounds of an operating blacksmith shop are pretty much relegated to the past.
Or are they?
Maybe not, thanks to a new class offered at Grape Day Park.

This might be an engaging lead in print, but it's probably too long for the average online outlet. Depending on formats, this lead might eat up the first two screens readers see, leaving them to wonder when the writer will get around to telling them what's going on.

A better lead for an online outlet might look something like this:

Phil Ewing can bend steel bars with his bare hands.
Is he a bodybuilder? A wrestler? A football player?
No, he's the instructor of a blacksmithing class now offered at Grape Day Park.

This lead takes a different approach, yet keeps the light tone of the previous lead. Most important, it gets to the subject of the story more quickly. It can be followed with similar details of how blacksmithing is a lost art now being revived.

The goal of writing a lead for online media is basically the same as in any medium—to grab readers' attention and inform them enough to make them want to continue reading. However, in the online world writers must be even more concise and clever to engage readers and make them forget about surfing somewhere else for a while.

GETTING YOUR FACTS ORGANIZED

Regardless of how good your lead is, you'll still need to make your remaining information flow together well. To do this, you must fully understand the different aspects of the information you're sharing—its strengths, weaknesses, surprises and unanswered questions—and convey those aspects in an engaging, logical way. More often than not, if you've done a good job of organizing your information, making the body of the story work is a matter of tying together your facts and quotes in a meaningful manner. Basically, your goal is to explain the story to the reader in a logical, concise fashion.

The inverted pyramid structure, which involves ordering information from most important to least important, is a good place to start when organizing your facts and quotes. Let's start with an example of an outline from earlier in the chapter:

Lead—two people seriously injured when westside home burned down this morning

Secondary information—time of blaze, address of home, names of residents

Interview with neighbor (eyewitness)

Quote from fire personnel about origin and possible causes

Damage estimates

Any other supporting information or interviews

An outline like this one breaks a story up into elements—not necessarily individual sentences or paragraphs, but clusters of information that are thematically grouped together.

There are several reasons this story has been organized in this way. At the top we've answered the most basic questions of the story—who (two people), what (house burned down, people seriously injured), when (this morning) and where (on the west side of town). In the secondary information, we've fine-tuned that basic information with details. Now let's say that the quote from the neighbor is as follows:

Arlene Ryan, who lives next door, notified the fire department and tried to awaken the family when she discovered the house was on fire.

"I was sound asleep, but our dog started barking," Ryan said. "I smelled something burning and looked next door and saw the flames in the back.

I called 911 and sent my husband out to see if he could wake them up.

I guess my son went out and turned the hose on."

This quote serves several purposes. It provides an eyewitness explanation of what happened, giving readers the kind of details they can't get from the bare facts of the story. It also gives readers a sense of the "How" of the story—it doesn't get inside the house that burned, but it gives the audience some notion of the sequence of events. It also puts the event in human terms—something that always engages readers.

The quote from fire personnel about the blaze's origins and possible causes is next because it provides the best available answer to the "Why" of the story. This is placed here because it's important but not as vital as the information before it because it's still speculative—firefighters will often say that the fire looks like it might have a particular cause, but that a full investigation will have to be done to confirm it. This quote is also less compelling than the quote from the neighbor, so it runs below the neighbor's comments.

The information that appears after this isn't unimportant, but it's neither as interesting nor as necessary as that which appears before it. Traditionally, this less important information is placed near the bottom with the expectation that it might be cut if the story runs too long—a custom that might not matter online with its lack of a **news hole** into which the story must fit. Still, placing such information below more important items makes sense in terms of how people read news—you don't want to bury your most important information.

The most important thing to note here is that even within a story using the inverted pyramid structure, elements can be moved up and down based on the degree to which they are more or less informative or compelling than other aspects. There is no single hard-and-fast order in which particular elements must be presented—it all depends on what's important and newsworthy in a given story. Although certain elements tend to be stressed in roughly the same order in particular types of stories, these are tendencies and not rules.

For example, as noted earlier, hard-news stories tend to begin with statements of the basic facts of a story, whereas soft-news stories (features and columns, for example) often begin with descriptions or anecdotes to set the tone for the details to come. But in each case, as the story goes on, there will be a mix of facts, quotes and other information based on the elements of that particular story.

The fire story is a good example of this. Changing different elements illustrates how information should be moved up or down within the story to increase its impact. Let's say that in addition to the neighbor's quote, we get this quote from the woman whose house burned down:

> "Everything's gone," a sobbing Sylvia Chandler said. "And if it wasn't for the neighbors' dog, we'd be gone too."

This is a poignant, dramatic quote, and it's from one of the people most centrally involved in the story. Because of these factors, you should probably place it higher in the story than you would place the neighbor's quote. You might not use it as the lead of the story, but it's so dramatic that you might well move it ahead of your secondary information, or at least make it the second or third paragraph after a summary lead. You probably wouldn't do this with a less dramatic quote, but this is so compelling that it deserves to be placed higher.

The examples thus far have dealt with hard-news stories, but features also require strong organization to work as news stories. True, feature leads are generally different from hard-news leads, and features generally use more quotes and descriptions than the average hard-news story. Structurally, however, features aren't that different. For instance, let's say you're writing a feature one year after the fire reported in the news story, and the Chandlers' uninsured home has been rebuilt thanks to donations of time and money from citizens and corporations in the area. This story might be well served by a contrast lead with a "then versus now" angle. Here's a possible outline:

> Lead—quote from Sylvia Chandler at the time her house burned, then new quote about it being rebuilt
>
> Secondary—brief information on when/how house burned and community effort to rebuild it
>
> Quote summarizing situation from family's priest, who was a prime mover behind effort
>
> More detailed information about rebuilding effort—how many people/companies involved, specifics on what needed to be replaced
>
> Quotes from some of the people involved on why they did it—start with friends of the Chandlers, then with Mark and Carol Matthews, who heard about fire through media and wanted to get involved
>
> Quote from Sylvia Chandler about surprise that strangers would help
>
> Information on when family's moving back in, what's changed about the house and their lives
>
> Wrap-up quotes from Sylvia about her gratitude and being back home again

This is a standard feature outline, and it could easily work well. It begins with the same dramatic quote mentioned earlier, then contrasts it with something new. It then works in assorted elements in a loose order of importance. This outline contains more quotes than the hard-news story did, yet they're placed in a particular order because of their perceived importance to the story and the degree to which they help explain things to the reader. For example,

- The quotes from Sylvia Chandler are placed at the top because they capture the contrasting emotions involved, which is a great way to hook readers of a feature story.
- These quotes are followed immediately by the most important basic facts of the story. This establishes the essential elements of the story quickly to inform the reader.
- The priest's quote is chosen next because of his role in the rebuilding effort, and because it sums up several things quickly. It also injects another voice into the narrative, which is an important aspect of feature stories.

The story then fills in the details of the rebuilding effort. In the original hard-news fire story, the lead introduced the reader to what happened, then the story filled in details about the specifics. The same thing happens here, but with a narrative or storytelling flow. Note that the story alternates between quotes and facts—this is a pacing technique common in feature stories and in some hard news as well.

Traditionally, hard-news stories don't require strong endings. However, given the storytelling nature of features, they generally require a more formal ending. This story ends with information about the family moving back in and quotes from Sylvia about the whole process; together these sum up the story well and give readers a sense of closure.

This structure might work, but there's always more than one way to organize and write a feature. Say, for example, that you thought the quotes from Mark and Carol Matthews were particularly good. You could completely reorganize the story and approach it from a different angle—from the point of view of a couple who heard about the fire in the news and felt the need to help. This perspective might result in an outline like this:

Lead—quote from Sylvia Chandler at the time her house burned, then quote from Mark Matthews about hearing it on the news and deciding to get involved

Secondary—brief information on when/how house burned, community effort to rebuild it, and on Mark and Carol Matthews, who volunteered to help a total stranger

Quote from Sylvia Chandler about surprise that strangers would help

More detailed information on rebuilding effort in general—how many people/companies involved, specifics on what needed to be replaced

Quotes from Mark and Carol on what they'd gotten themselves into, and from friends of Chandlers on working with them

Information on when family is moving back in, what's changed about the house and their lives

Wrap-up quotes from Mark and Carol about their effort, and from Sylvia on her gratitude

This outline would result in a completely different story about the same events. By reorganizing your information to stress different elements, you've overhauled the story entirely, yet it will likely still work. You might use some quotes from Mark and Carol that you'd have left out of the previous story, and you might move up other items about them, but most of the information is the same. It's simply a matter of choosing to stress certain elements and structuring the story based on those elements.

At this point, consider your options in audio or video clips from your interviews or other material. When you know the approximate structure of the story, you can determine what might be useful within that context. For example, video of the house before and after rebuilding might complement this story well, and audio clips from some of the major figures (Sylvia Chandler, the priest, the Matthewses) might spice up the narrative. Try to select small segments that you're not using otherwise—sometimes certain quotes sound better spoken than transcribed, and other times you'll simply find that one brief sound clip sums up a lot about a story. Also try to choose pieces that stand on their own; this usually works better to complement stories than relying on segments that require explanation.

In many ways, this makes you a cross between a print and a broadcast reporter—you learn to set aside certain clips because they work well as sound bites or video footage while using other segments within the story itself.

There are several points to remember when organizing your stories:

- There is no set formula for writing a story, whether it's hard news or a feature.
- In either case, organize the information in a way that explains the story to the reader, whether through facts or through storytelling elements.
- Identify the elements that need to be explained, and those that don't need explaining.
- By organizing these elements well, you'll make the actual writing of the story much easier.

SUMMARY

There's a lot to think about when writing a story for online consumption. As with writing any other news story, you need to write in a clear, informative and engaging style. Yet the online medium demands more. You also need to think of the physical aspects of news pages on the Web—how they appear on the screen, their strengths and weaknesses, their features and limitations. It's not always easy, but when it's done properly, you can tell a story online in ways that no other medium can match.

RELATED WEB SITES

Purdue University Online Writing Lab
http://owl.english.purdue.edu

University of Missouri's Online Writery
http://www.missouri.edu/~writery/

The Poynter Institute's Writing and Editing page
http://poynter.org/subject.asp?id=2

EXERCISES

1. Write a summary lead and nut graph based on the following information. Then write a feature lead and nut graph based on the same material.

   Open Debate is an Internet site devoted to conducting polls about all sorts of issues. The site lets users create online polls on any subject they want. The site handles all coding and tabulation and does things like breaking down answers by sex and age group. A bulletin-board discussion accompanies each poll. Sites like this one have been growing in numbers on the Internet in recent years. They allow Web users to conduct polls that can attract hundreds or thousands of respondents, though they often do not use many of the statistical methods of professional polls. Critics argue that this makes their validity questionable, but supporters say the polls are just for fun and not meant to be scientific in nature.

2. Write three suggested headlines for each of the following stories. Make the first one eight words or fewer and the second one exactly six words. For the third headline, give it both a headline and a subhead—a headline of six words or fewer and a subhead of eight words or fewer. Separate the head and subhead with a colon (as in "Senators to Vote on Tax Bill: Plan Would Reduce Rates on Capital Gains").

    A. Paul Sutton, longtime head coach of the Louisville State University basketball team, and his wife were killed Thursday evening in a three-car accident on Interstate 65 near Bloomington. Four other motorists were injured in the crash, which occurred at about 9:40 p.m. Witnesses said Sutton's 1998 Lexus was heading northbound and swerved from the far right lane across the other northbound lanes. Sutton's car was struck broadside by one car, then hit the center median and was struck by another car.

    B. Among America's many natural wonders, a lesser-known gem is Montana's Glacier National Park. The vast landscape covers 1,600 square miles and contains some of the most spectacular mountains, valleys and waterfalls in the United States. Mountain goats, grizzly bears and hundreds of other animal species freely roam the countryside. The park boasts more than 730 miles of hiking trails, as well as numerous campgrounds and scenic drives.

    C. A blacksmithing class is now being offered at Grape Day Park. Instructor Phil Ewing, a professional blacksmith for years at the nearby Bandy steel works, shows participants how to use traditional anvils, forges and assorted tools to create all sorts of items from steel. These include everything from candleholders to fireplace implements to swords and many other items.

3. For item A and item B in Exercise 2, write a lead and nut graph tailored specifically for online news. For each of these, explain the factors about online news and Web pages that caused you to structure the material as you did.

8

||||||

Revving Up
Your Writing

Whether online, on paper or on TV, you have to tell a good story. However, you must tell it in a way that fits the medium—something many in the online world have yet to master. To attract readers and keep them coming back, you need to learn good basic techniques to make all of your stories engaging to readers. This chapter shows how writers use assorted techniques to energize their writing regardless of the subject matter.

The traditional approach to putting together a compelling story is to write a punchy, informative lead, then assemble your information in some sort of logical manner as a single story that contains certain narrative threads for readers to follow to the end. In other words, you essentially lead readers on a guided tour of your information in a linear fashion. The information is presented completely, accurately and in an order that makes sense.

However, the online venue presents information in an entirely different way from any previous medium. With the addition of links to outside information, most Web pages are nonlinear—they encourage you to chart your own path, to latch onto one aspect of a story and read more about it. If a print story is a guided tour of a story's information, the Web is a *self-guided* tour of that information. Some people may walk through the front door and go through the first floor clockwise, room by room, whereas others may choose to go counterclockwise, and still others may take the elevator to the top and work their way down.

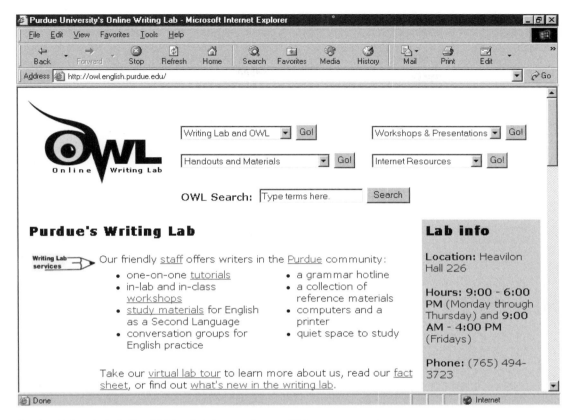

Purdue University's Online Writing Lab is one of many Web resources
for writers who want to clean up and energize their writing.

SOURCE: owl.english.purdue.edu (accessed September 25, 2003). Used by permission of the Purdue University Online
Writing Lab.

This is the way people interact with information online. The reporters who succeed in the 21st century will be the ones who best tailor their writing to this new
way of reading news. This is not an easy task—it requires mastering traditional storytelling techniques while also completely rethinking how stories are structured.

ACTIVE VERSUS PASSIVE VOICE

In the online world, you don't want to write stories that just stare back at readers
from their screens. Your writing must be vibrant and compelling. You want to
grab readers, to engage them, to help them zip from point to point like well-oiled
race cars.

This book isn't primarily concerned with teaching you to write a decent English sentence—you should know how to do that already. Having said that, using the **active voice** is an essential element to writing good leads, and it's just as essential for the rest of your story. Using the active voice means writing sentences in which the subject acts rather than responds. For example, the active phrase "people tire quickly of reading long blocks of text online" is tighter and livelier than the passive phrase "people quickly become tired . . .".

You accomplish two useful things by using the active voice. First, using the active voice energizes your writing—literally, your sentences come to life when their subjects are performing actions instead of having actions performed upon them. Lively, active sentences are less likely to bore readers. Second, active verbs are generally clearer because they directly explain who is performing the action. "The city council gave a contract to a manufacturer to supply paperweights" is less confusing than saying "to supply paperweights, a manufacturer was awarded a contract from the city council." The active sentence explains things more plainly—the subject performed this action for this reason.

In addition, using the active voice almost always results in using fewer words. Since the **passive voice** often includes a form of the verb "to be" ("is," "was," "am," "are" and so forth) in addition to the main verb, passive sentences tend to be longer than active ones. Here's one example:

> **Passive:** A 35-year-old Paramus woman was killed Wednesday morning when she was struck by falling debris near a demolition site in Newark.

> **Active:** Falling debris from a Newark demolition site killed a 35-year-old Paramus woman Wednesday morning.

This isn't an arbitrary rearrangement of information. The first sentence might not strike you as a bad one—it seems straightforward and factual. However, the second sentence gets across the same content in fewer words. You're trying to tighten your writing, and by using the active voice you've cut the word count from 21 in the first sentence to 14 in the second. Multiply this difference by the number of sentences in a story and you're suddenly writing a much tighter piece, which must be your goal in the online venue.

If you continue with the details of the story, you discover that the active voice isn't useful only in leads.

> **Passive:** According to Newark police, Lisa Clayton was standing on the northwest corner of Seventh and Doyle streets, which is adjacent to the site where a five-story apartment building was being torn down. Clayton was waiting to cross the street when a section of mortar near the top of the building gave way, which allowed bricks to drop on her from 40 feet above.

> **Active:** Newark police said that as Lisa Clayton waited to cross the street at the northwest corner of Seventh and Doyle streets, a section of mortar collapsed near the top of the five-story apartment building being demolished in an adjacent lot. This dropped bricks on Clayton from 40 feet above.

You need to explain a lot at this point in this story, but you accomplish it more quickly and effectively using the active voice. The passive example contains

PRECISION AND CLARITY

Using active verbs is one way to make your writing clearer. Another way is to be as precise as possible in your writing—to say exactly what you mean, no more, no less.

USE YOUR THESAURUS PROPERLY

Too many beginning writers use a thesaurus as a reference tool to find a word that will dazzle readers. Actually, the thesaurus is most useful when you recognize that a phrase or passage is weak or doesn't convey your exact meaning. By getting in the habit of opening the book (or starting the computer program, as the case may be), your working vocabulary will expand to include more precise words, not just more big ones. You'll also get in the habit of choosing words carefully.

DON'T USE WORDS YOU DON'T KNOW

Nothing's more embarrassing for a writer than misusing a word or phrase when trying to sound erudite and impress someone. This is obviously true when you mistake one word for another that sounds similar (for example, "epitome" for "epiphany," "repression" for "recession," "erroneous" for "erogenous," and hundreds of other examples). Look these words up and get them right. A sneakier problem is when you incorrectly use a word whose meaning is similar to what you want. Writing that a group "worked fervently" on a project, for example, or that someone was a "diligent admirer" of a particular person is less obviously incorrect but still reflects poorly on you as a writer.

BE SPECIFIC

To say that an official "gave information about how the companies made the deal" is a lot less compelling than to say he "explained how the companies would merge their computer and publishing interests." The more specific you can be, the more directly and efficiently you'll be able to explain the details of your story.

USE REAL VERBS

These days seemingly any noun can be made into a verb. People no longer eat lunch, they simply "lunch." They never play computer games, they engage in "gaming." They don't outfit their offices, they "office." Made-up verbs like these (and dozens of others) may be chic, but they're also weak. You're better off using a solid active verb even if it means using an extra word. One of the most common fake verbs is "impact," which is really a noun. You can "have an impact" on someone, but to say you've "impacted upon them" or that you "want to impact the process" is poor English. "Impacted" means your wisdom teeth came in crooked. If you're not sure if a certain word is really a verb, look it up.

USE REAL NOUNS

This is a bit less obvious than using real verbs. Students will sometimes write that "police are carrying out an investigation" when they should write that "police are investigating." By taking a verb ("investigate") and turning it into a noun ("investigation") you've *nominalized* the verb, creating a weak noun. Nominalizations tend to lead to dull and overly lengthy sentences because they use several words to do the job of one verb. Nouns ending in "tion" are generally nominalizations, and many times the words "made" or "make" will precede them. Don't write that someone "made a decision" when they've decided, "voted to approve" when they've approved something, or "made an adjustment" when they've adjusted.

63 words, whereas the active one contains 49. You've replaced "was standing" and "was waiting" with "stood," "was being torn down" with "being demolished," and "allowed bricks to drop" with "dropped bricks." In each case, you've replaced a passive phrase with an active one and slimmed down the story, drawing the reader through the story more quickly than in the passive voice version.

When you're first learning, it's often difficult to figure out how to make your sentences active. Even veteran news writers sometimes take time for thought when arranging sentences to eliminate the passive voice. Look at the previous example and see if you can identify several places where sentences were reorganized to make them active. In the passive example, the first clause—"According to Newark police"—contains no verb at all, and it's hard to get more passive than that. In the active example, this was replaced with "Newark police said," which is an active phrase that includes a verb.

Let's walk through an example of how you might turn a passive sentence into an active one. Here's a passive sentence that continues the previous story:

> Officials from Thompson Demolition Inc., the company that is in charge of the building's wrecking, said their workers had used yellow caution tape to block off the street corner earlier in the morning. They believe that someone else may have taken down the tape before Clayton got there.

How can we make this paragraph more active? Let us count the ways:

- The first verb, "is," found in the phrase "the company that is in charge" is passive and can be eliminated by shortening the phrase to "the company in charge." This works in the context of the sentence.

- The next item that should be changed overlaps the first one—the phrase "in charge of the building's wrecking" is passive. You could simply change it to "in charge of wrecking the building," but "wrecking" is a weak verb because it doesn't explain the action well. You could use "demolishing," but that would be repetitive because "demolition" is part of the company's name. Here is a good spot to use your thesaurus and come up with a useful active verb. In this case, "razing" would be a good choice. The phrase "in charge of razing the building" is active and a much better choice than its predecessor.

- The phrase "had used yellow caution tape to block off the street corner" employs two verbs, one passive and one active. How can we change or eliminate the passive "used"? In this case, we can get rid of "used" by simply reorganizing the phrase to read "had blocked off the street corner with yellow caution tape." The phrase "street corner" can also be shortened to "corner" since we've established it's a street corner. Together, this shrinks the phrase slightly—from 11 to 9 words—but more important, it makes the phrase much more active.

- In the second sentence, the phrase "someone else may have taken down the tape" is passive. "Taken down" is not as strong a verb as "removed," and it's two words instead of one, so it should be replaced. In addition, "someone else" can be shortened to "someone" because we learn in the next clause that the tape was removed before Clayton arrived at the corner. With these two changes, the phrase would read, "someone may have removed the tape."

- Finally, the verb "got there" is weak and can be replaced with a stronger one-word verb, "arrived."

After all this rewriting, let's compare the passive and active versions of the paragraph:

Passive: Officials from Thompson Demolition Inc., the company that is in charge of the building's wrecking, said their workers had used yellow caution tape to block off the street corner earlier in the morning. They believe that someone else may have taken down the tape before Clayton got there.

Active: Officials from Thompson Demolition Inc., the company in charge of razing the building, said their workers had blocked off the corner with yellow caution tape earlier in the morning. They believe someone may have removed the tape before Clayton arrived.

Here you've cut the paragraph from 48 words down to 40, and you've made it more active. If you were really obsessed with word count, you could shrink it still further by changing "the company in charge" to simply "the company," or "blocked off" to "barricaded."

Writing active sentences takes practice and skill, but you'll be surprised how quickly you can get used to it. Examine the verbs in your sentences—to see where passive verbs can be replaced with active ones—and look for phrases that can be rearranged to become more active. You'll find more tips for streamlining your writing later in this chapter.

STORY FLOW TECHNIQUES

Using the active voice is an important technique to help you achieve smooth **story flow,** but there are many others. Each is aimed at drawing readers through stories quickly—an essential element of online writing.

One useful story flow technique is called **pacing,** which involves writing sentences of varying lengths to create a rhythm within your stories. The best way to understand how pacing works is to see good and bad examples of story rhythms. Here are a couple of examples of poor pacing:

Consecutive long sentences: Clayton is believed to have been on her way to visit a friend when the incident occurred, as her car was parked less than a block from the scene of the collapse. Police have interviewed bystanders as well as workers who witnessed the event, and are not saying whether charges will be filed against Thompson Demolition. Under state law, Clayton's family could sue the company for criminal negligence if it is determined that workers were aware that the caution tape had been removed before the incident occurred and did not correct the situation. If individual workers are found to be at fault, both the demolition company and the workers themselves could be held responsible for Clayton's death.

Consecutive short sentences: Clayton had been on her way to visit a friend. Her car was parked less than a block from the scene. Police interviewed people who saw the event. Police may file charges against Thompson Demolition. Clayton's family could sue. This could happen if workers knew the tape had been removed. Both the company and the workers could be held responsible.

Both of these stories get across the same basic information, but they read completely differently. The first seems to drag because it contains too many long sentences in a row, and the second one seems clipped and abrupt because it's full of short sentences. The trick is to learn to balance long and short sentences to create a rhythm. Here's a better-paced example of the same material:

> Officials believe Clayton was on her way to visit a friend when the incident occurred. Her car was parked less than a block from the scene. Police have interviewed both witnesses and workers and have not said whether they'll file charges against Thompson Demolition. Under state law, Clayton's family could sue the company for criminal negligence. If workers knew the tape had been removed before the incident and did not correct the situation, both the company and the workers could be held responsible.

This is still a long paragraph, and it should be broken into two or three paragraphs using transitions (which are discussed later in the chapter). However, it reads better than either of the others because the sentence lengths vary. You needn't bend over backward to make sure that each long sentence is followed by a short one and vice versa, but you should be aware of the pace of the story. Some people in the business refer to this as how a story "sounds," and veteran journalists usually develop an ear for the rhythm and pacing of their stories.

One way to do this is by re-reading the story while paying attention to the cadence rather than the content. Some journalists read them out loud, others can do it in their heads. This is similar to the technique mentioned earlier of reading your lead aloud. As you write more and more, you'll find that you become more attuned to the rhythms of your stories.

Inexperienced writers sometimes get bogged down in **transitions**—points where your story shifts its focus or otherwise moves from one section to another. Transitions are often called the "glue" that holds the different parts of a story together, and this is a useful metaphor. Transitions are particularly important in online journalism where readers scroll or click from one section to another and can easily lose track of a story's connecting threads. Without effective transitions, stories online or off will seem disjointed and hard to read.

A transition can come in just about any size, depending on the context. Some are simply one word ("however," "later," "meanwhile"), whereas others are phrases ("on the other hand," "in contrast," "the next day"). In longer articles, whole sentences or paragraphs may serve as transitions from one section to another. In any event, transitions serve both to alert the reader to the change in focus and to logically and smoothly introduce the next subject.

An appropriate introduction to a new segment of a story expresses the relationship between the old and new segments. This is less complicated than it sounds—if the new segment contains information that seems to contradict the preceding segment, you need to use a transition that expresses this, such as "however" or something similar. If there is an unexpected similarity between two seemingly unrelated topics, your transition might include a word such as "yet." Here are a few examples of different types of transitions:

CREATIVITY

People often become interested in writing because it's a creative activity. Journalism, however, is a highly structured form of writing. Some people believe its structures inhibit their creativity; others claim that exercising creativity within those structures is a special skill.

Who's right? That's up to you to decide, but there are appropriate and inappropriate techniques, as well as good and bad times to use them. In general, you can take a few more liberties with feature stories, but even then there are limits to what most editors will accept. Here are examples of the right and wrong ways to use some common creative techniques in journalism:

- *Setting the scene.* In a novel, this is an immediate necessity—the writer needs to paint a verbal picture of the area in which the narrative takes place. In journalism, this technique can be used, but in a somewhat different way. In hard news, often the lead and nut graph provide the story's most relevant facts and outcomes, then succeeding paragraphs set the scene. From the point of view of a novelist, this amounts to immediately giving away the ending, but this is journalism, not fiction, and you don't have several hundred pages to tell your story. In a feature, you can sometimes begin your story by setting the scene, but you need to get to the point within the first couple of paragraphs. This is doubly true online—if you don't get to the point within the first screen, you're in danger of losing readers.

- *Foreshadowing.* Within hard news, dropping hints about what's to come is rather useless because your objective is to explain things directly. Only in longer feature pieces should this be considered, and then with good reason.

- *Imagery.* This is one technique that journalists should use regularly. Skillful journalists use imagery—bits of language that appeal to the senses—as a descriptive tool to convey the details of a scene to readers quickly. Rather than taking time to set a scene, a reporter will toss in a few descriptive words and phrases to give the reader some notion of what the scene was like. This is true in both hard news and features.

- *Alliteration/assonance.* Using repetitive consonant or vowel sounds (for example, "Teachers took a tech talk tutorial") is more likely to distract the reader than to get the message across effectively. Having said this, these techniques *are* common in headline writing (as discussed later in this book).

- *Anecdotes.* There's nothing at all wrong with using anecdotes in your writing, as long as (1) they're from someone featured in the story (not you, the writer) and (2) they're relevant to the story you're writing. Anecdotes are often an excellent way to personalize a story or to explain something in a compelling way. Be sure, however, that the anecdote you use serves the purpose of moving the story along. If it's used in a hard-news story, it should inform the reader; if it's in a feature, it can inform or entertain as long as it remains relevant to the story.

- *Figures of speech/clichés.* Whether in hard news or features, you should have a good reason for using well-worn phrases. Sometimes they're used to make a point or to grab reader attention, but stay away from using them regularly. People visit your site to read something new and interesting, not to discover that "that's the way the ball bounces," "the early bird gets the worm," or that "good things come to those who wait."

- *Figurative language.* This is where beginning writers often get sidetracked. Having been rewarded in their teen years for being able to turn a phrase, some writers enter journalism classes believing that mellifluous verbosity is the ticket to success in the field. As has been noted throughout this book, however, journalism is primarily concerned with telling stories quickly and directly. This doesn't mean that all figurative language should be abandoned—just reserve it for occasions when its use will actually help move a story along or tell it in a compelling way. In other words, in journalism, figurative language isn't the entrée, it's the spice.

The central rule of exercising creativity within journalism is this—don't get carried away. Pick your moments when a creative technique or a turn of phrase will strengthen your story without distracting from it.

Officials believe the caution tape had been removed before Clayton arrived at the scene. *However,* one eyewitness wasn't so sure.

Thompson Demolition officials denied any wrongdoing, *while* police officials withheld comment until after completion of their investigation.

Thompson Demolition was involved in a similar incident seven years ago, when a falling piece of molding injured a passerby at a Paterson site. *Yet* the company has been accident-free in recent years, even winning a citation from the Occupational Safety and Health Organization in 1999.

The first transition (However) acts as a bridge between contradicting narratives and will presumably be followed by a quote. The second (while) ties together two linked pieces of material from different sources. The third (Yet) differs from the first because instead of linking two significant sections of the narrative, it briefly introduces and links two isolated and seemingly contradictory snippets of information. This type of material is often used later in stories to offer background for the different sides of the issue.

If the contrast between two sections is great enough, using an entire sentence or paragraph for a transition might be warranted. Here's an example of a transitional sentence that would probably stand alone as a paragraph:

> While investigators tried to determine when the caution tape was removed, county inspectors wondered why a solid barricade was not used at the scene.

This transition links the details of the incident to larger questions, which will be addressed in subsequent quotes and other material.

The best writers accomplish a great deal with their transitions. On one hand, they provide readers with reasons to understand why the upcoming section is related to the previous one. On the other, they insert the transitions into the narrative smoothly and subtly, using a minimum of words if possible. Here's an example of a brief transition linking two disparate quotes:

> "In terms of legal action, the key issue here is the removal of the caution tape," said City Attorney Jack Sanders. "If she removed the tape herself, there's no case, but if it was gone beforehand, it raises lots of issues."
>
> *Legal strategies, however, provide little comfort for Clayton's friends and family.*
>
> "She didn't deserve anything like this," said Michelle Whittington, a long-time friend of Clayton. "She was just standing there and boom, she's gone. It could have happened to anyone. It's scary."

Aside from the ties to the same incident, the two quotes here have little in common. The first quote deals with details and laws, and the second deals with the emotions and questions that accompany the loss of a friend or relative. Yet this transition links the quotes by briefly addressing the conflict between the two aspects of the story. It alludes to both aspects quickly and provides the reader with a clear tie between one and the other. This type of transition—concluding the discussion of assorted details, then bringing the story back to its personal and emotional level—is often used near the end of stories.

The most important thing to remember for effective transitions is to keep them as simple and concise as possible. The purpose of transitions is to seamlessly shift the focus from one subject to another, not to draw attention to the transition itself. The more seamless your transitions become, the more easily your stories will flow.

One of the most important uses of transitions is to tie quotes from different sources together. Using too many consecutive quotes from the same person tends to bore readers—hearing different voices interacting makes articles more varied and lively. Most reporters employ a technique called **dialogue**—alternating quotes from different sources—to create a more diverse narrative.

This technique and the reasons for using it might not immediately make sense. You've undoubtedly read many articles that quote only one source and seemed interesting enough. The best way to understand the technique is to see examples where it improves an existing section. Here's a passage that doesn't use dialogue:

> Reviews among the paying customers were mixed.
>
> "I thought it was great," said Ronnie Wilson, 28, of Clifton. "It was really exciting from the start. I wasn't really a big fan of the first movie, but this one was a lot of fun.
>
> "The first part, where they were out in the desert, I thought it was gonna be boring," Wilson continued. "I mean, the effects were interesting, but it took a while to get going. But later, when they were in the water, it was really cool. Then later, the fight scene—that was awesome."
>
> Christine Taylor, 19, of Avon disagreed.
>
> "It was stupid," she said. "The first one was a lot better. I don't know why they bothered to make this one, except to make more money."

This might be somewhat interesting, but using the dialogue technique spices it up a bit. For example:

> Reviews among the paying customers were mixed.
>
> "I thought it was great," said Ronnie Wilson, 28, of Clifton. "It was really exciting from the start. I wasn't really a big fan of the first movie, but this one was a lot of fun."
>
> "It was stupid," countered Christine Taylor, 19, of Avon. "The first one was a lot better. I don't know why they bothered to make this one, except to make more money."

The second example is snappier, and not just because it eliminates the secondary comments from Wilson. It creates an immediate contrast in opinions as well as introducing different competing voices. People speak differently and use different phrases, and that diversity makes your stories more fun to read. Even when you're writing a story that's primarily about one person—a personality profile, a story about someone receiving an honor or award, or something similar—you should strive to talk to several people and work their comments into the narrative. This will make the piece sound less like an ego trip and more like a serious report.

When we use the term "different voices" in online journalism, we also mean it more literally than in the print media. It's more effective to have a mixture of interview audio clips from different people than just one voice discussing different subjects. An exception might be for an in-depth or Q&A interview story, but for the sake of keeping your audience engaged, strive to get usable material from many different sources.

STORY STRUCTURES

The trait that may change the most from print to online journalism is the structure of stories. Story structure involves more than just the order in which information flows best—it also must take into account the characteristics of the medium. Because reading a story on a computer screen is different from reading it on paper, online journalists have to structure their stories differently to make them work within the medium. Even after several years of daily journalism on the Web, however, no single structure is accepted as the best means for reporting a news story online.

At an even more basic level, the simple act of placing a story on a page is still an unsettled issue. Some outlets let their stories run at full length on one page, encouraging readers to scroll down through several screens of information. Others break up stories into smaller increments and ask readers to click to a second or third page. Some studies show that readers would rather click ahead than scroll down, but the issue is by no means settled. With this in mind, this section will look at some traditional story structures as well as some new ways of telling your stories online. For current examples of stories written within these structures, check this book's Web site at http://communication.wadsworth.com/craig.

As noted earlier, the inverted pyramid is the most common story structure used in traditional news. By reporting the most important information first, then continuing from the most important to the least important, you cater to both the reader who wants to know the essence of a story quickly and the reader who wants to learn more about the circumstances.

The inverted pyramid is the dominant style for hard-news stories in particular, both online and in other outlets. While it's closely tied to traditional news values, this structure is in many ways ideally suited for the online medium. Online readers are notorious for only wanting to read one or two screens' worth of information, and the inverted pyramid generally conveys a story's most vital facts within one screen of information. However, beyond hard news, the structure is seldom employed online because it's so closely tied to traditional news, and online audiences disdain anything even remotely stodgy.

Another common story structure is the **chronology,** which essentially recounts events in the order in which they occurred. Sometimes called a *narration,* this structure can give readers a strong notion of the chain of events that led to the incident in question. This is used in both hard news and soft news, though chronologies are most often used in hard news as secondary stories (more on this in the discussion on sidebar stories). In some instances, it's the only way to explain a complex event. Hard-news stories often contain sections that recount a sequence of events, but a stand-alone lead story is seldom written in this style.

Chronologies seem to be more common online than in print, if only because they're a different way to tell a story. Yet structurally they conflict with the online audience's seemingly fleeting attention span. Most industry research indicates that online readers tend to surf quickly through sites looking for interesting material, but once they find something that captures their interest, they will often read about that topic in great depth. This may account for the popularity of chronologies online.

For more in-depth stories, another common traditional style is known as the **Wall Street Journal structure.** Named after the venerable New York business newspaper, this style is characterized by a long, descriptive lead followed by a transition that ties the lead to the main details of the story. The story's details are then developed and tied together at the end, frequently by some reference to the subject mentioned in the lead. This style and its elements are common in features, whether in a standard soft-news story or a "news feature" (a serious feature story written about a newsmaker or event).

Consciously or unconsciously, many online writers use the Wall Street Journal structure in their stories, whether they're business oriented or not. In fact, though their writers and editors may be loath to admit it, many stories at online journals like *Slate* and *Salon* are written in Wall Street Journal style, or at least borrow heavily from it. While this style may not immediately convey the central information of a story, it often quickly personalizes the story and makes a reader want to continue. Even so, when used online, stories in the Wall Street Journal style often drop in a quick early reference to the main thrust of the story.

Rather than reinventing the wheel, many online outlets have chosen to use these traditional styles while adding new features that make those styles work better online. One such feature is subject heading links at the top of long stories. These links list the four or five main subjects the story addresses and allow users to click on those subjects to jump directly to the point at which the story deals with them.

For example, a story about the State of the Union address might contain an introductory overview paragraph followed by several graphs specifically addressing points made within the speech. If such a story contains subject heading links, readers can click one that interests them and immediately skip ahead to the section pertaining to that subject.

This feature has several consequences for you as a writer. Mainly, it encourages you to recognize and label your transitions from one subject to another. If you have this in mind as you outline your story, it should help to keep the material well organized. It also helps you learn to write each section as a readable standalone item. While writers hope that the audience will read the entire story, the fact remains that many in the Web audience will choose sections corresponding to their interests. Ideally, you'll learn to write stories that both flow well as complete pieces and contain sections that are readable on their own.

Subject heading links also work well when a piece covers more than one topic. Some columns and digests are collections of disparate bits of information believed to be important or entertaining for readers. Examples include news briefs, three-dot columns, "people" columns and countless others. Since information in these formats is already broken into sections by subject, it's a simple matter to create subject heading links at the top to enable readers to hop directly to the subject that captures their interest.

Another type of story treated differently online is the **sidebar** story. This is a secondary story that expands on one aspect of a major story and appears nearby for readers who want more information. Often these are brief profiles of a person or an agency involved in the main story, explanations of a complicated aspect of a story, or some other facet of a story that deserves further study.

Using the State of the Union example mentioned earlier, sidebars might be written on any number of related subjects. A sidebar might provide local or national reaction to the speech, details of some of the specifics outlined in the speech, the likelihood of the speech's proposals being approved by Congress, comparing the speech with those of previous years, or dozens of other possibilities. The key with any subject is to recognize when a particular aspect of the main story deserves its own "substory," one that might attract reader interest. If you find yourself asking several questions about a single aspect of a multifaceted story, that subject may well deserve a sidebar.

Sidebars present a logistical problem for online news outlets, however. In print, the placement of sidebar stories is easily accomplished—often the sidebar appears in an inset box near or within the text of the main story. On the Web, however, given the constraints of the computer screen, the act of wedging in a sidebar story while keeping the main story readable is challenging. This is especially true when there are many other elements already on the page (navigation buttons, advertisements, links and so forth). If a sidebar is short enough, it is sometimes placed in a narrow box to the right of the screen, which squeezes the main story to the middle. If the sidebar is a longer piece, it will sometimes occupy a separate page, with a small inset box to the right of the main story providing a link to the sidebar and encouraging readers to "See also . . .".

SUMMARY

There's a lot to think about when writing a story for online consumption. As with writing any other news story, you need to write in a clear, informative and engaging style. Yet the online medium demands more. You also need to think of the physical aspects of news pages on the Web—how they appear on the screen, their strengths and weaknesses, their features and limitations. It's not always easy, but when it's done properly, you can tell a story online in ways that no other medium can match.

RELATED WEB SITES

American Press Institute's Cyberjournalist.net
http://wwwcyberjournalist.net

Purdue University Online Writing Lab
http://owl.english.purdue.edu/

CUNY Writesite (City University of New York)
http://writesite.cuny.edu

Ohio State University Center for the Study and Teaching of Writing
http://www.cstw.ohio-state.edu

Colorado State University Writing Center
http://writing.colostate.edu

EXERCISES

1. Visit three of the biggest news sites on the Web—CNN.com, MSNBC.com
   and FoxNews.com—and select a major story (not a wire service report)
   they all have in common. Then write an outline of the story as it appears
   on each site and discuss the similarities and differences in structure between
   the three stories.

2. Rewrite the following sentences so they are tighter, more precise and use
   active voice:

   a. According to witnesses, Peterson was struck by a motorcycle that was
      going west on 59th Street.

   b. Williams was arrested Friday night after he allegedly was trying to escape
      from police who were chasing him.

   c. Officers were quoted as saying Cruz was in the bank when the robbery
      happened, but they didn't think he did it.

   d. Bryant's son Danny did enjoy the show, and when asked said his favorite
      character was the tiger.

   e. Though she was not expected to be finishing in the top 10, Shelley
      ended up finishing in second place among the women who were in
      the race.

3. Select a lengthy major story from an online news outlet of your choice and
   print it out. Locate as many transitional words and phrases as you can in
   the story, and mark them with a highlighting pen. Then rewrite the story
   using the same material but a different story structure. When you're finished,
   highlight your own transitions.

 4. Select a lengthy major story from InfoTrac College Edition or an online
   news outlet of your choice. Using material from this story and material from
   other online resources, write a brief sidebar to the story on a related topic.
   Be sure to cite all the sources for your information.

9

||||||

The Last Minute(s)

The scenario of a print or broadcast journalist working and working to fine-tune a story right up to the last minute before the deadline is one of the images most often associated with journalism. In the online world, however, things are different. Some journalists argue that in the online medium there's no such thing as the last minute; others believe that *every* minute is the last minute. Because of the constant updating of online news sites, most online reporters don't have the luxury of one or two set deadlines per day. This chapter discusses some of the items online reporters must deal with as they complete their stories and prepare for future updates. It also examines the ways in which putting the finishing touches on a story means something very different for an online reporter than for newspaper and television reporters.

When major news events occurred during the first half of the 20th century, Americans didn't gather in front of their TV sets or computers to see what had happened. Since they didn't yet have these technologies, and early radio news was spotty at best, Americans in both urban and rural settings often gathered outside the offices of their local newspapers, waiting for the latest news. The newspapers posted brief updates on message boards outside their offices and produced extra editions with the detailed information. Most metropolitan dailies produced multiple editions throughout the day to keep readers as well informed as possible.

At CNN.com, as with any news outlet, when a major story breaks, there's no waiting around for later editions. Reporters must act immediately.

SOURCE: CNN.com (accessed October 15, 2002). Used by permission.

While instant coverage of breaking news events is now available through cable television and elsewhere, for many readers online journalism represents a return to quick, well-written analysis updated regularly, rather than lots of footage with sketchy explanations. The best online news outlets usually post bulletins on breaking news almost immediately, with more in-depth information available within an hour or so.

Many of online journalism's biggest fans are people at work who don't have televisions available but who can check online sites to get updates as new developments are reported. Thanks to the high quality of deadline reporting by major online outlets such as CNN Interactive, MSNBC and the wire services, these days the online audience has come to expect a lot from online news as a medium. Online news readers expect the depth of print reporting with the speed of broadcast.

For the reporter, this is challenging—how do you deliver depth without compromising speed, and vice versa?

DEADLINES

Perhaps the biggest single difference between the job of the online journalist and that of other journalists is the deadlines involved. The notion of being able to update stories instantly and regularly is a major change from most traditional reporting.

While early to mid-20th century newspaper staffs produced multiple editions throughout the day, in recent decades newspapers have generally produced only one main edition per day. This means that reporters have based their work on a 24-hour news cycle—they've had one main deadline and have worked on their stories all day with an eye toward that time. This has given newspaper reporters the opportunity to do quite a bit of work developing their stories before submitting them for editing. Television reporters have generally had multiple deadlines corresponding with the times of newscasts aired by their stations or networks. While this sometimes requires them to file updated reports throughout the day, for many nonbreaking stories only one report is deemed necessary.

This single-deadline day emerged from the technology of producing newspapers. When thousands of newspapers must be printed and delivered, it's more cost-efficient for most papers to print only one edition. Deadlines must be met to keep the whole process on schedule—to assure that press and delivery personnel can perform their tasks on time. Late stories translate into workers waiting around on the clock to do their jobs, which results in your news outlet paying them overtime. While this has little to do with scooping your competitors, it hits your news outlet in the wallet. In the online medium, the lag time involved in printing and delivering disappears, as does the cost of printing new editions. This gives online outlets the potential for a continual, round-the-clock news cycle, and deadlines have shifted accordingly.

Cable news is a medium with deadlines similar to those in online journalism. With the emergence of CNN, MSNBC, Fox News and other cable networks devoted exclusively to news, it has become feasible to update a story immediately. For reporters, this means staying on top of a story and reporting new details as they become available. However, since a TV channel can only cover one story at a time, major breaking stories are generally the only ones updated more than once or twice a day. It's true that these networks can "crawl" updated information across the bottom of the TV screen, but these brief updates don't require the amount of work involved in a full story update. Full-time news radio stations also have similar deadline structures but are without the ability to convey visual information or to supplement coverage with a crawl.

In online journalism, where any story can be updated at any time, reporters know that there is a constant or "rolling" deadline. In this medium, sometimes getting a scoop on your competitors is not a matter of hours but of minutes. Still, like so many other aspects of this medium, your own experience with deadlines will depend entirely on your publication's standards, goals and audiences. For example, if you work for the online site of a print outlet, you may adhere to traditional once-a-day deadlines unless you're covering a breaking story. Many print outlet sites update online stories only when a major story is breaking. This might be different for the online site of a broadcast outlet, where content is often updated with each newscast.

The number of outlets that update continuously, however, is growing and is likely to continue to grow for the foreseeable future. So you need to be prepared for the unique challenges of a constant rolling deadline. While this sounds nerve-racking, reporters and editors in the online world have adjusted to it and developed skills at quickly analyzing the facts that are absolutely necessary for publication and those that can be confirmed later for updates.

In all likelihood, in the online medium your deadlines will vary according to the timeliness and importance of the story you're covering as well as the nature of the story. As more information becomes available, you'll get used to writing story updates as new information warrants rather than waiting for the deadline for your next edition or newscast.

In many ways, writing for the online medium is a lot like reporting for a wire service such as Associated Press or United Press International. These organizations provide information for news outlets worldwide with deadlines at every hour of the day, and wire services must update their stories constantly to accommodate these deadlines. Their subscribers—news organizations—expect round-the-clock coverage. Online outlets may or may not have subscribers, but their audiences generally expect regular updates. In this ultra-electronic, superfast era, people don't have time to wait around. Online news sites have to meet their audiences' deadlines, not their own.

DON'T BELIEVE YOUR MOTHER

Having established the elastic nature of online deadlines, you should recognize that the most important aspect of getting stories posted quickly is getting them right. This means that, like any journalist, once you have your story prepared, you need to conduct a final round of fact checking. This should not be a cursory glance—you must analyze all the assertions in your article and determine whether they have been confirmed and attributed properly. The oldest adage in the reporter's vocabulary is, "If your mother says she loves you, check it out." Since you're in the information business, you need to make sure that your stories are reliable.

The best approach is to verify anything at all that might be disputed. How you go about doing this will vary according to the specifics of your article. If you're writing about a specific event—a crime, a meeting, a speech, a ballgame—most of the substance of your article will be based on straightforward facts about that event. Even when disagreements arise within articles like these, you can generally

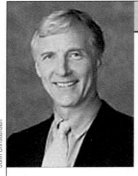

|||||| **FROM THE FIELD**

John Christensen
Freelance writer
Former Senior Writer, CNN Interactive

John Christensen was familiar with deadlines when he came to work at CNN Interactive in 1997. That doesn't mean he was quite prepared for the online definition of deadlines.

"It's a pretty intense job," he says. "It's very demanding. If we have a plane crash or a press conference that we can monitor, we've got to have something up very quickly, within an hour or so, or whatever it takes, depending on how big a story it is and how much material you've got. You need to get something online pretty much right away, and sometimes you'll have a producer or an editor who will write just a couple of graphs and we'll post that, just so we have something up until a longer write can be finished and posted."

Christensen says that his best preparation for the job was working at an afternoon newspaper where deadlines were in the morning. "The last newspaper I worked for was in Honolulu," he explains. It was an afternoon paper, and our deadlines were very early. So basically, you hoped you got your story done the day before, or you came in extremely early and pounded something out."

Since the online field was so new, CNN hired him in spite of a lack of online savvy. He had plenty of reporting experience, but no online experience at all. "None!" says Christensen with a laugh. "Not even Web surfing. I was not Web-conversant at all. I admit to feeling bewildered at times—I was learning new terminology, and getting into various queues and that sort of thing on the computer."

verify facts about them fairly easily. If all your sources have spoken on the record and you're working with official documents—police reports, minutes of meetings and so forth—you can simply attribute statements to the people who said them and facts to the documents that contained them. If there are disputes over numbers or specifics, be sure to report the facts as each side sees them, and also do your best to verify them independently. Above all, if anything seems even slightly questionable, do a little more digging and try to confirm it.

When dealing with stories of a less concrete nature, fact checking is both more difficult and more necessary. If the facts themselves are in dispute, and there are no official sources or public records to rely on, you need to be especially careful to confirm the details. For example, if your story revolves around a dispute within an organization—allegations of misconduct, mistreatment of employees, unjustified firings or other touchy subjects—tread carefully. Make sure you understand the dimensions of the dispute, and find out who is on which side of the issue. Your object should be to gather solid information as well as comments from people

While Christensen learned about computers from some of the younger staff members, in return he taught them a lot about core journalistic values. "When I started here," Christensen says, "I realized there were people from other disciplines in the newsroom, and that because they didn't have a journalism orientation, they didn't have the obsession with accuracy and precision and timeliness that journalists do. In the same vein, some of them must surely have wondered why on earth I was so dense, why I had such a hard time with some of the technical things I had to learn."

Being a little older than some of the people he was working with, Christensen seemed to particularly appreciate the technological wonder of producing online news. "Newspapers—some of them have been around for 100 years or more," he says. "When you go to a place like that, there is an established structure, an established business. And you become a component, you fit into it. But you're very conscious of the fact that this is an established business, with an infrastructure and a momentum all its own. Here, everything is so new, five years ago it did not exist. So I look around the room, and I think, it's astonishing to me that everybody is acting as though it's normal."

Christensen worked on deadline at CNN Interactive for three years, but these days most of his work is on the site's special projects. This included helping to write and assemble material for its huge millennium package of 1999–2000. It was produced in conjunction with the television network's miniseries on the events of the preceding 1,000 years.

"It was interesting for me—I used to love history when I was a student in high school," says Christensen. "That's quite a time span. There were all kinds of different ideas of what we could do each week. I wrote the timelines for 9 of the 10 centuries. That's kind of grunt work, but I found it kind of interesting and a challenge. For some reason, graphically we were restricted to 12 entries per century. In fact, on some of them I only had 8 or 9, so I had to come up with 2 or 3 more. Keeping those to 70–75 words, which I found was about the right length, that was a challenge. Taking something like Leif Ericson discovering Nova Scotia or Newfoundland and doing that in 70 words was quite a challenge."

on all sides of the dispute. Submit your story only when you're comfortable that you've confirmed as much as you can and represented the different points of view.

Obviously, you need to confirm the status of the major players in any story. Make sure all names and job titles are correct and that any references to people involved in legal proceedings are accurate. One area where inexperienced reporters sometimes get into trouble is with causal relationships. There's a tendency to write things like, "Because of faulty wiring, the house burst into flames," without backing it up with sufficient evidence. This is the sort of thing that can cause lawsuits, and nobody wants that. Even when you have confirmed a cause, you need to report the source of that evidence (for example, "The fire department's investigation concluded that because of faulty wiring the house burst into flames.").

This vigilance for confirming facts is essential even in opinion pieces. Your attitudes and beliefs are entirely your own, but if you express them based on flimsy information, you're committing an irresponsible act. The best opinion writing backs up its arguments with facts wherever possible and with other informed opinion (for example, "An article in the August 6 edition of *Newsweek* called the decision 'outrageous and ill-timed'."). This gives your piece the added weight of journalistic credibility—it's not just what you think, it's a well-considered and informed opinion.

The process of fact checking also goes beyond simply verifying individual pieces of information. Sometimes in the process of organizing a story facts may be presented in misleading ways. Sometimes important pieces of information depend on lesser facts that get edited out by mistake, or assertions from sources make their way into the story without verification. This is simply a product of trying to assemble a lot of information into a readable story. This is also why your final read-through of a story is the most important step in fact checking. Make sure that all facts are both confirmed and clearly stated, with no loose ends or areas for possible misinterpretation.

This may sound like a time-consuming procedure, and it certainly can be. However, when you get in the habit of it, the fact-checking process simply becomes a common aspect of reporting, just like interviewing and writing. The need to get a story done as soon as possible should never supersede the need to get it right. If necessary, submit a shorter story with all its details confirmed, then update it later when you verify more facts.

TWEAKING FOR THE WEB

Now that you've checked your facts, you need to address one more aspect of the story. As mentioned in earlier chapters, in the online world simply writing a compelling story isn't enough. The best online stories often contain links to audio or video clips, previous related stories or even to home pages of people, agencies and companies mentioned within the story. You'll need to identify various aspects of the story that would be enhanced by links or multimedia.

In general, you should identify useful audio and video clips early on, before you actually write a story. Once the story is largely finished, however, take a little time to review your chosen multimedia. Sometimes while you're writing a story you'll receive new information or get an additional interview that will cast the story in a new light or give it a new angle. If this happens, your audio and video choices might no longer seem appropriate. Don't be afraid to make an occasional last-minute change; your main goal is to make the entire package work. Also be sure you check over any sidebar stories, fact boxes, pull quotes or other additional material that accompanies your story.

At this late stage, go back through your story and look for items that might provide useful links. (Depending on your site's protocol, you may even perform this task while the copy desk is reading your submitted story.) Look for references to companies or agencies that have their own Web pages and provide links to them. If you referred to an earlier article about the same subject, also note that for a link. In addition, some sites have prewritten profiles of newsmakers within their geographical or subject areas. These special pages are often linked with the first reference to this person in the article. As you continue to write for the online medium, you'll get used to noting possible links as you write, but you should still double-check your stories for them when you're finished writing.

Every site has different rules about placing links on story pages—some link only to related stories from their own publication, others will link to outside sites, and some others will include links to the home pages of every organization or company mentioned in a story. In addition, some place these links at the end of the story, while others simply embed them within the story itself, allowing users to click on the names as they appear throughout the story. You'll need to learn your outlet's standards, then consult with your editors to develop a sense of what works and what doesn't. This should lead you into effectively being able to define link material without much effort. (This is discussed further in Chapter 13.)

An important element of this, however, is making sure that your links point to the proper sites. As part of your fact-checking routine, check the Web to locate the URLs for the pages to which you want to link. While the URL for a corporation might seem obvious—www.microsoft.com, for example—you can't simply count on this. Take the time to make sure your links work because there's nothing Web users hate more than broken links.

This is especially true for links to previous related stories on your outlet's own site. As noted in Chapter 6, you should have some idea of your outlet's previous coverage of a topic before you write a story. If you've done this, you can easily provide links to related articles at the end of the one you're finishing. This is a popular feature with readers, and one that is unique to online outlets. If your outlet allows free access to previous articles, you should definitely take advantage of this feature. If your outlet charges for access, at least links like these will alert readers to the availability of other interesting and useful articles on the same or similar topics.

At this stage, with the writing essentially done, review your work to be sure your article provides a complete package for the online reader. Make sure you've maximized the online potential of your story by making it textually, visually and interactively appealing. Remember, you don't want just to create a dressed-up print article. You might use some standard writing techniques along the way, but ideally your piece will be so tightly integrated with its medium that readers won't be able to imagine it any other way.

DEVELOPING STORIES, UPDATES AND FOLLOW-UPS

If television is the best format for covering an individual public event, and newspapers are the ideal medium for a story that resolves itself in one day, online journalism is likely the perfect outlet for a story that carries on over a period of days, weeks or even months. By both keeping readers updated on the latest details of a story and linking to previous stories to fill in background, the online medium works perfectly for stories whose details are revealed over a long period of time.

For an online reporter who has adjusted to the medium's ease of updating, the notion of a story playing out over weeks and months is just an extension of the approach to most stories. However, you should learn the right way to finish a story that will likely be updated later.

When you cover a one-time, stand-alone event—a fund-raiser, a concert, or a meeting—there's a good chance you'll only write one story about it. However, lots of stories aren't like this—you won't know all the details about some stories right away. Stories in which the details unfold over a period of days or weeks are called developing stories. These are common in criminal investigations of all sorts as well as in many other kinds of stories.

If you're covering a homicide, for example, you'll often publish your initial story using only the sketchy details immediately apparent within the first few hours after the crime is committed. Perhaps police have not yet identified a suspect, but you can report the details of what is known. As a suspect is identified, then captured, then charged, then eventually tried on the charges, a reporter will write a new story for each new development in the case.

This process involves some special techniques in writing stories, both before and after you learn new information. If you're writing a story on a murder that occurred within the last few hours and there are still many unanswered questions, don't simply ignore them. You don't want to leave loose ends in your stories. Note the elements that are still unexplained and state them in the active voice. Here's a poorly worded, passive example of this:

> Motives for the crime are not known, and a suspect in the case has not yet been identified by police, though it was reported that witnesses saw a white male of medium build running from the area. Witnesses are being interviewed in hopes of creating a composite sketch of this man.

Here's a much better, more active example:

> Police have not yet identified a suspect and do not know of any motives for the crime. However, investigators said witnesses saw a white male of medium build running from the area. Police are interviewing witnesses in hopes of creating a composite sketch of this man.

This type of information alerts the reader to the fact that more information will be forthcoming in future articles. It also sets the stage for the stories you will write when more information becomes available.

This sort of thing isn't only used in articles about crimes. Let's say you're announcing that a local concert venue has booked Sheryl Crow to play a concert in April but the particulars have not yet been announced. Here's an example of how you can be specific about things that are unknown:

> Promoters have not yet set the exact date and time of the concert. A spokesman said they would release this information, along with ticket prices and seating options, sometime in the next few weeks.

Sometimes you'll simply rewrite an existing story if new information comes in quickly, or add a quick sidebar. These are referred to as **updates**—not a complete rewrite of the original story but an addition to it. This is often simply a case of plugging in information in the place where you'd previously stated that the information was unavailable. Different sites have different policies on this type of updating—many require that an updated story be noted as such at the bottom, with the time and date of the update specifically stated.

However, you'll often write a completely new story if you get new material a few hours later or a day or two after the original event. Appropriately, these are called **follow-up stories.** They have two main purposes—to provide new information about a previous story and to bring readers who didn't see the previous story up to date.

To write follow-up stories well, you need to get across the new information but also quickly summarize the main points of the previous story. Here are the first three paragraphs for a follow-up to the homicide story:

> Police arrested a Detroit man early Thursday morning on suspicion of murder in the death of Eric Minton.
>
> Thomas Walters, 23, who was charged with one count of first-degree murder, was alleged to have shot Minton in a dispute involving Walters' girlfriend.
>
> Minton was shot and killed Monday night in a Novi trailer park. Police said witnesses saw a white male of medium build running from the scene, though no suspect or motive was identified at the time.

Notice how the third paragraph summarizes the previous information so that readers who missed the original story know the essential details. Depending on the amount of information previously known, this summary can stretch far beyond one or two sentences. Indeed, for complex stories, you may need to use two or three paragraphs to explain the important details of the story up to this point.

Though the online venue allows readers to look back at previous stories, you still need to provide a summary of information from earlier reports. You shouldn't force your audience to go through previous stories to get up to speed. However, you can link to previous stories for assorted purposes, especially if a previous story contains something useful, such as an in-depth interview with one of the main people involved in the story or multimedia elements that readers might enjoy.

SUMMARY

Is there a "last minute" in online journalism or not? The answer probably depends on your point of view, but it's clear that the notion of completing a story by a given deadline has been radically altered in this medium. To succeed, reporters must be able to both write stories quickly *and* get their facts straight. They must also learn to make adjustments as they write and appeal to both those who have followed the story all along and those who are reading about it for the first time. In the online medium, rather than writing isolated individual stories, reporters leave a trail of stories that users can follow from the beginning if they like. More than in any other venue, online stories are often more of an ongoing process than a finished product.

RELATED WEB SITES

CNN Interactive
http://www.cnn.com
CNN special millennium section
http://www.cnn.com/SPECIALS/1999/millennium/

EXERCISES

1. Go to a local newspaper's online site and select a major story it has covered recently. List three suggestions for multimedia (audio or video clips) and three suggestions for links to outside Web sites. Also, provide a sentence or two explaining why each choice is appropriate and what it would add to the story.

2. Write a lead and nut graph based on the following information, stressing what you know rather than what you don't know:

    You are writing in January for an outlet based in St. Louis, Mo. The Commission on Presidential Debates has announced that a presidential debate between the Democratic and Republican nominees will be held in mid-October at Washington University in St. Louis. The event is tentatively scheduled to be held in the school's basketball arena, the Washington University Field House, but could be moved to the Samuel B. Edison Theatre. Provisions have been made for anywhere from three to five presidential debates and one vice presidential debate. Other cities that may host debates include Boston, Mass., Danville, Ky., Winston-Salem, N.C., Madison, Wis., and St. Petersburg, Fla.

3. Write the first three paragraphs of an update story based on the following information and the material from earlier in the chapter about the death of Eric Minton:

    It's been 10 days since Eric Minton was killed. Last night police arrested a second suspect in the case, 22-year-old Gerald Stacy, as an accessory to the murder. Police believe Stacy drove Thomas Walters from the scene of the crime and helped him hide from police. Stacy, of Flint, Mich., is believed to have known about the attack in advance. Both Stacy and Walters have prior arrest records for petty theft.

 4. Using InfoTrac College Edition, search the archives of a newspaper outside your local area to find a topic that's been covered for a long period of time. Select two stories about the topic that were published a week or more apart. Print both stories and identify all the new information found in the later story. When appropriate, indicate when each new detail was revealed. Submit both your findings and the printouts to your instructor.

||||||

PART III

Editing
for Online Journalists

For editors, the basics of style, spelling, fact checking and headlines haven't changed too much. However, the lack of space concerns and the availability of multimedia and links can add new dimensions to online stories. The chapters in Part 3 prepare editors for both traditional and new editing tasks.

10 An Uphill Battle: Online Copyediting

Some of the copy that appears online is truly dreadful. The Web has long been a haven for bad spelling, grammar and style. This chapter addresses elements of these problems as well as the changing vocabulary brought about by the Internet.

11 The Online Editor/ Utility Infielder

An online editor these days truly needs to be a jack-of-all-trades. This chapter looks at all the different skills an online editor should possess, including managing pages, links, story content and interactive features. It also looks at questions driven not only by the content of stories but by the unique ergonomics of Web pages and browsers.

12 Multimedia for News

Using audio and video on Web sites is all the rage, but is it too much trouble for a college newspaper? This chapter discusses the available formats and their best uses. It also examines what multimedia really adds to the pages of an online news outlet.

13 Basic Online Layout

Forget anything you've ever learned about standard newspaper or magazine layout. Here you will learn the parameters, constraints and terminology of the online medium and become familiar with the most common elements of online news layout.

10

||||||

An Uphill Battle:
Online Copyediting

The Web is a great outlet for free speech. It's too bad so much of it is nearly unreadable. The very freedom that spurs the creative and freewheeling atmosphere on the Web also produces some truly ghastly writing. It's not just the atrocious grammar and spelling and the endless inaccuracies—Web writers often show a complete disregard for the conventions that make language understandable. While all of this might be tolerable in chat rooms, online news outlets have too often been known for letting their standards slide. It's true that the rise of the Internet has added whole volumes of new phrases to our collective vocabulary, but that shouldn't result in online news outlets publishing third-grade-level writing. Against this backdrop, the copy editor becomes a very important person, particularly because many Web copy editors do a lot more than proofread pages. This chapter looks at some of the tasks involved and addresses elements of the common problems in online writing.

In David Shenk's 1997 book *Data Smog: Surviving the Information Glut* (San Francisco: HarperEdge), Shenk coined a term that neatly summarizes a phenomenon we've all come to recognize in the age of cable, the cell phone and the Internet. "Data smog" refers to the information with which we're overloaded every day. Shenk argued that data smog is made up of not only the material we dislike—junk mail, unsolicited e-mail, endless advertisements—but also the information we enjoy. In other words, people become so caught up in all manner of information—

good and bad—that they end up wasting large portions of their lives plowing through it.

There's an awful lot of smog on the Web. Part of the reason all that data is so smoggy is that it's so poorly written. A huge percentage of Web material is dashed off quickly with little regard for whether it's readable. This is troublesome for several reasons, the most obvious being that it can create a "dumbed-down" environment in which complex thoughts are not valued, rewarded or expressed. Perhaps more important, however, such careless writing practically begs to be misunderstood. With all of the raw nerves on the Web just waiting to pounce on anything potentially incorrect or misstated, and all of the "flame wars" that start based on some ill-considered statement, it's very easy for one slipshod message to contribute whole new clouds to the haze.

In online journalism, you should be out to eliminate data smog, at least in your own publication. The best way to combat it is with clear, accurate, readable stories. However, not every reporter writes this way, and not every section editor has this in mind while editing. This is where a skillful copy editor can turn into the most important person in an online news organization. Some might see the position of copy editor as a low-level job, but in fact it's vitally important. The professionalism of many news organizations rests as much on their copy staffs as on the skills of their writers. In a developing medium such as online journalism, this is especially true.

SAVING THEIR BUTTS

A common misconception about copyediting is that it's all about proofreading. The stereotypical image of a copy editor is an uptight dweeb who has little in life to enjoy beyond gleefully pointing out your mistakes. In fact, a good copy editor is a reporter's best friend. While it's true that proofreading is a major portion of the job, copy editors have to catch much more than the occasional misplaced comma. They're the last line of defense against any errors the reporter may have made.

Keep in mind that reporters can make all kinds of errors beyond simple misspellings. They shouldn't, but they do. (After all, not every reporter has read this book.) While copy editors are expected to catch spelling or grammar errors, they also look for factual errors, misleading passages or items that might get the paper into legal trouble.

Section editors should catch these mistakes, but they are often distracted by concerns about specific aspects of the story. Their primary concerns might be whether particular officials are quoted accurately and presented in a balanced fashion and how high certain elements of the story are played. Because of this, other elements sometimes slip through the cracks, and a good copy editor will catch them. This means that in addition to knowing all the rules of language, the best copy editors also have a lot of general knowledge about assorted subjects. Part of this comes with experience—as you read more material in your daily job, you

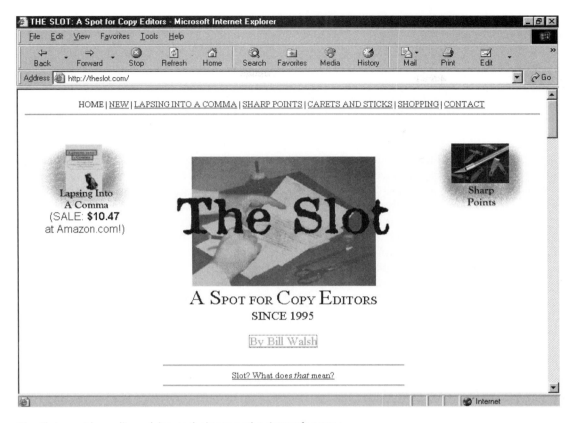

The Slot provides online advice, techniques and pointers for copy editors of all levels of experience.

SOURCE: theslot.com (accessed September 25, 2003). Used by permission.

learn a lot. It's often said that a journalist is a generalist, and this is a fine example of how wide-ranging general knowledge can help you. Conversely, you should also recognize the limitations of your knowledge and know where to look to double-check facts. Increasingly, the ability to quickly search the Web to verify information is a useful skill for copy editors.

In addition to the skills needed by most copy editors, regardless of medium, online copy editors have a bigger job. Because of the reach and potential audience of the Web, consistency and accuracy are even more important online than in print or on TV. Yet many news organizations give their Web operations short shrift. With the exception of online-only outlets and a few progressive print and broadcast sites, online staffs are often small and must process huge amounts of information. This often includes the text of an entire day's newspaper or news broadcast plus any breaking stories or other Web-only content on a site. Some sites don't employ separate online copy editors at all—they simply post material that's been edited for print.

In contrast, many savvy outlets see the differences between the Web and other media and recognize how important copyediting for the Web can be. Because of the assorted elements unique to the Web, an online copy editor needs additional skills. The most crucial of these is the ability to check links to stories and multimedia and to correct them if necessary. There's nothing more dispiriting for readers than to click on a link, anticipating an interesting story, and end up with a big, fat "NOT FOUND" staring them in the face.

The dead-link phenomenon is particularly troubling if your site links to off-site pages. Since Web sites are constantly being redesigned, a link that worked in January may no longer work in April. Furthermore, some sites—particularly those that charge for use of their archives—change site URLs after a page has been online for a certain period of time. So you should make it a general rule to double-check any links that you believe might have changed for any reason. Again, the more experience you gain, the better your instincts about these and other similar matters will become.

The purpose of all this is to present the most professional product possible. Often a good copy editor will save an editor or writer untold headaches by recognizing an inconsistency, a set of numbers that doesn't add up, an erroneous assertion or some other embarrassing error. Mistakes like these might seem unimportant at the time, but catching them can rescue a reporter from a flood of mail and dozens of phone messages. Remember, athletes aren't the only people who make great catches.

A FEW GENERAL POINTERS

Whether online or off, some techniques tend to work well when copyediting, although the Web requires a few extra procedures of its own.

The copy editor's job involves both proofreading stories and checking for content errors. Accordingly, as a general rule, you should read each story twice—first for mistakes in spelling, grammar and link text, and second to catch anything incorrect or misleading within the content of the story. This makes sense. The first time through, you're paying so much attention to mechanical errors that you may not actually absorb many details of the story. The attention to every last letter that is inherent within the first read-through also makes it the perfect time to check the URLs in any links on your page. Once you're sure everything is spelled correctly and stated clearly, you can double-check the facts. While not every copy editor follows this procedure, it's a sensible way to make sure you don't neglect one aspect of copyediting for the other.

During the first read-through, it's important for copy editors to follow along in the story word by word. This cannot be stated strongly enough—if you don't look at each individual word as you go along, you'll find that all kinds of mistakes creep into the stories you edit. Your brain will instinctively "connect the dots" if you read quickly, glossing over misspellings or inserting articles and conjunctions ("and," "it," "the," "or") when they're missing. You need to read at the speed of your eyes, not your brain.

One way to make sure you do this is to read the copy aloud. Copy editors frequently say each word out loud to themselves as they read—it's not uncommon for someone walking into a newsroom to see copy editors poring over printouts, reading them aloud quietly to themselves. Another common technique to assure you read every line is to slide a blank sheet of paper down the page, covering up subsequent sentences as you read. Still another way is to read from the last sentence to the first—sentences should flow logically together in either direction.

In the online world, copyediting procedures vary from one news outlet to another. Some copy editors only read stories before they are placed on pages, others only read them after they've been placed, and still others do both.

Certain kinds of mistakes tend to crop up frequently in any sort of news story, and copy editors need to get in the habit of spotting them and fixing them quickly. Here are a few tips to identify the most common errors.

Mechanics

Make sure subjects and verbs agree. If your noun is plural ("sisters"), the verb needs to be plural as well ("are"). Errors in subject-verb agreement tend to crop up in complex sentences where another noun appears between the subject and the verb.

Wrong: "The bill with five amendments **were** ratified by the assembly."

Right: "Anderson, accompanied to the station by his children, **was** taken into custody."

Watch out for "they" and "their." This is by far the most common mistake involving pronouns. Inexperienced writers frequently misuse the word "they" when referring to a singular organization. This is common in daily conversation, so many people think it's grammatically correct, but it isn't.

Wrong: "IBM announced that **their** third-quarter profits held steady."

Right: "The Justice Department announced **its** plans for prosecuting the case."

Watch out for "that" versus "which." The general rule for using these two words is based on the absence or presence of a comma beforehand. If a comma immediately precedes the word, it should be "which"; if not, it should be "that." An independent clause (a section of a sentence that can stand as its own sentence) generally will not contain "which," whereas a dependent clause (a section of a sentence that expands on material from another section) often begins with "which" in referring to the earlier clause.

Wrong: "The trial **which** followed captured the public's attention."

Right: "The verdict, **which** caused endless speculation, came Friday morning."

Wrong: "Trials such as these, **that** grab the public spotlight, are becoming common."

Right: "The incident **that** happened 18 months ago shocked the town."

Watch out for "farther" versus "further." The important difference between these two words is that "farther" deals with distance whereas "further" basically means "additional."

Wrong: "She drove **further** than anyone else to attend the meeting."

Right: "He asked if there were any **further** objections."

Wrong: "He said he would not pursue the matter any **farther.**"

Right: "The home run traveled **farther** than any in recent memory."

First references. In general, refer to people by their first and last names only on the first reference to them in the story; refer to them exclusively by last names thereafter. In the process of editing, a first name sometimes gets cut, leaving no reference at all to the person's first name. This can easily slip by if you've read another story recently about the same person.

Courtesy titles. News organizations all have different policies on the use of **courtesy titles** ("Mr.," "Mrs.," "Dr." and so forth). This can present problems when using wire or news-syndicate stories that use different standards than you do.

Content

Does the lead misguide the reader? Sometimes reporters get so carried away with crafting a punchy lead that they write something that will mislead readers about the rest of the story. Sometimes a lead overstates certain aspects of the story just to grab readers, and at other times it simply doesn't reflect the true nature of the story. Work with the reporter or your editor to better inform the reader while retaining the elements that might make the lead interesting.

Don't convict a suspect. A simple slip-up that leaves the impression that a suspect is guilty could possibly cost your organization thousands or even millions of dollars in lawsuits. Make sure that anyone who has not been convicted of a crime is referred to with the correct legal status, whether it's "Being sought in the abduction of . . . ," "Charged in the death of . . . ," "On trial for the theft of . . ." or whatever may apply. Also, remember that until someone confesses all aspects of a crime are *alleged* until proven in court, and all victims are also alleged.

Double- and triple-check headlines. Since they're the most prominent feature of any online story, you need to make sure that all headlines are factually accurate, spelled correctly, grammatically correct and contain no double-entendres that will come back to haunt you. A common rule is to examine every headline and subhead for at least three to five seconds to make sure it works.

Do numbers in the story add up? Maybe you got into journalism to avoid math, but that's why we have calculators. It's usually a simple matter to double-check the figures in stories, and it can save untold headaches. If the numbers don't add up in a story based on amounts of money spent within a budget or something similar, it casts doubt on the entire story, and officials will happily point this out.

Web-Specific Items

Double-check links. Copy editors are often working too quickly to stop and verify the text of every link on a page, but they can usually test links to see if they lead where they should. It's much better for a copy editor to find an error than for a reader to complain that a link doesn't work properly. When time permits, copy editors should scan URLs to identify anything questionable. For instance, if a story links to the Web site of the Sony Corporation of America, and you notice that the link text says "http://www.sonny.com," you should alert the editor to the probable error. If you notice that a link to a QuickTime video clip lists a file extension of ".mob" when it should be ".mov," alert the editor. (See Chapter 12 for more on multimedia and file extensions.) Even if some items you believe to be errors actually turn out to be correct, this practice will head off any potential problems for readers.

Check all supporting elements. A good online copy editor should request to see stories after they're placed on pages to make sure headlines, links, tables, sidebars, photo captions and any other related material are all correct and consistent with the content of the story itself. When putting together a package full of links and multimedia to accompany a story, it's easy to get facts crossed up and wind up with contradictions between the story and some of its supporting materials.

While these pointers will help you, this is by no means a comprehensive list of errors you might find or ways to guard against mistakes. There are literally hundreds of other grammatical rules and procedures you should know. This book is not a grammar text—if you have problems in this area, there are many useful books and Web sites on this subject (see the Related Web Sites listed at the end of this chapter for a few good sources).

Perhaps most important, get to know your own weaknesses as a copy editor and work to correct them. We all have weak areas, as both writers and editors. Do you tend to overlook missing pronouns or articles? Are there a few particular words whose misspellings you tend to miss, or do certain grammar rules cause you trouble? It is important to identify these weaknesses and to work on fixing them. This is often done with the help of a colleague, either an editor or another copy editor. If you're confident about your command of the rules of language, you'll work more effectively and efficiently. Your bosses will also be glad to see that you're willing to work on shoring up your weak areas.

THE SPELL-CHECK PROBLEM

A few years ago, a Southern California newspaper switched from a very old computer system to a new one. One of the new system's features was the spell-check function, which alerts writers to possible misspelled words. Shortly after the installation of this system, a reporter sat down to compose a story about the trial of a local financier named Richard Silberman. When the reporter was finished writing, he decided to run spell-check on the story. However, he was still somewhat unfamiliar with how the spell-check function worked. At one point, the reporter inadvertently clicked on the "Replace All" button instead of the "Skip" button. When he was done spell checking, he submitted the story to the copy desk. Here are the first three paragraphs of the story as the copy desk received it:

> La Jolla financier and local Democratic Party figure Richard T. Superman was sentenced yesterday to 46 months in prison for his participation in a money-laundering scheme.
>
> Superman, the estranged husband of city council member Susan Golding, was convicted in March on two felony counts for helping launder money he believed came from a Colombian drug cartel. In fact, Superman was dealing with an undercover FBI agent who was posing as the cartel's financial adviser.
>
> Superman, 56, showed no expression as federal Judge William B. Enright handed down the sentence.

This is not to say that spell-check always causes problems. In fact, astute writers (and astute students) can fine-tune their spelling skills by paying attention while the function runs or when the program underlines potential misspellings. However, too many writers have come to use spell-check as a crutch rather than a tool.

This has created an epidemic among young journalists. To put it bluntly, most of them can't spell. This is the single most common complaint about young writers in newsrooms (as well as public relations firms and advertising agencies) across the country. This should be a major concern for all students—it sends the message to potential employers that either you don't care enough to spell things correctly or that you're just not very bright. Neither of these is a message you want to send to someone interviewing you for a job.

While working through high school and college, many students seem to rely on spell-check as a cure-all. Everyone knows it's not perfect, but the function does a good enough job that students can effectively make it through high school and into college without needing to know how to spell. If those students manage to become professional reporters, they've already acquired the bad habit of letting the computer spell for them. This is particularly a major problem for those students who rely heavily on computers—in other words, the ones most likely to end up in online journalism.

Such carelessness makes the copy desk's job more difficult because the reporters don't know enough about proper spelling to avoid making the same mistakes over and over again. This builds up resentment among the copy staff, particularly because copy editors are in the business of being accurate. Plus, if someone at the copy desk just happens to miss the error, the story is published with an error that makes the writer look bad. While one copy editor might miss an error, an audience of thousands (and potentially millions on the Web) will certainly spot it immediately, and many of them will let you know about it.

The spell-check problem can work two ways. Most often, it will ignore incorrect spellings because they resemble a different word. This can manifest itself in a near-unlimited number of ways. If a writer isn't careful, it can also change cor-

SPELL-CHECK HOLES

Like the computer itself, spell-check is a marvelous tool that can help save you time and effort. However, writers should beware—spell-check has its quirks and limitations. If a reporter misspells a word, but the misspelling inadvertently creates an unintended word, spell-check won't detect the error. For example, a common typo turns the word "from" into "form," as in "The charity received the donation form the company." Spell-check won't catch this mistake because it doesn't make spelling decisions based on logic.

If reporters aren't careful, this quirk can cause them to turn in stories containing mistakes that are difficult for copy editors to catch. Like all readers, copy editors recognize obvious misspellings more easily than misspellings that accidentally create words. Here are some common types of mistakes that elude spell-check—see if you can catch them the first time through:

WRONG WORD

The store is open seven days a weak.

The accident cite has been sealed off by police.

"'We did are best," said the Little Leaguer.

WRONG FIRST/LAST LETTER

The movie surprised dome people who expected a comedy.

The children disagreed about the candy they liked vest.

Police took the suspect it for questioning.

OMITTED LETTERS

Parents can chose from several options.

Some onlookers believed the police took to long to respond.

The mayor indicted that no new action would be taken.

ADDED LETTER(S)

The border collie took Beast of Show honors.

Pop culture items from the '70s are know popular again.

The accident was at the cornered of Fifth and Market.

LETTER(S) IN MIDDLE

There were few clues, but polite questioned one witness and sought others.

The witness didn't knew the exact time of the incident.

The election results were so close that a recount was a string possibility.

To avoid mistakes like these, reporters need to carefully proofread all stories. Most spell-checkers give you the right to agree or disagree with the proposed spelling before changing a word, but a careless click can cause all sorts of problems. Copy editors need to get in the habit of reading each story aloud, word by word, to make sure that they catch even mistakes masquerading as correctly spelled words. Spell-check is only detrimental if reporters allow it to lull them into believing they don't need to know proper spelling.

rect words into improper ones, as in the "Superman" example. These imperfections can allow all sorts of otherwise unimaginable copy to make it into your publication—everything from foul language to misleading words to lies and incorrect statements. Even the best copy desk will not catch every error, particularly if there are a lot of them in a story.

There's an additional headache related to spell–check that is specific to the online medium. Most online news outlets use standard word-processing programs (Microsoft Word, Word Perfect and so on) for their copy, then transfer the edited stories to HTML layout programs (Adobe GoLive, Macromedia Dreamweaver and others). However, these days many HTML programs contain their own spell-check functions, which may differ in important ways from those in word processors. One program may miss a certain word, while another one won't, and vice versa. In a worst-case scenario, mistakes made by one program may be compounded when transferred to the other program.

Here's a nightmarish example. The following paragraph contains two proper names and many Latin-influenced titles, with all items spelled correctly:

> Carvin Hendricks, 36, was charged with the bludgeoning death of Manolo Bejar, 29, outside his apartment in the Villa Norte complex on Caminito de los Hermanos in San Ysidro.

After running this paragraph through a word processor and an HTML program, both using spell-check's "Replace All" function, this is the result:

> Craven Handpicks, 36, was charged with the bludgeoning death of Manila Bear, 29, outside his apartment in the Villain Norse complex on Comminute de loss Herman's in San Isidro.

Neither program inflicted all this damage on its own, but even more unsettling, the resulting paragraph was checked again and sailed right through spell-check in both programs with no errors reported. This is more than a little scary. It's not likely that a reporter would click "Replace All" twice by mistake, or that all these errors would somehow slip by a copy desk, but with such obvious imperfections in the technology, the potential for trouble remains.

None of this is meant to dissuade editors, reporters or copy editors from using spell-check as a tool. But it is important to recognize the limitations of spell-check and to learn to look for the types of errors it doesn't catch. It's vital for everyone involved to learn how this function works and to know its strengths and weaknesses. Thoroughly knowing the commands and procedures of your word-processing and HTML software will help immensely in avoiding embarrassing errors.

HEADLINES AND CUTLINES

In most traditional newsrooms, copy editors are also in charge of writing headlines and photo captions. Reporters are sometimes encouraged to suggest headlines, but it's often a copy editor who must write them. Many copy editors find this the most enjoyable part of the job—it's their opportunity to exercise a little creativity. Headlines are often the first item a reader notices about a page, whether in print or online, and a compelling headline is the catalyst that convinces the reader to look at a story.

The primary goal of a headline is to quickly tell the reader the gist of the story. In many ways, it's like writing a lead, but tougher, because you have fewer words to work with. The headline identifies the story's important point or points and conveys them in a brief phrase. As with lead writing, you need to use active verbs, both to make the headline forceful and to keep its length short—phrases with strong verbs are almost always shorter than those with weak ones.

In print news, headlines must both inform readers and fit into a specified area on the page. This has made good headline writing for newspapers something of an art form. In the online medium, it's long been assumed that there are few if any space limitations—you can fit a fairly lengthy headline across the top of a screen, and most online sites have few if any rules about multiple-line headlines. However, headlines are uniquely important in the online medium. On many news home pages, headlines serve as the text that links readers to stories. It's often the only reference to a story on the page, and thus the only source of information about the story that most readers will see. This reinforces the need to get across a lot of information very quickly—as a reader scans the home page, your headline must stand out among the menu of stories.

There's also one new consideration for online headline writers. These days more and more readers are using their cell phones to Web surf. This means that your headlines are frequently being read on extremely tiny screens, with users scrolling through all but the shortest headlines. In many ways, this marks a return to writing headlines to fit in small spaces, and it means you have to work extra hard to get the point across quickly.

Since you're trying to grab readers' attention, you should think creatively when writing headlines. Having said this, it's awfully easy to get carried away. Not every headline should be funny or even clever because the primary goal is to explain the story. A story about a fatal car crash, for example, is not usually a good place for a deft turn of phrase—your headline should match the mood of the story. For all headlines, a good rule to follow is this: A headline can entertain readers, but never at the expense of informing them.

Beyond simply thinking creatively, there are some general guidelines to follow when writing headlines. Your main objective should be to get the gist of your story across as completely as possible in four to six words. It should summarize the most important points and match the tone of the article without stealing from the lead (which will anger reporters and disappoint readers). Above all, it should lure readers into looking at the story. If the story subject is appropriate, you can write something clever, but it shouldn't detract from the story.

If your job doesn't generally include writing headlines, you should still know a good one from a bad one. If a reporter or editor has provided a suggested headline, it's a copy editor's job to note whether it is misleading, inaccurate, inappropriate or otherwise ineffective. Editors or reporters often write clever headlines that have relatively little to do with the story; it's the copy editor's job to step in and make sure readers are informed, not just amused.

Writing photo captions—"cutlines"—also has a lot in common with writing leads. It seems simple enough—you identify the people, places and actions in a photo. However, it's a bit trickier than you might think. First, you need to describe what's going on in a photo without stating the obvious, which is often harder than it might seem. For example, if a photo depicts two people obviously posing for a picture, the easy way out is simply to say that they're posing, which is quite passive and states the obvious. If you can get information from the story that accompanies the photo, you can briefly state the significance of the event shown—for example, "Joe Smith and Fred Jones met Friday to finalize their working agreement." As with this example, you should also aim to write cutlines in the active voice. Sometimes it's difficult, but use the tips from Chapter 8 to make sure your cutlines are active.

Your information should provide as complete a description of the photo as possible—try your best to identify all persons clearly visible in the picture (unless it's a crowd photo), and try to write words that match the tone of the photo. If the photo accompanies a story, avoid using information from the lead or the headline of the story in your cutline—you want to avoid repetition if at all possible. The best cutlines—whether for stand-alone photos or pictures accompanying a story—are independent sentences, almost like tiny story leads.

STYLE

When journalists talk about **style,** they're not discussing the perfect wardrobe. They're referring to the accepted set of spellings, grammar rules and other guidelines followed by news organizations. Style guides—books that define a given set of linguistic parameters—are commonly used in all forms of creative and professional writing. (Please note that this book is *not* a style guide and assumes you will either acquire one or use one belonging to your news organization.) Some of the most common style guides are William Strunk Jr. and E. B. White's *The Elements of Style,* fourth edition (Boston: Allyn and Bacon, 2000), the *Chicago Manual of Style* (Chicago: University of Chicago Press, 2003) now in its 15th edition, and the *MLA Style Manual,* second edition (New York: Modern Language Association of America, 1998).

By far the most widely used style manual in journalism is the *Associated Press (AP) Stylebook and Briefings on Media Law* (Cambridge, MA: Perseus, 2003). Alone among the major style guides, it's tailored to the needs of journalists. It addresses all sorts of journalism-specific problems, questions, usages and all manner of minutiae related to journalistic writing.

Most newsrooms adhere pretty closely to AP style, but every organization seems to have its own peculiar exceptions. For example, some outlets use modified punctuation rules for headlines, and others amend particular rules based on commonly used terms in their geographic areas. One way or the other, editors need to make sure that reporters and copy editors are acquainted with any exceptions that apply to their newsroom.

For online publications, AP style can be a thorny issue. While the style guide contains entries for assorted online-related terms—Internet, World Wide Web, Web page and so on— many holes remain. There are literally dozens of common online terms whose usage isn't addressed in the AP style guide, such as DOS (Disruption of Service) attacks, hacking and cracking, and many online editors feel the need to go beyond AP to find something authoritative on the subject. A style guide often used for this purpose is *Wired Style: Principles of English Usage in the Digital Age* (San Francisco: HardWired, 1996), which is produced by the staff of the well-known high-tech magazine *Wired.* This book is backed up by a Web site featuring many new post-publication entries. Still, it is by no means the only book of its type, and there is no single online style Bible just yet. Style choices are often a combination of traditional news styles and adapted terminology that can vary from one organization to another.

Beyond the grammar and spelling choices found in style guides, however, every news outlet has layout-oriented aspects of style—that is, standard fonts and sizes for headlines, cutlines, photo credits and body type. In online news, layout style often extends to standards for placement of advertisements and links, standard uses of color and graphics, and other elements that should remain consistent throughout the site. A good copy editor should be able to catch any breaches of these elements of style in addition to typographical and content errors. They'll know assorted specific rules for their publications on one-line headlines for different browsers, dual bylines, inclusion/exclusion of dates and many other seemingly trivial items.

As with spell-check, in the area of style, computers both giveth and taketh away. Not long ago, most print publications' pages were laid out on dummy sheets and pasted up by hand, which added an extra step in quality control but slowed the process of producing pages. These days, most print news organizations lay out their publications on computers, using templates and libraries to speed the process. As might be expected, online publications are even more template driven, and styles for headlines, bylines, captions and so forth are generally built right into the templates or style sheets.

This sounds like a breeze for copy editors—all elements of a page are simply plugged into pre-existing style sheets, so all the formats should be correct, right? Well, anyone who's worked with computers for very long knows that every so often something gets fouled up. For whatever reason—someone clicked the wrong button or hit the wrong function key—formats do get fouled up. The most valuable copy editors know their organizations' styles well enough to catch when a photo caption is showing up in the Helvetica font instead of Times New Roman. They know when it should be bold and isn't, or when it's showing up at the wrong size. They'll also notice when a photo or box isn't lining up properly, or when the ads that belong on the left have been laid out on the right.

SUMMARY

There's plenty of "smog" on the Web, emanating from chat rooms, discussion groups and even online news outlets. As a copy editor, your job is to clear the air at your own publication—to make sure the writing that passes through your computer is filtered clean of linguistic impurities. The existence of sharp-eyed, well-trained copy editors gives the best publications in any text-based medium their reputations for quality, consistency and professionalism. While the Web may be awash in third-grade-level spelling, grammar and prose, there's no reason an online news outlet can't present as classy a product as any other medium.

RELATED WEB SITES

A Spot for Copy Editors
http://www.theslot.com/

Purdue University Online Writing Lab
http://owl.english.purdue.edu/

Yale Web style guide
http://info.med.yale.edu/caim/manual/

Strunk and White style guide online
http://www.bartleby.com/141/index.html

WiredStyle
http://hotwired.lycos.com/hardwired/wiredstyle/index.html

EXERCISES

1. Identify the "spell-check proof" errors in each of the following sentences:

    a. The golfer shot five under oar for the round.

    b. Prof. Jones was named the new faulty advisor to the school paper.

    c. At the fair, your likely to find a variety of booths.

    d. The cars raced though the intersection at a high rate of speed.

    e. The parents where relieved to discover their daughter was safe.

    f. The crowd recognized the them song from the TV show "Friends."

    g. The fire department assisted in the recuse.

2. Fix the mechanical errors in the following sentences:

    a. Procter and Gamble announced their third-quarter earnings Thursday.

    b. The brothers, on the advice of their lawyer, was not speaking to the press.

    c. The prosecutor accused Mr. Green of selective amnesia.

    d. The project was one which Patrick had planned for years.

    e. The team, whose members fought injuries and a tough schedule, were valiant in defeat.

3. Write three suggested headlines for each of the following stories. You can be creative, but remember that you should first inform, then entertain:

    A. MINNEAPOLIS—According to a poll released today, Minnesota Gov. Jesse Ventura's approval rating has plunged since a controversial interview in Playboy *magazine.*

    A Minneapolis Star-Tribune *poll found 54 percent of Minnesotans approve of Ventura's overall job performance, compared with 73 percent last summer. Almost three out of five Minnesotans said they do not think the governor is a good role model.*

In the interview, the former pro wrestler called organized religion "a sham and a crutch for weak-minded people," and suggested that the perpetrators in the Navy's Tailhook sexual harassment scandal were misunderstood. Ventura also told Playboy *that he would like to be reincarnated as a size 38-DD bra.*

B. ATLANTA — Spacing your kids 2½ years apart may be ideal for producing healthy, full-term babies, according to a study that found a sound medical basis for what many women are doing already, for altogether different reasons.

A study by the Centers for Disease Control and Prevention found that while having babies too close together can be bad for an infant's health, having them too far apart may be even worse. Both situations raise the risk that the new baby will be premature or small, which can cause long-term health problems, even death.

C. NEW YORK — A new product claims to be able to more realistically cover bald spots than wigs, weaves, implants and hair-in-a-can.

Made from wool fibers, Toppik is sprinkled onto the scalp with a shaker. The fibers adhere to thinning hair with static electricity and create a fuller look. It costs far less than other remedies, and the manufacturers claim that it will adhere until shampooed out.

4. Read through some news content on any Web site and try to find examples where article titles or link text are misleading. (For example, if you click on a link that says "Consumers to receive thousands in rebates," then you discover that only a few hundred people who bought a specific product are eligible, that's a misleading headline.) Discuss why the headlines are misleading and suggest better headlines.

11

||||||

The Online Editor/
Utility Infielder

The menu of duties for print newspaper editors is often full yet somewhat limited. They must assign stories, work with reporters, assign spaces for stories, perform final page checks and see that pages are completed on time. Online editors are expected to do all this and more. In many ways, an online editor must be a jack-of-all-trades, knowing a little bit about everything from writing the perfect lead to using JavaScript to figuring out why a link won't work. This chapter examines questions driven not only by the content of stories but by the unique ergonomics of Web pages and browsers, and it provides information on the habits and preferences of the online audience.

In many ways, being an editor at an online publication is very different from working in any other medium. Online editors work in an environment with the following expectations and constraints:

- The product looks slightly different to every user (from one machine and browser to another).

- Any necessary content changes can be made immediately.

- Audience response can be registered instantly.

- It is expected that breaking news will be covered immediately.

- Changes made at other outlets must be monitored to avoid dead links.

- The range of content includes print, video, audio and interactive elements.

- There are few if any limits on any aspect of online stories.

- All news stories can be archived easily for public use.

- The potential audience is limitless and ill defined.

These circumstances—and the possible uncertainties that accompany them—would drive many traditional news editors crazy. Yet this is the milieu in which online news editors operate. On one hand, it's exciting and challenging to work in such a vibrant new medium. On the other hand, you're often juggling an awful lot of things all at once.

Many online news editors have compared the job to being a utility infielder in baseball—someone versatile enough to play many different positions competently when needed. An online editor wears many hats and performs many disparate tasks. Some days you may find yourself simply editing content, whereas on other days you may be designing an interactive feature or editing audio or video. One way or another, professionals agree on one thing about being an editor for an online news outlet—it's not boring!

HOW DO I EDIT WHEN THERE'S NO NEWS HOLE?

Newspaper editors have often turned the *New York Times'* slogan, "All the News That's Fit to Print," on its head. Given the constraints imposed by the newspaper's physical properties and the number of advertisements sold for a given day's paper, "All the News That Fits" is often more appropriate. A large percentage of the job is based around the fact that everything must fit within that day's **news hole**—the amount of space left on a page after room for advertising has been blocked out. Stories must be edited to fit the space available, photos must be cropped and resized, and graphics must be formatted to conform to that day's specifications.

At least theoretically, no such space limitations exist in online journalism. Since each story occupies its own separate page, it can literally be as short or as long as necessary. This forces a different approach to editing—rather than focusing on making a story fit into a hole, editors must decide on the optimum length for the story based on its merits. Does the story simply run too long, or is there value in material later in the story?

This is a particularly important question when working for the online site of a print newspaper. Suppose a story was originally 25 column inches in length but was cut to 15 inches in the paper due to lack of space. Should you run the story at its original length because you can? Should you run it at the print length for the sake of consistency? Or should you edit it to a length you feel is appropriate? Editors throughout the industry answer these questions differently.

One issue on which all online editors agree is that there's a lot more to the job than just worrying about a story's proper length. From the start, online editors need to think beyond the text of their stories. They need to consider the placement of assorted layout elements—ads or links in the margins, any sidebar boxes, links to previous or related stories and other items that may appear on the page (see Chapter 13 for more on layout). Even more important than placement, however, is the content of these additional items. Do all these elements support one another, or does one contradict another? Would one element be better served by placing it on a different page? Will all the elements be ready when it's time to post the story? All of these are questions faced by editors in some of the best online outlets today.

Of course, this assumes that all of these features are available. Though news on the Web has been around for a few years now, not every news organization has fully embraced it. Although most print publications now have online editions, many of them simply post stories as they appear in the day's paper. More often than not, online editors find themselves with little beyond text and a photo or two to work with. This is likely to change over the next few years, but it remains common in today's media marketplace.

REPURPOSING

Editing stories to their proper length is just one of the online editor's varied tasks. If you work for the online edition of a print outlet, you'll also need to learn about repurposing. Using a print medium's content as the basis for the online product is a very common practice among local newspapers that have small online staffs. Many scholars and editors at more cutting-edge outlets refer to this derisively as "shovelware"—that is, "shoveling" the text of stories onto the Web with little concern for the unique qualities of the Web environment. Editors at many smaller newspapers counter that they don't have the budget to hire a larger staff to produce Web-only content. They also point out that Web editions of most major newspapers are loss leaders and that almost none has yet turned a profit.

For editors with limited budgets, however, the argument really doesn't matter. They face the reality of producing an interactive multimedia product with a staff and protocols based on putting out a print product. They must figure out how to most effectively transform print stories—the lifeblood of the core product—into something palatable for Web audiences. To use a phrase popular among such editors, they must "think outside the box"—look beyond the standard parameters of print news and come up with innovative ways to supplement the story itself with material that enhances it and makes it more appealing.

Under these circumstances, smart editors see repurposing as an act of transformation rather than simple shoveling. They work with reporters and get them in the habit of thinking about multimedia elements and links to add to their stories on the Web. While the reporter is writing a story, these editors might look on the Web to find related URLs for links or interesting sites that tie in to the topic of the story. Perhaps they might think of questions to pose for chat or discussion groups on the outlet's site.

Wherever possible, rather than simply creating a story, online editors seek to create a **story package**—an in-depth menu of information that allows interested readers to delve more deeply into the details of a story. Sometimes these details are available on the outlet's own site, and sometimes links take the interested reader to a different site where the subject is pursued further. While editors don't have time to create a detailed package for every story, they can include a few elements— links, discussions, multimedia or other features—that make the story into something that goes beyond what's available in the day's newspaper. This is a truer notion of repurposing, or transforming a standard text story into something unique to the online medium.

This works best when the reporter is thinking of the needs of the online environment from the beginning. At online-only outlets, reporters must understand the nature of the online medium from the start. At outlets that are primarily print or broadcast, however, you'll often run into trouble with reporters who are trained first and foremost to provide content for the core product. Sometimes veteran reporters will resist the notion of providing different kinds of content for the Web site, and others will simply forget or have trouble fitting it into their established routines and procedures. If you'd been a print reporter for 20 years and suddenly someone was asking you to tape your interviews for audio clips, you might resist or feel threatened.

Gaining the cooperation of reporters and editors from the core business is vitally important in making the online side of a print or broadcast outlet work well. Often they simply are unfamiliar with the Web or aspects of it, aren't acquainted with how Web layout works, or haven't been shown the benefits of putting together a well-rounded story package. It's important to approach these people with respect and to convey the benefits of providing rich, in-depth content for Web use. The sooner they start providing you with suggestions for audio, video, links or other items, the easier your job will be and the better your site will be overall.

If you work for the online site of a broadcast outlet, the notion of repurposing may differ considerably because your core content will be so different from a print outlet. The biggest advantage for broadcast outlets is the video or audio footage produced by the main business—you can generally provide audio or video of news stories pretty easily. Sometimes entire newscasts will be archived, while in other situations individual stories or raw footage will be available on the site. Yet by itself, this isn't really enough to make up a full story package. Most broadcast outlets provide print stories to go along with their news footage, in spite of the fact they don't have the same volume of text as a print outlet. Sometimes on-air scripts are rewritten for this purpose, and at other times writers or editors compile stories from reporters' scripts and notes as well as from wire service

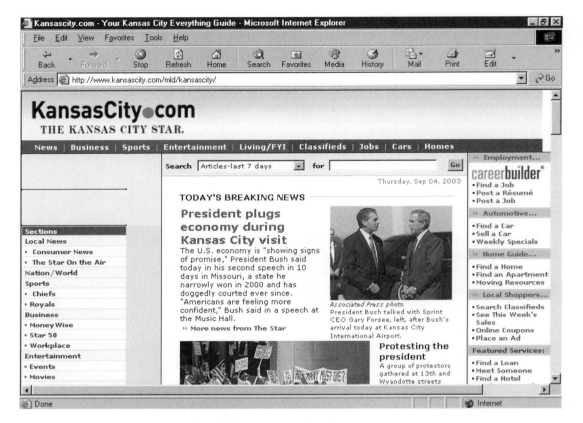

The *Kansas City Star* newspaper works with local partners in radio, television and other community institutions to produce Kansascity.com.

SOURCE: kansascity.com (accessed September 2, 2003). Used by permission.

information. When possible, other elements are added to create a well-rounded story package.

An important aspect of repurposing—and of every other aspect of the news business—is to know your audience. In the online world, the better you know your audience, the more effectively you can serve its needs. If you're going to modify the content of your core print or broadcast product, you'll need to know what modifications will best enhance the product and best accommodate the preferences and expectations of your audience. You want to fashion something specific for that audience, not just post something generic online.

For example, if you're working for the online site of a local newspaper, your primary audience might be made up of people who have moved away from your city but regularly check your site to keep tabs on the old hometown. Since the potential audience for Web news is global, some editors might view online coverage of a major breaking story from a big-picture point of view, opting away from the local point of view and reporting with more of a national news approach. However, if the audience looks to your site primarily for your local reporting, you'd be better served to go ahead and report the local angle. Your readers can go to dozens of national and international sites to get the global overview but only to your site for the local perspective. Your site has its own point of view—its own purpose— and as long as you keep that in mind, using the site's capabilities to enhance a print story doesn't have to be simply an exercise in copying and pasting text.

LINKS

If online editors must master repurposing, they must also master one of the main tools used in the process—the hypertext link. Most of this book has reinforced the notion that online news differs from print and broadcast in meaningful ways. The most obvious way in which this is true is through the use of links on news pages. No other medium allows the reader to quickly jump to another story, perhaps from another day or even from another outlet, or to go directly to a related non-news site. By linking to related stories, editors allow readers to pursue the subjects of their stories rather than simply moving on to the next story in a section. Online audiences appreciate this feature and have come to expect it from all online outlets.

At a fundamental level, the inclusion of links changes the way people read the news. The standard print newspaper leads the reader along a fairly ordered path. It's understood that the front page contains the items deemed most important, laid out top to bottom in descending order of importance, with succeeding pages continuing the process of reporting lesser and lesser stories. Themed sections—local, sports, business, features and so forth—continue this orderly process. Readers are loosely led down the page and through the sections, and though there is no rigid order in which one must read the stories, there is a suggested hierarchy of information. This organized process encourages linear thinking—following along a prescribed path from one story to another.

As noted in earlier chapters, however, the subtraction of the ordered newspaper layout and the addition of links on the Web encourages nonlinear thinking— following whatever subject strikes you at the moment rather than any prescribed path. Since readers expect this from online outlets, it's up to online editors to think ahead and determine where readers of any given story might want to go as a result of that story. This is an essential part of including links on a site—they don't just appear there on their own.

Some aspects of this are easier than others. If you've edited a site for a while, you'll often be quite familiar with the previous related stories that have run on your site. Linking to these is simple enough. In addition, linking to sites of companies and agencies mentioned in the text is not usually much of a problem. If you

|||||| **FROM THE FIELD**

Stan Austin
Online Managing Editor
Kansas City Star

The *Kansas City Star* might not immediately leap to mind when you think of the nation's great newspapers, but only if you haven't seen its Web site. The Midwest daily won the 1998 Digital Edge Award for Best Online Newspaper of 150,000 circulation and above, and the man behind it all was Stan Austin.

"I've been at this newspaper company for 15 years," he says. "Actually, there used to be two papers—the *Times* and the *Star*. The *Times* was the morning paper and the *Star* was the afternoon paper. I started working for the *Times* in 1985, and stayed there until the papers merged in 1990. I came over to the online side in 1995."

That was the year KansasCityStar.com was launched. The paper had already invested in early home-access services—it had one of the country's first AudioText telephone information services, which continues today. A team had been assembled to move into a new technology called ViewText when the Web began to cause a stir in 1995.

"I had been an assistant business editor for special projects," Austin says, "and had an interest in computing and an interest in the Web. I applied for the job I have now, and came over that fall. We hired a few folks, and we just literally went down in the basement and built a Web site."

The site went online late in 1995 but wasn't formally unveiled right away. "We did a soft launch," Austin says. "We were out there, we were live, we were updating it every day, but we weren't promoting it. The original plan was that we were gonna be out here for about a month, and then we were gonna do a big promotional blitz. That was targeted for Valentine's Day 1996. Well, between January 1 and the end of January, the publisher at that time, Bob Woodworth, a very smart person with a lot of business savvy, began to think, 'How are people going to use the Web five years from now? Is the newspaper model going to satisfy the needs of Web users down the road?' He was really ahead of his time there.

"Out of the discussion that followed came the idea to create a parallel site, a sister site, called KansasCity.com, that would be what at that time we called an umbrella site. It had a strong civic presence—had the chamber of commerce, the convention and visitor's bureau was an affiliate, had sports teams like the Royals as affiliates. And interestingly, it had the TV stations

don't already know the URLs involved, a Web search can usually take care of the problem in a minute or two. Choosing any additional sites that relate to the subject matter of the story can be a little trickier. You can search the Web to find related sites, but selecting one or two to reflect the story's subject is a touchy matter—you don't want to appear to choose sides by virtue of your selections, or to misrepresent a particular point of view.

here in town—the ABC, NBC, CBS and Fox affiliate stations were all affiliates. KansasCity. com went on to become a portal site—we didn't know what a portal was in those days—and that's how we got it off the ground."

Austin's role as a supervising editor has been largely to oversee the work of online editors (content producers). In that capacity, he has tried to go beyond simple repurposing of print material to provide something more for his readers. "We're interested in helping a user learn more about a topic that becomes a story. We're looking to provide context. We're looking to provide an opportunity for them to interact with other users about this particular story topic, or interact with us."

The site's many special projects have been reader favorites and played a large part in winning the Digital Edge Award. "We try to pick our spots and look for niches," says Austin. "We put a lot of effort into giving a good treatment to the investigative pieces and the more in-depth profiles that are produced in the newsroom. And with a lot of those, we try to look for Web-only elements that we can add to them."

One of the most successful of these was called "Money Games: Inside the NCAA," which examined how money had corrupted the college athletic association. "It was about an 18-month reporting effort by the newsroom's projects team," Austin says.

"This organization had gotten so far away from its original mission in so many areas, from executives lining their own pockets to looking the other way on academic violations and so forth. But our project team's database editor was able to pull the NCAA's database of enforcement records—how its bylaws were enforced over the years—and put that into a Web-compatible format. The result was that people coming in to use that site could go in and look at enforcement records for every school in the NCAA for a particular period of time. It was pretty amazing."

Even when his site runs repurposed material, Austin tries to provide the reader with something extra. "We generally do not do any editing on stories once they get over to the server," he says. "So if they send us 40 inches on a story, then 20 inches gets cut out in print, it's going to run 40 inches on the site. I think that's great for the reader. Readers notice it—there are some diehard readers who will maybe come online first because that's more convenient, then they'll get to the print side later, and say, 'Okay—I'm glad I got that extra 20 inches.'"

Austin candidly notes, however, that readers aren't the only ones who like the extra material. "Reporters love it!" he says with a laugh. "They're always glad to see their words uncut. That's something we work to our advantage in trying to get support across the newsroom, and getting reporters to give us heads' up on things. So, yeah, the vanity angle really works with reporters."

Even before this stage of the process, editors must make many decisions relating to the placement and functionality of links. First, the actual placement of links is a subject of debate. Some outlets link from within the story, turning the text's references to agencies, companies or organizations into links to previous articles about those people or agencies, or to their own home pages. Other outlets choose to place such links at the beginning or end of stories.

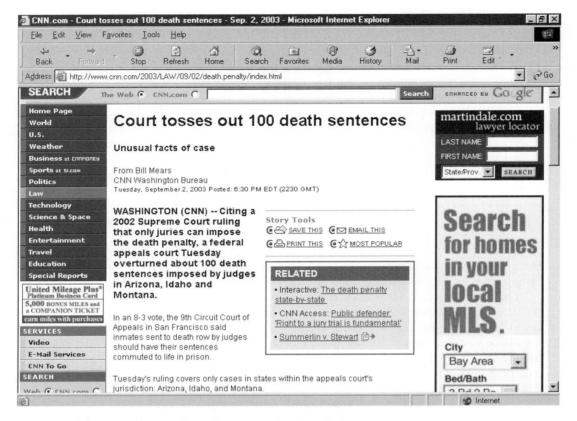

To create a full story package, online editors must often look for items to include as related stories as shown here on CNN.com.

SOURCE: CNN.com (accessed September 2, 2003). Used by permission.

For example, the end of a story at one site might use links as follows, with underlined text denoting a link:

> Microsoft Chairman Bill Gates indicated that no further agreements were planned with Dell or IBM, but that the company was keeping its options open.
> Related sites:
> <u>Microsoft Corporation</u>
> <u>IBM</u>
> <u>Dell Computer Corporation</u>
> Profiles:
> <u>Bill Gates</u>

Another site might embed links within the same text like this:

> <u>Microsoft</u> Chairman <u>Bill Gates</u> indicated that no further agreements were planned with <u>Dell</u> or <u>IBM</u>, but that the company was keeping its options open.

There are arguments in favor of each approach. Those who prefer to embed links within the text of stories often say that this allows users to click on anything that interests them as they read—they don't have to scroll down to the end of the story or sift through other content to get to what they want. Those who place links at the end usually argue that embedded story links encourage people to abandon stories before they've finished reading them, and that people who are really interested in the linked pages can easily locate the links at the end of the story.

If you choose to embed links within stories, you also must decide whether to turn every reference to the agency or company into a link or just the first reference. Some argue that you should make every reference a link for consistency's sake, and also because if a reader is deep into a story, scrolling back up through the text to find the link is a pain. Others argue in favor of first-reference links simply because if too much of the text is made up of links, it can distract readers from the article's content.

A different issue is whether to link to off-site pages at all. Some sites don't do it, fearing that this encourages people to leave their sites and never come back. These sites only link to other pages on their own site that may contain previous articles or preformatted searches for articles about the particular company, agency or person. Other outlets link to off-site pages as a service to readers and to save their own people hours of extra coding trying to replicate information available elsewhere.

As if this weren't enough to keep an online editor's head spinning, some links behave differently than others. Many outlets that link to outside pages encode their links to open a new browser window rather than loading the linked pages into the current window. This means that when readers are finished with off-site pages and close the new window, they are returned to the original story. This is particularly common among sites that embed links within stories—it makes people more likely to come back to your site and finish what they've started. However, it can create problems for users with older computers or older browsers, and the last thing any online editor wants is to create a page that will freeze a user's computer. That's the surest way to permanently lose a reader.

Finally, online editors have to worry about dead links. If freezing a user's computer is the last thing an editor wants, the next-to-last thing is a link that doesn't work. This is usually caused by one of two things. First is a typo in the URL, which you or a copy editor should catch before publishing. Second is the "familiarity factor." When you link regularly to a particular site or page, you or your reporter may know the URL off the top of your head. This is fine as long as the site you're linking to doesn't go through a redesign while you're not watching. If this happens and you end up with a dead link, readers will usually let you know pretty quickly, but it can be a major headache to fix depending on the specifics of your outlet's design.

MANAGING PAGES

Another hat worn by online editors is that of traffic cop. By managing the site's pages well and including features that make navigation easy for users, your site's online traffic will move smoothly and efficiently and won't leave readers stranded and looking for a way out. Good online editors keep in mind the hierarchy of the pages on their site and know how to most efficiently guide readers to different areas through assorted site features.

Every print newspaper has its front page, and every online news outlet has its equivalent—the **home page** or "index" page (see Chapter 13 for more on this pivotal page). The home page must accomplish a great deal—it must feature the day's major stories while also serving as the place to find links to section pages (local news, sports, business and so forth) and to any archives that may be available. Some home pages look much like the front pages of newspapers, and others serve as portals for businesses beyond the news industry.

If you become an online editor, you'll likely inherit templates or style sheets used to create index and story pages. This doesn't mean that you should simply take what you're given without trying to improve it. Good online editors look at a lot of other online outlets and note the features that work well, perhaps compiling lists of items that could be tried on their own sites. As the graphical standards of Web pages become more and more sophisticated, the expectations of readers increase. This is why smart editors fine-tune their pages regularly and redesign them every year or two to incorporate new features. If you find something on a Web page you might be interested in using, you can use your browser's "View Source" command to look at the HTML code that makes it work. Many times it will involve JavaScript, style sheets or other advanced items you may not be familiar with, but you can at least get an idea of how to approach a similar feature on your site.

Producing these index and story pages daily requires an organized approach. Many online news outlets create new master directories for each day's product. For example, if this book's Web site were actually an online news outlet, the day's output for October 19, 2002, might reside at the following address:

http://communication.wadsworth.com/craig/2002/10/19/index.html

All pages from 2002 would go into subdirectories corresponding to their month and day in the "2002" directory. All pages from October 19 would be saved in the "19" subdirectory, and the next day's pages would be placed in a subdirectory called "20." Different news outlets organize their files differently, but for the sake of managing files well, you'll need to establish a system that makes sense to everyone concerned.

A feature that makes online news unique is the ability to put together an archive of past stories that can be used by readers. By setting up your directory structure in a logical way, this can be as simple or as complex as you want it to be. You can simply allow readers to pick a past date and browse that day's product, or you can create separate pages for certain writers (often columnists) or certain major news events. If you want to create a more functional archive, install a search function to enable users to search past editions by typing in keywords. This is usually a more complex process involving programs called CGI scripts, which take input from the browser and process it on the server. These are generally in place at most online outlets, and you'll need to learn the specifics of your publication's scripts if you work with them. One way or another, it's a popular feature with readers, even though at some outlets users must pay to access archived articles.

STORY CONTENT

It may seem like an afterthought here, but online editors also need to worry about the content of their sections' and outlets' stories as much as any other editor. Obviously, online information must be accurate and informative, but it must also work within the online medium. Online writing must get information across very quickly, particularly if your site doesn't show much text on the first screen of news stories.

The notion of creating a story package means that the writing is just one aspect of an online story, albeit an important one. In creating a well-rounded package, every element must complement every other one—all text, photos, links and multimedia must contribute to the same story. (This excludes items in the page's margins such as ads, section links or "top stories" links, which are clearly not elements of the story package.) Inconsistencies within news story pages are common at many online news outlets, but you should strive to set higher standards. While links might take a reader to a story that takes the subject in a different direction, all the information on any one page should contribute to the overall theme of the page.

This all works best when you and your reporters have a collective notion of the most important elements of a story and how the story will be presented. While working on a story, reporters can keep their eyes open for items that would enhance its Web presentation—they're the ones venturing out of the office and doing all the interviewing. You can call this a shared vision or simply good communication, but as you work with reporters, the more rapport you can build with them, the better their stories will be and the more your outlet will benefit. If you'll pardon the expression, online journalism works best when reporters and editors are on the same page.

Even if you trust your reporters, however, you need to be vigilant about making sure that the information you're publishing is accurate. Fact checking is always important, but particularly so in the online venue. Your product is visible worldwide, and if people think you've made a mistake, they can easily go to other Web sites to see if you're wrong. Ideally, your reporters should share this ethic and do a lot of this type of work on their own, but you should double-check anything that seems even slightly fishy. A good idea is to have your reporters give you their lists of sources for each story including Web and database sources used to verify information. If a mistake does slip through, you can then correct it as soon as you're aware of it. Some outlets simply make the correction without any other changes, whereas others note the change and the time it was made at the end of the story.

Although stories can run just about any length online, different outlets use different formats for longer stories. Some simply let the story run on one long page, and others break it up into multiple pages. The latter allows readers to read a few screens of text (usually three), then click to go to the next section of the story. Most outlets that do this also include links to all the succeeding pages, both to allow readers to skip ahead and to alert them to the length of the story. Research has indicated that past a certain point readers would rather click to a new page than scroll down the same one. Having said this, clicking through multiple pages has its problems as well. If there is heavy traffic at your site, loading subsequent pages can take a long time, whereas a single page is there to be read in its entirety as soon as it's finished loading. Plus, printing a long story is much more of a pain when you have to click to several pages and print each one of them rather than clicking the Print button only once. Some sites create two versions of each story—the reader-friendly version spread over a few pages and the printer-friendly version, which eliminates ads and places the story on one long page. Still, at this point designing two different versions of each story is beyond the means of many online outlets.

Rather than regularly facing this choice, the best approach is to keep things as concise as possible. Regardless of the lack of any rigid length restrictions, people generally don't enjoy reading huge blocks of text online, whether they're on one page or spread over several. The only real exception to this is when a reader takes a deeper interest in the subject of a story and wants to read more about it. In this case, your links and archives should allow readers to immerse themselves in your past coverage of a topic as well as any off-site pages pertaining to it. Thus, you don't have to tell every aspect of every story with each new report. If you've organized your site well, you can simply point users in the right direction and turn them loose.

INTERACTIVE FEATURES

One final function an online editor must perform is that of ombudsman, acting as a liaison between a news organization and the public, investigating complaints and taking suggestions from subscribers, viewers or readers. Readers can quickly alert you to problems such as dead links via e-mail, but they can interact with your site in other ways as well. As noted in Chapter 2, interactivity is a distinctive characteristic of the online medium, and it's one of the most appealing facets to most users. More than simply being an avenue to pester editors when they make mistakes, interactive features give online news readers more of a feeling of participation.

Many online news sites these days contain discussion forums, in which site users can post messages exchanging views on assorted topics in the news. These are useful for people who want to talk about local or subject-specific issues that don't have their own Google discussion groups or other venues for debate. Many times, in the wake of a major local news event, the busiest part of a local news out-let's Web site is the discussion forum where people share opinions, gossip, ideas and theories, or sometimes celebrate or grieve. While not technically an area within the realm of editorial content, smart editors keep their eyes on these dis-cussion groups to see what readers are talking about and perhaps to get a story idea or two or to refocus coverage of a particular event. Every once in a while, the con-tent of these discussions is a story in itself. Either way, discussion forums are use-ful and popular at the outlets that provide them.

A logical extension of this feature is the chat session. Many local and national outlets boast this feature, where newsmakers (and occasionally reporters) stop in to interact with the readers and answer their questions. Everyone from public officials to celebrities to sports stars seems to be doing chat sessions these days, and news outlets can often attract figures who are well known to their readers. This offers a lot to all concerned. First, readers get a chance to ask questions of some-one they admire (or disagree with), which likely wouldn't happen otherwise. It's often good for the news organization because a well-publicized chat session with a noteworthy guest can increase the traffic and create new interest in your site. For the guests, it's also generally good because it offers the chance to get a little posi-tive publicity and seem open to the masses without many of the risks posed by public appearances. If the guest would be mobbed in public (for either positive or negative reasons), a chat session avoids the commotion. Furthermore, since it's all done in text, guests' responses can be carefully worded and well thought out, un-like situations where they must answer questions with cameras rolling. Clearly, there are several potential benefits to these sessions—the only downside comes if there aren't many respondents. If you've done your homework, you'll probably have a good idea of what to expect.

One way to find out who readers would be interested in chatting with is to ask them via an online poll. Many major Web sites have discovered that running informal online polls is popular with users and relatively easy to do. These days online outlets will ask anything from "Who will you vote for?" to "What do you do if your blind date has bad breath?" Sometimes the questions are more interest-ing than the answers, and other times the results are downright shocking. Readers always like to know what other people think, and to add their own two cents' worth as well.

Web polls, however, do have a serious downside. First, they're not scientific in nature—an important point for all journalists to recognize. Web polls make no pretense of using random samples or accurately representing populations, so their results cannot be analyzed using traditional poll analysis techniques (such as mar-gins of error and so forth). Most Web polls also make no provisions for prevent-ing the same user from voting over and over to influence the totals. In other words, as true measures of public sentiment, they're useless. Essentially, they are only done for the purposes of entertaining users. As long as this is understood and Web poll results are not taken seriously, they're a harmless and popular diversion.

A more useful interactive feature is the Frequently Asked Questions (FAQ) page. This is easy to create and is very useful for readers. Literally, editors should begin compiling a list of frequently asked questions (and the answers to them) as soon as a site goes online and build on it from there. These can include anything from "How did your site get its name" to "How do I apply for employment with your organization?" and everything in between. Deciding how extensive your FAQ page should be is entirely a judgment call. It should be long enough to answer questions relevant to most readers yet not so long as to boggle their minds. There are also many formatting choices available, from a single long list of questions and answers to a high-tech, XML or JavaScript multimedia wonder with collapsing headings and all sorts of bells and whistles. It's up to you and your readers to decide what works.

Of course, all those questions have to come from somewhere. As noted at the beginning of this section, virtually every online news site contains e-mail links. Literally, this is a link users can click on to send e-mail messages to given editors and reporters. The text that appears on the screen for most e-mail links is the address itself. This is a good idea because some users don't have their browsers configured to automatically send mail and others prefer to use a separate mail program that isn't linked to the browser. This allows users to copy down the address and use it however they choose.

At large sites, e-mail links create huge volumes of messages, which are often first answered with an automated response, then followed with a personal message. The backlogs can be substantial at times, yet online news editors consistently say that one of the ways their sites improve is through user comments. In this way, an online site is a reflection of both the editors and the users—less a prepackaged product than a collaborative effort between medium and audience.

SUMMARY

Some in the traditional media look at online editors as purveyors of shovelware, yet not many traditional news editors have to master the disparate sets of skills of a good online editor. From knowing the audience to knowing journalistic standards to knowing the ergonomics of Web pages, you need to be a very well-rounded journalist to be a good online editor. You need to have a clear notion of the strengths of the online medium and of how your outlet can make the most of its resources to serve the wants and needs of readers. Because of the interactive nature of the medium, an online editor must listen to the readers more than most traditional editors are accustomed to doing. This produces a unique product—one that no print or broadcast editor can fully duplicate.

RELATED WEB SITES

Netscape's Web development page
http://developer.netscape.com

Kansas City Star
http://www.kcstar.com

EXERCISES

1. Select a story from the front page of any section of the print edition of your local newspaper and clip it or photocopy it. Write a summary of how you would present it online as a story package. Would you edit the story for length? What types of photos, audio or video would you try to get to supplement the story's coverage? What types of Web pages would you link to? Include your copy of the story with your summary.

2. At home or at school, videotape a local or national news broadcast. Select a story from that broadcast and write it up as a print story of at least one double-spaced page in length, using any resources you can find on the Web or elsewhere for additional information. Then list other elements you would use to convert this to an online story package—provide details of photos or video you would use, and list the names, subjects and URLs of at least three related Web pages.

3. Go to the Newslink Web site's list of online papers by state, at http://newslink.org/statnews.html. Follow the link to your state, and pick three different outlets. Go to each site and examine its home page. Write a summary of the similarities and differences between the home pages of these sites, and rank them according to your assessment of their usability. How are they organized visually and textually? Is one easier to use than the others? Is one more visually engaging than the others? Be sure to thoroughly explain why you believe the aspects of one page are more or less appealing or useful than others.

12

||||||||

Multimedia for News

Multimedia on the Web has become both a buzzword and an enigma. It's hard to define, but people know it when they see it. Using audio, video and other appealing features on Web sites is a necessity these days, but how do you make it all work? More important, for news sites does multimedia have a purpose beyond simply showing off? This chapter looks at the assorted formats available, discusses their use, and examines when multimedia truly adds something to a story and when it's just a gimmick.

There are lots of definitions of multimedia out there, but one student's summation typifies most young people's descriptions: "It's the extra stuff that makes Web pages cool." Most of us have become familiar with the elements of today's Web pages that move, talk, play music and otherwise entertain us. Everyone agrees they can make a page stand out among the crowd, and most people find multimedia elements very appealing.

In the midst of all the animated intro pages, audio and video clips, pop-up windows and photo spreads, one question about multimedia on the Web is rarely addressed: "So what?" So it catches your attention and makes you look a little longer at a page. So it's visually or sonically interesting. So it's cool. So what? Does it inform you? Do you learn anything from it? Is it thought provoking? Does it have any influence on you at all? Or is it just eye candy?

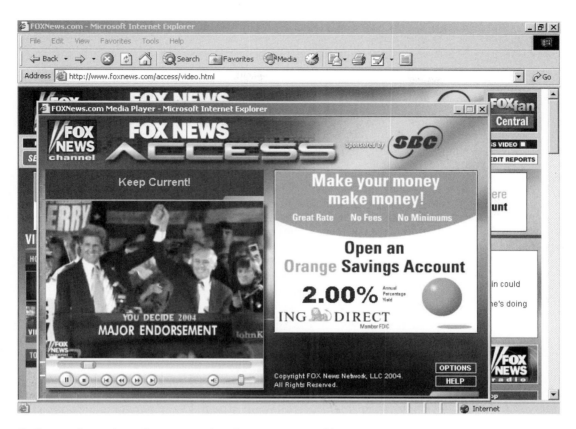

Similar to other major online news outlets, Foxnews.com provides
links to streaming video of breaking news and other reports.

SOURCE: foxnews.com (accessed September 25, 2003). Used by permission of Fox News Network LLC.

This is a serious question for everyone on the Web but particularly for journalists. It's true that in the online medium you want your news product to stand
out among the crowd. The problem is that there's a tremendous temptation to include multimedia elements on your site simply to catch people's attention. There's
not anything inherently wrong with that except that journalists' ultimate goal
is to inform the public, to give people information they can use in their daily
lives. The challenge in the online world is to put together a site in which readers
are both entertained and informed, where multimedia elements enhance a story
rather than distract from it. Ideally, you can create a visually and intellectually appealing site that tells a story in a way utterly unique to the online medium, taking
full advantage of each element's best qualities to completely satisfy a reader's

interest. It's not easy, but it can be done, and if you want your news site to stand out and thrive online, it *must* be done.

DEFINING AND
CONCEPTUALIZING MULTIMEDIA

Before we can create this harmonic convergence between form and function, we have to know what we're talking about. We have to figure out what we mean when we use the term *multimedia*. Technically, **multimedia** simply refers to the use of multiple types of media within a presentation. This can include anything from straight text (or hypertext) to photos, graphics, audio, video and animation.

The problem with this definition is that it's too broad. According to these standards, television qualifies as multimedia because it incorporates audio and video. The definition would also include almost every Web page in existence because they usually include some sort of photos or graphics in addition to text. It also raises a worthwhile question: Is anything that beeps or flashes multimedia? That would include a lot of things on today's Web pages, from text that "lights up" when the mouse cursor passes over it to animated icons to advertisements that flicker with persuasive messages.

For years, before the Web existed, multimedia primarily applied to in-person presentations that made use of slides, overheads, audio or videotape and other elements that would appeal to the audience. When sound cards, speakers and graphics-enhancing video cards were first added to computers, machines outfitted with these features were called "multimedia computers." These elements allowed for graphically rich programs and utilities as well as for games with realistic sound and video. With the rise of the Web, however, multimedia has gradually acquired a new meaning.

These days, multimedia generally refers to elements that add sound, video or animation to Web pages. Modern Web browsers are equipped with programs called "plug-ins," which allow different elements to play within or be displayed by the browser. If your browser doesn't have a particular plug-in, it will usually offer you the option of downloading the plug-in, which will then make the given element work. Many pages containing audio, video or animation allow the user to select items to be displayed and to click buttons to start and stop a given display. This is interactive multimedia—something that puts the user in control of the feature.

There's no question that multimedia elements can make a Web page more attractive and grab users' attention. The union between news and multimedia is an uneasy one, however. Too often veteran journalists see the use of multimedia as putting style before substance, of sacrificing journalistic integrity in favor of flashy graphics. The content of the news should never be compromised, period. However, journalists should not fear multimedia—indeed, they should look at the

Web's multimedia capabilities in terms of how those capabilities can best maximize their outlets' ability to cover the news.

To better understand this, let's return to the question raised earlier: Is anything that beeps or flashes multimedia? For journalists, the answer is "no." Journalists need to conceptualize multimedia as sound, video or animated graphics that enhance a story. The second part of this definition is as important as the first. Multimedia should never be used simply as a toy: don't use multimedia elements unless they will add something unique to a story. (More on this later in the chapter.)

AUDIO FORMATS

The Internet has become a noisy place. What used to be a quiet outpost for students and scientists now contains all sorts of music, voices, and assorted sounds in various formats, volumes and languages. The content can run anywhere from high-quality recordings of sophisticated music to all manner of poorly recorded material of dubious value. While online journalists might wince at some of the uses of sounds online, it's important for them to know some of the most common formats and their strengths and weaknesses.

To begin with, users must have computers that support sound reproduction. Many office workstations and older PCs do not have sound cards or speakers. These days, most audio content requires such equipment. There are also various settings on every user's machine that determine the compatibility of assorted formats, as well as the volume, tone and other qualities of the sound the machine will produce. This makes creating sound for Web pages a risky proposition, but some formats have gained near-universal use in modern computers.

The most widely accepted audio format for all computers is the "Wave" format. Files of this type generally have the file extension ".wav" and can be played through almost any modern computer, including some without sound cards. The Windows Sound Recorder program, which is included with the Windows operating system, also saves files in Wave format. Wave files can also be played on most Macs of recent years using the Windows Media Player or other similar programs.

Wave files are just about everywhere. The system sounds on newer PCs—the sounds they make when starting up, shutting down, asking you a question and so forth—are Wave files. When programs play a sound as they load, they're almost always Wave files. This is because on one hand Wave files have been around for a long time, at least on PCs. On the other hand, the format allows anything from scratchy monophonic recordings made with a single flimsy microphone to CD-quality stereo masters. In fact, some professional digital audio recording programs save songs to Wave files. Clearly, the format is very versatile.

The downside to Wave files is that they're large. Even at the lowest level of quality, a one-minute Wave file can easily be about one megabyte in size. In these days of 300-gigabyte hard drives, that may not seem like much, but it still takes a

Brock Meeks

|||||| **FROM THE FIELD**

Brock Meeks
Chief Washington Correspondent
MSNBC.com

In many ways, Brock Meeks is on the cutting edge of journalism. Covering Washington, D.C. for the ultra-high-tech MSNBC, reporting on technology and policy, he has found himself at the heart of the action in the computer age. Not bad for a guy without a journalism degree.

"I don't even have a college degree," says Meeks. "I just got busy writing and never looked back. I started writing freelance, then eventually I went to work for the *San Francisco Chronicle*."

Meeks' freelance work took a turn toward technology when a friend showed him how to use a modem. Soon he discovered he could tap into publicly available corporate and government databases to get the story behind policies. "I started writing about how you could use this information, how you could tap into this information, and use it from a social activism standpoint," says Meeks.

"The typical example is the 'fight the nuclear reactor, not in my backyard' type of thing. So I started writing about how you could tap into these databases. And once I figured out that all this information was out there, I also figured out that, wait a minute, this could not only be used for good, but it could be used for evil too. There were all sorts of privacy concerns, who's getting my info, what information can other people get on me, is the government snooping on my information, and all that. And in addition to that, I became painfully aware, back in 1984 when I started doing all this, that the electronic world I was inhabiting was painfully white and male. And I started to worry about the social aspects of it—what about minorities? What about women? How come they're not online? Is there anything being done to increase that access? So I started writing about all of that."

Once he began using the Internet, Meeks discovered it allowed for a new kind of journalism. "I adopted this kind of alter ego persona," he says, "and I was writing an outlaw publication that was solely distributed in cyberspace via mailing lists, called CyberWire Dispatch. I kind of took on the gonzo journalism mantle of Hunter Thompson and just converted that

while to download. On most computers, you must download the entire file before you can listen to it, which results in a lot of sitting around before you can hear the content. Higher-quality stereo Wave files can easily take up 10MB for every minute of sound, which will make for very long download times, even on fast connections. In an age when people want everything right away, telling someone to wait two minutes to download a one-minute audio clip is a losing proposition. So while compatibility is a major plus for Wave files, they aren't without problems.

Two widely accepted alternatives to Wave files have emerged. One format into writing about cyberspace issues, and doing that all online. So I have this straight job that I do for money, and then I have this labor of love called CyberWire Dispatch which has since won me journalism awards and some pretty good recognition, that I do online and I do for free. And that's gotten me where I am today."

Where he sometimes is today—to his surprise—is on camera on the MSNBC cable channel. "When I joined MSNBC," says Meeks, "I learned that not only would I be functioning as a 'print' journalist, but they were going to throw me in front of a camera without any training and see if I could handle that. That's how I became an on-air correspondent for the cable channel."

Meeks' most prominent recent reporting, both on TV and on the Web, has been his coverage of the long Microsoft monopoly trial. He says it is a good example of how his company's Web site can make use of multimedia to integrate many elements available to MSNBC but also of how reporters have to exercise some restraint.

"We don't have any artificial constraints as far as space," says Meeks. "Theoretically we could write as much as the servers would hold. But people's reading habits won't allow that— you can't write 4,000 words on a relatively small story. So what we do instead is this. Let's say for example I'm covering the Microsoft trial. After the courtroom proceedings at the end of the day, both sides would come out and do a standup on the courthouse steps, which would be taped by the folks at CNBC, our sister cable station. So instead of taking down everything verbatim that was happening during that question-and-answer, I would often just make notes about particularly salient questions that were asked and particularly good answers. I would tell my video folks to grab that piece of video and I would just allude to it in a couple of sentences in my story, rather than having to write 200 words about it. I could just refer to that in a couple of short sentences in the story, with a link, referring people to look at the video itself."

Thus, multimedia is worth a thousand words, or at least 200. "It saves me space and time in a story, so I can go on and get the other things," Meeks says. "It allows me to cram much more into my daily story than I could have otherwise. We could just pull in that video and just refer people to that, or we could just pull in a specific audio portion of that, where people could click on that. People could just click on that video or audio clip, and it saved me a lot of time, and saved me a lot of space in my story."

These days, Meeks might sound like a multimedia whirlwind, yet he admits his computer knowledge has come more from on-the-job experience than vocational training. "I have no formal technical background," he says. "I still can't program my way out of a paper bag."

stresses fast access, and the other stresses quality. The first of these is **RealAudio.** This format—which uses the file extension ".ram" or ".rm"—offers near-immediate access to audio content. RealAudio uses streaming audio technology, which allows users to hear the audio as it downloads. This technology also allows for live, real-time coverage of all kinds of events, from speeches to games to disasters.

The more recent RealAudio players can reproduce very high-quality stereo sound. The player has become so commonplace that it's included in the installation of some browsers and is available as a plug-in for others. The format has allowed radio stations to broadcast on the Web, creating a mind-boggling array of content for listeners to choose from. RealAudio users can also get sports, news and assorted Web-only content with little trouble. The format has created something of a new industry in Web radio.

RealAudio's downside is sound quality. While the player is capable of receiving and playing high-quality audio, listening to anything more than a snippet of such sound requires a high-speed Internet connection. Users with home dial-up connections usually have to settle for monophonic, AM radio quality sound. While this is fine for listening to a ballgame, it's not ideal for audiophiles. Also, because the files play while they download, any congestion on the Web can cause content to pause, become distorted or stop playing entirely. Finally, most RealAudio files can't be saved to the hard drive, meaning that a user must come back to the same site to listen again.

The second, more quality-oriented format is **MP3.** This format's file extension is its name—".mp3"—and it's a descendant of the MPEG audio/video format (discussed later in the chapter). It takes CD-quality audio and compresses it to a fraction of its original file size. This is terrific for people who want to download music—indeed, MP3 has exploded in popularity in the last few years. Portable MP3 players now let people take downloaded music with them wherever they go. With this popularity has come controversy, and the music industry has taken assorted legal steps to curtail the practice of sharing copyrighted songs. Regardless, the MP3 format is now everywhere.

There remain drawbacks to using the MP3 format on news sites, however. Unlike RealAudio, you must completely download files before listening to them, which can take a while. Even compressed, a one-minute track can take quite a while to download, especially via home dial-up or other slow connections. The file sizes remain large, slightly larger than a low-quality Wave file. Plus, the format is not as widely supported as the Wave or RealAudio formats, so if your material doesn't need to be in near-CD quality, such as an interview clip, there are disadvantages.

These are the most common sound file formats, but you will occasionally run into others, particularly some older formats no longer in wide use. For example, you may find files on the Web with the extension ".au"—literally, for "audio." These were popular in the early days of the Web because they were very small files. They'll still play in most browsers, but their sound quality is very poor. A long-time Macintosh audio format was the ".aiff" file, which will still play on most Macs, but its sound quality is also generally poor.

For Web designers, one advantage of Wave files is that they fit seamlessly into Web pages. They can be embedded into the code of the page and played automatically upon loading or when the user clicks a button. (The latter is generally preferable—when you make a sound play automatically, it creates the scenario of a user trying to secretly Web surf at work, only to have his cover blown when some silly sound blurts out of his computer before he can stop it.) They can also be linked to a page to be played on demand or downloaded to be played later. The newest browsers also support some of these functions for RealAudio files, but Waves are by far the most common file format for this purpose. This may change as the other formats and players become more widely used and as browsers become more and more sophisticated.

VIDEO FORMATS

Despite the increasing popularity of broadband connections in the home, video remains less common than audio on the Web. The reason for this is simple— video requires more space for storage and more bandwidth for downloading. However, it's becoming more and more of a staple of news and entertainment sites as people get faster computers with faster modems and larger hard drives. Among all types of video files, the common trade-off is between file size and picture quality and resolution (size on the screen). Almost without exception, better-quality video with larger images means bigger files and longer download times.

Video on the Web is also found in several formats, which differ in terms of benefits and compatibility. Probably the most universally compatible format is **QuickTime,** originally developed by Apple but now found on most modern PCs as well. Files of this type—usually bearing the extensions ".mov" or ".qt"—can provide full-color, full-motion video (with audio) of varying quality and image sizes. These files can be played on most PCs and Macs—almost all new computers come with either QuickTime software or the QuickTime browser plug-in installed.

If compatibility is a strong point for QuickTime, in many cases quality is something of a weakness. Generally QuickTime movies are relatively small on the screen—occupying one-quarter of the screen or smaller. Though these files can be shown at double their original resolution or even bigger sizes, the picture quality becomes very grainy when enlarged. This is particularly true of older QuickTime files. More recent releases of the QuickTime software are more sophisticated and offer better picture quality and larger resolution, though as noted previously, the file sizes are much larger. When handled by the browser plug-in, QuickTime movies can be viewed while downloading, but this generally only works cleanly with a T1 or faster connection. With home dial-up, the movie will play sporadically as more and more of it downloads. If you save it to your hard drive, however, the movie will play uninterrupted after saving.

A format almost as widely used as QuickTime is **RealVideo,** the visual cousin of the aforementioned RealAudio. As with RealAudio, RealVideo is a streaming technology—the video is displayed as it downloads, and it allows for live coverage of events. These files, which generally have the file extensions ".ram," ".rm," or ".rv," can be played just about immediately upon opening the player. Because of its dominance in streaming live video, RealVideo is virtually always the technology used for webcasts, the popular live video or audio broadcasts of everything from press conferences to academic lectures to concerts.

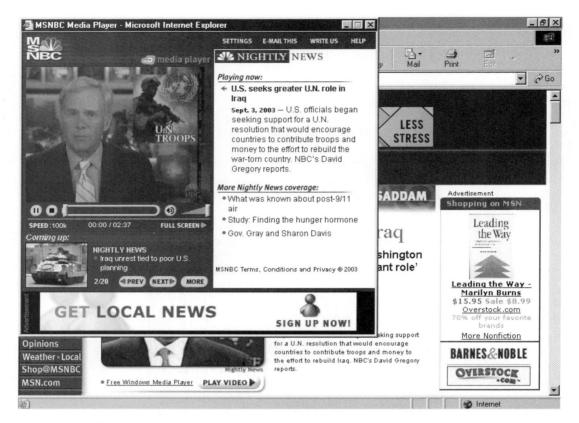

As a partner with Microsoft, MSNBC's streaming video content uses
Microsoft's Windows Media Player to display reports.

SOURCE: msnbc.com (accessed September 3, 2003). Used by permission.

The weaknesses of RealVideo parallel those of RealAudio. Unless you have a
fast network connection, quality is a problem. For home dial-up users, the video
is very grainy, often jerky and hard to follow. The audio that accompanies the picture is of low quality and can also be choppy. Furthermore, unless you have a fast
connection, the picture is generally very small on the screen. It's also prone to delays due to heavy Web traffic, and users can rarely save content to their hard drives.
Still, at this point there's no major alternative for live video on the Web, and as
with RealAudio, there are dozens of "channels" all over the Web full of content
unavailable in other formats.

A third well-known format is **Windows Media,** the format created by
Microsoft. As might be gathered from its name, this format is native to the Windows platform, though it will display on many Macs and in many browsers. The
streaming version is a descendant of the original Video for Windows, or AVI,

format. The **AVI** format is an integral part of the majority of Windows video-capture software—the programs that create movie files. Often files will be captured from live video or a VCR in the AVI format, then compressed into a different file type. Depending on a computer's graphics and video capture hardware, AVI files can provide CD-quality stereo audio and high-quality video at resolutions all the way up to full-screen size.

Once again, the trade-off for all this quality is file size. A raw (uncompressed) AVI file can easily be more than 100MB in size, depending on the screen size and length of the video. In fact, longer AVIs can easily fill an entire CD-ROM disc. This doesn't mean the format is useless—far from it. Professional film editors often use the format for editing and outputting video, but they have advanced hardware and huge hard drives that can handle the immense files involved. For Web use, however, large full-screen files are basically impractical, though some Web outlets have used small-resolution AVIs for video clips, which is why the streaming version is far more popular online.

A video file format that many Web users favor is the **MPEG** format, which stands for "Motion Picture Experts Group" after the group that developed the format. These files—with the extension ".mpg"—use data compression to try to achieve a happy medium between high quality and resolution and small file size. MPEGs can achieve excellent picture quality—they're a more rudimentary version of the mp2 format, which is the file format used for DVD movies. With MPEGs, the file size is usually about one-tenth the size of an uncompressed AVI file. Most modern computers (1GHz or faster) can display MPEG files at full-screen size with high-quality results.

A downside to MPEGs is that they're not as widely compatible across platforms and browsers as the other formats mentioned. While Windows Media Player is common on recent PCs and will play most MPEGs, often Mac users must use the QuickTime player, which temporarily converts the files to QuickTime format to play them. Some browsers will play MPEGs, some won't, though there are plug-ins available to make them work. In addition, even though MPEGs are smaller files than comparable AVIs, they're still large files that take a long time to download for nonbroadband users. Anything at a 320×200 resolution (half the standard VGA screen size) at a minute in length will still approach 10MB in size. While this is an improvement on 100MB and the quality is very good, it's still not feasible for most Web users. Plus, the entire movie must be downloaded before it can be played.

For Web use, video files are more cumbersome than audio files, due to both size and compatibility issues. Unlike sound files, video files are almost never embedded within pages and played automatically upon loading. Almost all video elements are linked from standard Web pages, to be played by the browser plug-in or displayed in a pop-up window. In addition to being large files and taking a long time to download, video files also eat up a lot of memory, which can slow any other tasks to a crawl or even occasionally freeze the user's machine. Video is a worthwhile element, but it should be thoroughly understood before it is used.

OTHER FORMATS

Online journalists may want to use multimedia elements beyond standard audio and video to enhance presentation. Some of these incorporate elements of audio and video, but each has aspects that set it apart from the formats mentioned previously. Some are fairly simple, and others are quite complex.

Among the simplest and most widely used of these formats is the animated **GIF** file. GIF stands for "Graphics Interchange Format," and the files have the extension ".gif." The nonanimated GIF file is a common format for photos and graphics on the Web. The animated GIF is a special kind of graphic file—it's actually a compilation of multiple still image files displayed in a set order to create an animated effect. This is the format used for the animated ads that are so popular with Web advertisers (if not with users).

These files can be created with assorted different graphics programs and can be configured in a number of useful ways. Designers can set the number of images to be included, the amount of time each of the compiled images is displayed, and whether the animated display will run continuously in a loop or only one time through. These are useful for eye-catching yet limited animation in a format that produces far smaller file sizes than full-motion video. As noted, the most common Web use is in advertisements, but GIF files are also popular on Web pages for children as they allow cartoon characters to run or jump or hop across the screen.

Animated GIFs work best when only a few images are used because that keeps file sizes small. More images means a larger file and a longer download. These are not recommended for a full-motion video effect, which works better in a true video format.

A common file format for music is the MIDI file (short for Musical Instrument Device Interface), which is not technically an audio clip. Rather, it's a piece of electronic code that is played on a keyboard (or other MIDI device) and saved, then downloaded and played by your computer's sound card. There are several things to like about MIDIs. First is that the files are *tiny*—a three-minute song can easily be 30K or less, which is a near-immediate download even over a home dial-up connection. Furthermore, they can easily be embedded within Web pages or linked to provide music behind a page. They're also almost universally compatible.

The bad news about MIDI files is related to their electronic-music origins. First, they are not realistic depictions of a band or group—they do not accommodate vocals and rely entirely on the musical skills of the programmer (which can vary dramatically). Second and perhaps more important is that they often sound different from one machine to another. Not every sound card is the same—different manufacturers use different "soundbanks," which assign certain tones to certain bits of code. This changes the "tone color" of each note. In fact, MIDIs can sound different on the same computer if played using two different MIDI-compatible programs. These files are seldom used in the news business, but they are common elsewhere.

A slightly more complicated format is the interactive slide show. This usually uses HTML code to create a pop-up window, smaller than the full browser window, for the purpose of looking at a series of photos. Often these will include buttons to go to the next image or the previous one, or to allow users to jump ahead or back to particular photos. Many of these use advanced JavaScript or Flash coding, which produces a smooth, professional look and many unique functions.

These presentations don't take nearly the time to download as a piece of full-motion video, but they aren't without their problems. First, slow dial-up connections can make the process of waiting for photos to load very frustrating. Second, while JavaScript and Flash coding work very well on most modern browsers, there are some compatibility and cross-platform issues. Some older browsers can't use JavaScript at all, and even some newer ones produce shaky results. Some newer machines require downloading a plug-in to play Flash video. Plus, if users have set their screen resolutions to different sizes or their screen fonts to unusual sizes or typefaces, it can cause problems making text and images line up properly. On the whole, online slide shows are fun and can be quite informative, but they must be used with care.

The Flash presentation, a complex format developed by Macromedia, Inc. that merges video, audio and animation, can incorporate pieces of assorted multimedia elements into an interactive window. As users see animation or video in a window, they can click on a button or designated area to start a program, go to another subject or otherwise interact with the program. Some of the most professional-looking Web presentations are done with this technology—indeed, Hollywood movie studios have recently started producing interactive Flash versions of their movie trailers exclusively for Web audiences. These formats can create a fuller multimedia experience than many previous technologies—they allow interactivity and incorporate many of the most compelling elements of the Web.

One of the most remarkable aspects of this technology is its ability to compress high-quality content into relatively small files. However, most Flash files still take some time to download—a relatively simple 30-second clip may still take a minute or so to load for nonbroadband users. While these files may begin to play as they download, as with RealVideo there can be delays due to Web congestion. These formats also require the user to download and install plug-ins, which are not always standard features of the major browsers.

SMART MULTIMEDIA FOR JOURNALISTS

One of the unique aspects of online journalism is the opportunity to make use of some of the interactive technologies discussed in this chapter. You can use all kinds of technologies to take your stories beyond the simple text of a newspaper or a TV news story that zooms by in 45 seconds. The key concern for a journalist is to think of function first—how will this item improve the whole story presentation? Would it really add something, or would it simply be multimedia for its own sake?

Until very recently, many factors limited use of multimedia in newsrooms. In addition to bandwidth concerns, the equipment necessary for reporters to regularly record video for the Web was too expensive for newsrooms on limited budgets. However, as technology has improved, some newsrooms have begun to buy small video cameras for their reporters to take on assignments. As the cost of even high-quality cameras dips well below $1,000, more and more newsrooms are likely to purchase them for their reporters. The notion of a reporter becoming a "one-man band"—providing audio and video in addition to a print write-up of a story—is no longer unheard of, but most reporters for online outlets don't yet carry cameras regularly.

If your organization uses this technology, you'll need to pick up a few extra skills. While staff photographers often do the actual shooting, reporters and editors need to be able to anticipate elements of a story that would translate well to short video clips. With a set event, such as a press conference, this is generally easier than with breaking news. A reporter needs to get a sense of what makes a good, useful video clip and what doesn't. Again, the main criterion for selection should be whether or not a piece of video tells a portion of the story in a unique way—does it enhance the story and offer something truly different and worthwhile? As technology improves, the use of digital cameras for this purpose will undoubtedly increase, and development of these skills will become more important.

If you're working in the broadcast media, taking a camera along on assignments is second nature. Traditional print reporters, however, still vary in how they capture interview material—some tape-record interviews, but many still jot down notes by hand. As noted in Chapter 5, the ideal scenario is to make an audio recording of the interview while jotting down notes—it's the best of both worlds, giving you the experiential learning from notetaking as well as the backup accuracy of taping. In the online world, recording affords you the option to select audio clips for posting on the page with your story. Most nonbroadcast outlets do not yet use video of interviews, though that will likely change in the next few years.

With phone interviews, there is also the option of recording the interview straight into a multimedia-equipped computer. There are assorted means of doing this, some using hardware and others using software. Some computer programs use your computer's modem and sound card to record conversations digitally and save them on your hard drive. There are also devices that use a special connector that fits a phone jack or handset and plugs into an input on your computer's sound card. (These can be purchased at electronics and computer stores or directly from several manufacturers.) Recording this way is useful because it generally saves conversations in a format you can easily use later on your news outlet's Web site. It also eliminates the hiss that comes with analog tape recording. As noted in Chapter 5, however, be sure to notify your interviewee at the beginning of the interview that the conversation is being recorded—it's not just the right thing to do, it's the law.

In most cases, the available content should tell you whether you have the raw material for useful multimedia. If a story is particularly visual in nature—a fire, a campaign rally, a game-winning home run—then a piece of video or a slideshow might be in order. Another useful case would be a circumstance where you can demonstrate a point by using an animated illustration. This can apply to many types of stories, whether it involves showing what the proposed new City Hall will look like once it's erected or illustrating how the shoulder joint works and how the local star pitcher's rotator cuff will be repaired by surgeons.

If a staff photographer has gotten a series of excellent still photos of an event, a slide show might be in order. Just because there isn't room to print all the pictures in the day's paper doesn't mean you can't show them online—they can provide a unique online-only angle to the story. For audio clips, try to use material that isn't quoted in your story—there's nothing particularly interesting about hearing the same comments you've just read. If someone uses an interesting turn of phrase that doesn't fit in elsewhere, it may be a candidate for an audio clip. If a particular piece of audio gets across an emotion, a point of view or a feeling that might not translate through its text alone, consider using it to help create a fuller picture of the story.

This type of content, however, is common to television. Online journalists must go beyond thinking simply of standard TV news elements. Is there an aspect of this story that might benefit from an unusual use of one of these multimedia technologies? A good place to use slide shows and some of the other formats discussed here is in an in-depth series of articles. Online sites have tended to specialize in serving as archives for special reports about all manner of topics, both national and local. Some of the more creative Web designers have used slide shows of archived photos with excellent effects. In other cases, Flash presentations have been used to create impressive TV-like opening sequences for the reports. Animated GIFs have also been used for this purpose, using a few still images to create an introduction that intrigues readers and makes them want to read on. An example would be a tableau of the photographs of people killed by drunk drivers, with photos appearing one by one.

Some may argue that elements like these are more about entertainment than information, but this misses an important point. As long as presentational aspects such as these engage readers and make them want to read more—to interact more with the stories—they constitute good journalism. Remember, anything that gets the audience engrossed in a subject and opens people's eyes to the content of a story isn't simply eye candy.

SUMMARY

Like any other means of telling a story, multimedia in online journalism has pluses and minuses. The pluses are straightforward—multimedia can help you provide audio and video on demand, it gives the audience richer content, and it adds another element to news presentation. The minuses can depend on the user's situation—there can be compatibility problems, the content can slow a user's machine down to a crawl, and download times can be interminable. A savvy online journalist will know the strengths and weaknesses of the different multimedia formats before using them and will be able to provide options that users will appreciate. Journalists should look to multimedia to enhance their stories with new dimensions, not as an end in itself. If approached correctly, multimedia can help you provide all the depth of print journalism and the audio and video of broadcast. Just remember: don't use multimedia because you can; use it because you should.

RELATED WEB SITES

Yahoo's multimedia listings
http://dir.yahoo.com/Computers_and_Internet/Multimedia/

Listings of local U.S. TV station sites by state
http://www.100000watts.com/tv-listings.html

Listings of local U.S. newspaper sites by state
http://newslink.org/statnews.html

EXERCISES

1. Choose two among the CNN, MSNBC and Fox News Web sites. Visit the sites and compare how they use multimedia with their stories. Use the home page and at least one story from each site to compare how they use audio, video, animation or any other multimedia elements. Which file formats do they use, and what variations do they offer (that is, choices between formats, bandwidths and so forth)? Summarize your findings in one to one and a half double-spaced pages.

2. Go to the Web site of one of your local TV stations. (Many stations can be reached via their call letters, for example, "wxyz.com," but if that doesn't work, use the URL provided in the Related Web Sites to find a list of local TV stations by state.) Compare how the TV Web site uses multimedia with how the Web site of a local newspaper uses multimedia (again, a URL is listed to locate newspaper sites). Does the TV outlet make full use of its video resources or use other multimedia elements to distinguish itself? Does the newspaper site use different multimedia elements of its own? Is the newspaper site affiliated with a TV news site, or vice versa? Write a one to one and a half page summary.

3. What types of multimedia do you like the best on news Web sites? Visit a few of your favorite sites and discuss the multimedia elements they use to engage and inform the user. Explain why you keep coming back to these sites and discuss how they integrate multimedia elements in the story package.

13

||||||

Basic Online Layout

Multimedia elements may make your site stand out, but good layout elements help readers to see what's there. As with newspapers and magazines, well-designed page layout makes it easy for readers to follow stories and to discover new ones. Yet the procedures for online layout are very different from those in the print media. In this chapter you will learn the parameters, constraints and terminology of the online medium, as well as the most common elements of online news layout.

ONLINE LAYOUT:
A COMPLETELY DIFFERENT ANIMAL

In both the print and online media worlds, page layout has the same general goals. Editors want to capture readers' attention and make it easier for them to identify, select and read stories. The simpler it is for readers to move through a publication (or a site), the more they'll be able to read and the more likely they'll return for your next edition.

Because of this, there are numerous classes and books and entire paradigms of thought about the most effective ways to lay out pages. As computerized layout became the norm throughout the 1980s and 1990s, publishing programs such as QuarkXpress and PageMaker became staples of every newsroom, and skills in using these programs became an asset for any editor. By the beginning of the 21st century, being conversant in the use of these programs was as important as knowing how to use a percentage wheel, a pica ruler or a dummy sheet had been in earlier times.

A Web page is not just what you see on the first screen. Here we have a banner at the top of the page, section links to the left, story links in the middle, text links at the bottom and advertising throughout. This page contains about three screens' worth of information.

SOURCE: the spartandaily.com (accessed September 4, 2003). Reprinted with permission.

To lay out pages for the Web requires the same basic design sense as any other type of layout. However, designing a print page using a desktop publishing program (or a paper dummy sheet, for that matter) is not adequate preparation for putting pages together using the HTML programming language. Online editors must take into account many factors that make layout for the Web completely different from standard print layout.

First, the HTML language wasn't really designed for news. If anything, it was more specifically designed long ago to add some interactivity and interesting elements to term papers posted by researchers. Most publishing programs for print media contain all sorts of news-friendly features—keyboard commands and libraries that allow for customization and quick formatting of headlines, bylines, photo captions and dozens of other elements. In contrast, HTML layout programs don't have these features built in because they're designed for general use and because they're limited to the commands and tags available within the HTML language.

Second, as has been mentioned frequently in this book, news Web sites present news differently from any other medium, print or otherwise. You must approach laying out the home page of a Web site from a very different point of view than a section front in a newspaper or a table of contents in a magazine. Aside from simply appearing on a screen as opposed to in print, Web pages have very different functions and goals.

Third, the online editor has many things to worry about that are markedly dissimilar from the concerns of a print editor. Web editors must worry about all the traditional layout elements (hierarchy of stories, clarity, graphics and so forth) plus a whole host of Web-specific issues. They must think about how quickly their pages will load, whether to split a story into successive pages, whether to include off-site links, whether to make links open new browser windows, and scores of other concerns particular to the medium.

Given these differences, it's important to understand both how to use HTML to lay out a page and also what you're trying to accomplish when you do it.

GENERAL POINTERS

At this point, you should forget almost everything you've ever learned about standard newspaper or magazine layout. Obviously, rules regarding writing and editing stories still apply, but in terms of layout, only these few rules carry over:

- News pages should look professional and be easy to read.
- Stories on a section front or home page should be listed with the most important stories at the top, followed by other stories in descending order of importance.
- Stories should generally have headlines and bylines, as well as photo captions and credits where necessary.
- Advertisements should be made as unobtrusive as possible.

Believe it or not, that's about it. Beyond these few elements, newspaper layout and online layout have next to nothing in common. Most newspaper pages contain several stories apiece, whereas most online news outlets have a home page containing listings of stories and sections. While different sections (local news, sports, business and so forth) may have their own front pages both online and off, each story generally occupies its own page online.

Accepting this, an editor laying out online pages must be aware of some of the parameters of computers in general and of Web pages in particular. Those who have worked in newspapers are usually familiar with measuring elements in inches or picas (one-sixth of an inch), but Web pages are measured with a much smaller unit—**pixels.** Short for "picture elements," pixels are the "dots" of various colors that make up everything displayed on a computer screen. When using any HTML layout program, you can specify the size of assorted elements in pixels.

The reliance on pixels adds a huge complication to online layout. If everyone's monitor were set to the same resolution, all pages would display in the same fashion. However, as noted earlier, not every computer or monitor is set the same. Many 1990s PCs came with monitors that would only display at the resolution of 640 pixels wide by 480 pixels high. As technology improved and monitors got bigger, however, more users took advantage of the ability to crowd more material onto their screens and began setting resolutions at 800 × 600 and 1024 × 768. These days it's not uncommon for users to have resolutions set at 1280 × 1024. While this offers variety and high-detail images onscreen, it creates giant headaches for anyone trying to design uniform Web pages.

This means that if you're not careful, a page that looks perfect on a display set at 640 × 480 or 800 × 600 will look tiny and compressed on a display at 1024 × 768. It means that text that looks huge on some screens will look just fine on others. In the print or broadcast media worlds, you'd never have to worry about cross-platform compatibility—the product looks the same to every user. Online, however, hours of work are put into designing pages that will look good on the majority of screens at the most popular resolutions.

With this in mind, most online news sites keep general layout on their pages pretty simple and straightforward. That is, there isn't a lot of complex formatting designed to make each page look letter-perfect as there might be on a print page. This also means there usually aren't a lot of large graphics or images or complex scripts built into the page. The fewer complex or unusual layout aspects there are on a page, the less likely something could appear horribly misaligned or poorly formatted on individual machines or browsers.

Another factor that leads most editors to keep their pages simple is that simple pages load more quickly. While modems are getting faster and high-speed home Internet connections are becoming more common, there are still an awful lot of users who dial up from home. These users can get quite upset if they have to sit around and wait a minute or two for a single page to load. There are exceptions to the "keep it simple" doctrine—several national and international news sites, such as CNN Interactive, MSNBC and Fox News Online, have created very graphically rich front pages to act as guides to their sites. On the average news site, however, the best advice is to think in terms of clear, straightforward design that is formatted cleanly and loads quickly.

These two screens are displaying the same page. The top screen is set at the resolution of 640 × 480. The screen at the bottom is set at 1024 × 768.

|||||| **FROM THE FIELD**

Retha Hill
Vice President for Content Development, BET.com
Former executive producer, WashingtonPost.com

How would you like the task of coordinating the news content at the Web site for an entire television network? That was the task Retha Hill took on in 1999 when she joined BET.com a few months before its launch. Fortunately for everyone involved, Hill was the right person for the job.

"You do have to conceptualize news differently, and you have to conceptualize the product differently," says Hill. "You need to get information across in a new way."

Hill helped put the *Washington Post* online in 1995, after eight years as a print reporter there. Unlike some print journalists—especially at that time—she knew that this was a medium that required a different type of presentation.

"You have to say, 'How do I take the same basic information and tell the story in a way that works on a Web page?'" Hill says. "You have to take the information and turn it on its head—actually, you have to turn the method of storytelling on its head—then tell the story taking advantage of the new technology. You can't approach it in the same way if you want it to be effective."

At the *Post*, Hill had the wherewithal and the resources to go far beyond simple repurposing of content. "I was the local editor," says Hill, "and expanded that to create a local portal of everything that had to do with living in Washington. There was kind of a national/international component to WashingtonPost.com, and then a component for people who lived in

You have many choices when establishing the best formats for your news outlet's pages. One device that is widely accepted is placing a logo or other identifying element on every page of the site. Given the nonlinear nature of the Web, readers can easily drift far away from their original point of entry, and by placing a logo on each page, your readers will always know when they're still on your site. This establishes visual continuity among the pages on your site, which both establishes an identity and makes readers comfortable navigating through it.

DESIGN ELEMENTS

Some of the most important design elements of Web pages were discussed in earlier chapters. At this point, however, it's useful to revisit these elements to see how they best serve your purposes when putting together news pages. If you thoroughly understand the uses, strengths and weaknesses of various elements, you can avoid a lot of future headaches.

the metropolitan area, 80 percent of whom had already read the *Post* that day. My challenge was to provide content that would encourage them to come online and interact with the newspaper a second time. So that content included all local arts and entertainment, and a robust federal community, where federal workers could deal with their issues and correspond with Mike Causey, a longtime federal government reporter and columnist."

While this was worthwhile, Hill's vision extended farther. "We had an area for the 13 or 14 colleges and universities in the metro area," she says, "where they could exchange books, find rides, find a date, get their news and info up, get linked in to other college students, etc. Of course we had the metro news, and we also had train schedules, transportation, commuting, anything you needed to know."

Hill recognized that seeing a newspaper's site as a Web portal—a central hub for all kinds of information rather than just the text of the day's newspaper—allowed a whole range of possibilities. For example, she took the *Post*'s Style section and transformed it for the Web. "I moved over as the Style editor," Hill says, "to create a more robust arts and entertainment area called Style Live. It had information from the newspaper, but also additional content that was aimed at what do you do that night, where do you go this weekend, what do you do next week."

Hill recognizes that not every outlet has the resources to take on projects like these. "I think it's important for your students to realize," she says, "that it depends on the size of the publication in the same way it depends, in the print world, if you work for a small weekly or you work for a large metropolitan daily."

That doesn't mean, however, that even a small outlet can't be creative. "You have to look at it like this," says Hill. "How are you going to take what's in the newspaper that day and use the technology to enrich the users' experience? It's all about taking advantage of the new technology. If you can't do that or you're disinclined to do that, then you're not being an effective online journalist."

Every online outlet uses HTML layout software and page templates to speed the process of cranking out news pages for the Web. An important thing to realize when using this software is that it's not performing some strange magic to create Web pages—it just automates the creation of an HTML page and the placement of tags and other codes to make it look like you want it to. **HTML tags** are pieces of code that tell a browser what to do. They're denoted within the code of Web pages by angle brackets ("<" and ">"). For example, the code that turns on boldface type is <B>. A forward slash ("/") within a tag turns the given property off, so to turn off boldface requires a </B> tag. This chapter does not include a comprehensive HTML tutorial, but it is helpful to familiarize yourself with the language. That way, if there are problems, you can "get under the hood," look at the source code and perhaps fix them. Any Web page composing program will have a setting to allow you to look at the page's source code, and most make it as easy as clicking a tab or button.

The simplest design element within HTML is probably the series of typefaces used throughout the page. Today's browsers can display all sorts of typefaces (fonts), but professionals know that you can't assume too much about all your users and their browsers. Some users have older computers equipped with older browsers that won't handle anything but basic typefaces. This is why, at least in terms of fonts, most news organizations play it safe and go with the most common fonts and settings. This doesn't mean they simply go with the browser's default fonts. Body text generally defaults to Times (on Macs) or Times New Roman (on PCs) at 12 points, but users can easily change these selections, which can throw entire pages out of whack. So designers must specify their chosen fonts, even if they're common.

Some Web-only outlets defy the play-it-safe approach, unabashedly aiming for a higher-tech audience and assuming that readers have the latest browsers. This allows them to experiment much more freely with unusual, eye-catching fonts and other items and features. If you're using an advanced HTML editing program, you can specify a special font and a more common backup font.

While typefaces can cause problems, you can experiment more freely with the size and color of type. Even the oldest browsers recognize the tags for larger and smaller type and for many colors. Most traditional news organizations' Web sites don't go too crazy with colored type, but they often use many different sizes of type to make pages look more visually appealing. As with the layout of any newspaper page, certain sizes and styles of type are selected as the site's default for various aspects of the page. For example, if your site uses the Heading settings and tags (<H1>, <H2> and so on), headlines may be set for Heading 1 or 2, bylines for Heading 3, photo captions for Heading 5 and photo credits for Heading 6. These are fairly common settings. (If you're unsure of your site's settings, examine the source code of one of its pages and search for <H1>, <H2> or <FONT> tags within the code.)

If your site uses the <FONT> tags and settings for layout, things can vary slightly more, mainly because the Heading tags automatically make the type bold. If you don't want bold type, you'll have to use <FONT> settings. HTML editing programs generally have a small drop-down menu of seven point sizes (8, 10, 12, 14, 18, 24 and 36 point) that make type larger or smaller using the <FONT> tag. The code for these is based on the base font of 12 point: the two smaller sizes are written into the code as SIZE = "−2" and SIZE = "−1" and the four larger ones are written as SIZE = "+1" and so forth on up to +4. You can also boldface, italicize or underline text formatted using the <FONT> tags. (While the Heading tags are automatically bold, you can use the italics and underline functions on text using the Heading tags.)

HTML editing programs make it easy to change the size of type, and also its color. In most cases, you simply select the text, click a color button (or a menu entry for "Character Properties" or something similar) and select a color. This inserts a hexadecimal code into the page—a six-character sequence of letters and numbers—that the browser then reads to display the color. (For example, the code for white is "#FFFFFF" and the code for purple is "#800080.") With most HTML programs, the same command can be used to create colored backgrounds for various page elements and even whole pages.

When you're writing your own code, most browsers will recognize the names of common colors (blue, red, yellow and so forth) within the <FONT> tags using the COLOR switch. However, you can be more specific and creative to a point. Even the oldest browsers will respond correctly to the codes for certain colors, while others will be displayed differently from one machine or browser to another. There are 216 colors that have been deemed "browser safe," and many HTML editing programs let you pick from these colors. Some allow other color choices, but you should be aware that different browsers and platforms might make them look different than you'd intended. (To find the codes and charts for these colors, visit http://www.lynda.com.)

Giving your page a colored background is usually an easy process. If you're using an HTML editing program, usually you'll click a color button or go to a menu item for page properties and choose a color. In Microsoft FrontPage, for example, you would look under the "File" menu, then select "Properties" (or right-click anywhere on the page and select "Page Properties") and pick your chosen color under the "Background" tab. If you're writing your own code, within the <BODY> or <TABLE> tags you use the switch "BGCOLOR=" followed by your chosen color, though if you don't have a table of Web-safe colors, you'll have to stick with the basic hues (red, blue and yellow, for example).

The element that makes the Web most visually interesting is images. These can include photos or graphical illustrations and can be in any of several formats. Two of these formats, however, are most commonly used by news organizations, and they're identified by their file extensions. For photographs, news outlets usually use the JPG (or **JPEG**) format. It produces very detailed photos in a compressed format that keeps file sizes small but quality high. The only downside of JPEGs is that the browser must decompress them, which takes slightly longer than the quicker-loading GIFs. The GIF format is most commonly used for graphics because it tends to work well in representing flat colors in browsers. GIF images have a limited color palette just like browsers do, and thus they generally display accurately within most browsers. (As noted in Chapter 12, certain programs can also produce "animated" GIF images, which are often used for advertisements.)

One way or the other, the larger the file size of an image, the longer it will take to load, which is why news organizations tend to keep the images on their pages small. Some online sites allow readers to click on these small images to see enlarged versions. This requires two versions of the image—the smaller one (called a "thumbnail," as in a thumbnail sketch) is located on the main page and is linked to the larger one. This is a nice feature for readers, but for the news outlet it takes up a lot of disk space and bandwidth. Nevertheless, most news outlets find it's a worthwhile trade-off in helping to attract readers.

As with a color, you can use an image as a background for your pages. In HTML editing programs, the process is usually the same, except you specify an image file rather than a color. In Microsoft FrontPage, for example, you follow the same procedure as setting a background color, but instead of selecting a color in the "Background" menu you select the box that says "Background Picture" and fill in the picture's URL. If you're writing your own code, inside the <BODY> or <TABLE> tags you use the "BACKGROUND=" switch followed by the file name of your chosen image file.

When using an image for a background, however, you should pay attention to a couple of potential problems. First, your background image can easily take away from the content of the page. This is why most background images use muted

USING TABLES

The HTML language was designed primarily to facilitate putting term papers online. It was never intended to help people create graphically rich Web pages, much less the multimedia extravaganzas we see today. As such, HTML is an imperfect and often frustrating design tool. It had (and still has) no commands specifically designed to divide pages up into sections, boxes or columns.

Luckily, early Web designers discovered they could use an existing tag to get around this omission—the <TABLE> tag. This was originally put into HTML to enable researchers to put spreadsheet-style tables into their pages. Fortunately, the <TABLE> tag can contain a secondary command (BORDER=0) that makes the borders of the table invisible. This has allowed designers to use the <TABLE> tag to divide up pages in all sorts of ways without the tables' border lines making the whole page look like a bunch of boxes.

The coding for tables can get complicated—in addition to creating a table and specifying a border width using the appropriate tags, the user has to create rows (using the <TR> tag for "table row") and columns (using the <TD> tag for "table data") and place content within the correct areas. Fortunately, HTML layout programs keep that formatting behind the scenes, generally allowing a user to drag and drop a table into a page, then format it from there.

In most layout programs, table attributes can either be set through menus or through right-clicking the table and selecting "Table Properties." Here are some of the attributes designers need to set for their tables:

- *Width.* You can specify width of the table in either pixels or percentage. (Users can also click and drag the border of a table to the desired width, but most designers prefer to set precise widths using menus.) Setting a table's width to "75%" means you'll create a table that is 75 percent of the width of the user's screen. Most designers recommend this method because people using different screen resolutions will always see the table displayed at the same relative width regardless of resolution. However, this means that table cells will hold more at some resolutions and less at others. Setting an absolute width in pixels allows greater control of the appearance of the items in the table, but it can cause problems for users with different screen resolutions.

- *Height.* This attribute is usually set in pixels, though it often goes unused. If there is no value set for height, the table simply expands to hold the material placed inside it. Designers sometimes use the height attribute if they're using tables to create something graphically precise, such as a block of color.

- *Border.* Most tables on Web pages have no visible borders, which allows material to be placed around a page without a "boxy" appearance. This is accomplished by setting the border to 0. However, if you want to create an actual table for displaying data, visible borders can be useful. Borders can be set to any number of pixels in thickness, though most visible borders are simply set to 1. Designers can also assign colors to their borders, and on some newer layout programs they can actually set a "light" border color and a "dark" border color, which can create some interesting shadow effects.

colors that do not distract the reader. Second, if you use an image that doesn't take up the whole screen, the browser will automatically "tile" the image across the screen—arranging it repeatedly across the screen as if it were tiles. This can create a very busy background that boggles the eyes, which will drive readers away quickly.

In addition, whether using an image or a color as a background, you must be careful to assure that the type and other elements on your page offer sufficient contrast to be read easily. In other words, don't use black type with a dark background. This is a particular problem in news when there is a lot of text to read. You need

USING TABLES, *continued*

- *Alignment.* This attribute tells the browser where the table will appear—to the left, right or center of the page. This is sometimes also called the "float" of the table. The alignment of the material within table cells is controlled by another attribute.
- *Cell Padding.* This attribute sets the amount of space between a table cell's border and content. It defaults to 1 but can be set to any number of pixels to create an indented effect within table cells.
- *Cell Spacing.* Rather than the space between borders and contents, this attribute sets the actual space between cells within the table, creating thicker "walls" throughout the table. This defaults to 2 but can be set to any number of pixels.
- *Background.* This is used to create a graphical backdrop for the entire table. Designers can specify either a color or image to serve as the table's background, but you should be aware of a couple of issues. First, if you set a background color for the table, then set different colors for cell backgrounds within that table, it can create a visual cacophony that's hard on the eyes of viewers. Second, using an image as a background can also create something hard on the eyes, but another trait causes bigger problems. Images used as backgrounds usually "tile"—they repeat in rows and columns until they cover the entire space, which can create some truly stomach-turning effects.

Having set these attributes for tables, designers also frequently need to specify some details about cells within those tables. To make content within cells behave the way you want it to, you often must tell the cell what to do rather than the item itself. As with full tables, in most layout programs cell attributes can either be set through menus or through right-clicking a cell and selecting "Cell Properties." Here are some of the attributes you can set for individual cells:

- *Width.* As with tables, you can specify the width of a cell in either pixels or percentage. Setting the width to "75%" means you'll create a cell that is 75 percent of the width of the full table; setting the width to 300 means the cell will be 300 pixels wide. Be aware, however, that in setting the width of a cell, you also set the width of the entire column in which your cell is located.
- *Horizontal Alignment.* This sets whether the content of your cell will appear to the left, right or center of the cell. You can also set this to "Justify" if you want justified text in the cell.
- *Vertical Alignment.* This is a handy command that allows you to set whether you want your cell's content to appear at the top, center or bottom of the cell. Either "Center" or "Middle" will work as an option here.
- *Border.* Cells will always have the same border thickness as the table they appear in, but colors can be set for individual cell borders. You can set "light" or "dark" border colors for cell borders as well.
- *Background.* As with tables, individual cells can have background colors and images, though some of the previous warnings about overusing them apply to cells as well as to whole tables.

to make your page as easy to read as possible, or you won't capture readers for any length of time. Young page designers tend to get carried away with making pages wildly colorful, with bright backgrounds and text, which is fine for your own personal Web site. (You probably have friends whose Web pages are bright and colorful but next to impossible to read.) However, when your audience is supposed to read many pages of news on a professional site, you're generally better off keeping it simple. There's nothing wrong with black text on a white background highlighted with images and color elsewhere on the page. Indeed, this is the way most news Web sites are set up.

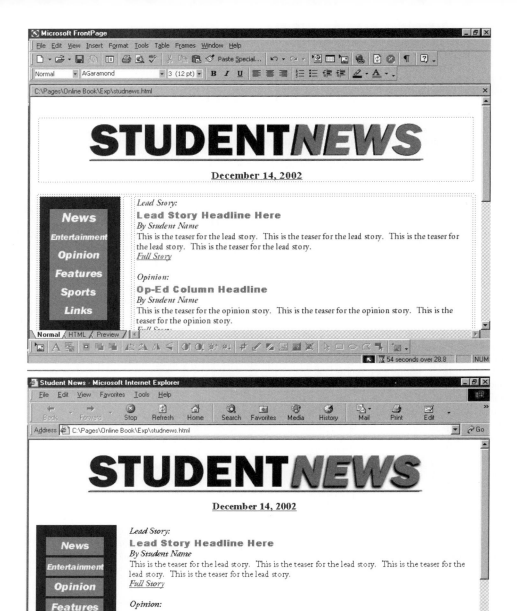

As with other Web layout programs, Microsoft FrontPage uses tables to arrange information on pages. The top screen shows a page being designed in FrontPage; although the table borders are set at 0, they are visible during layout as dotted lines. The bottom screen shows the finished page as it appears displayed in a browser.

Probably the most important design element is one that the reader doesn't even usually notice—the table. Most of the online news sites you've seen use tables extensively to divide up pages into areas for advertisements, links, story text and other elements. Just about any time you see columns of information in an online news page, the formatting has been done with tables. Since tables are the main way to do this, you'll need to familiarize yourself with the ways they work. Be advised that since tables were not originally designed with news in mind, they have some quirks that must be circumvented. The box titled "Using Tables" explains some of these idiosyncrasies, as does this book's Web site (at http://communication .wadsworth.com/craig).

THE HOME PAGE

A news home page has a somewhat different function than a personal home page. While personal pages can highlight whatever they want, news pages must attract readers in particular ways and drive them to story pages within the site. Not every news site handles these tasks the same way, but there are certain common threads among them.

The majority of home pages on the Web have the file name "index.html" or "index.htm" because the Unix operating system defaults to those names. (Some Windows servers default to "default.htm" instead.) For online news outlets the notion of an "index" page is useful because the home page generally serves as exactly that—the index to the stories currently on your site. Online news outlets' home pages generally showcase the day's big stories and provide links to other sections of the site. The headlines of the featured stories usually serve as link text— you click on a headline that looks interesting to go to its story.

For those accustomed to newspapers, the home page is the equivalent of the front page, but in many ways a home page has to accomplish more than a front page. While both promote the biggest stories of the day, the home page is the avenue for all other usage of the site. Newspaper users can ignore the front page entirely and skip right to the sports or business sections without much trouble. Web users, however, must either locate a link to the lead sports or business story or to the given day's sports or business page. Rather than simply serving as the first page of news, the home page is the universal jumping-off point for an online news outlet.

Because it's the central gateway to your site, the home page needs to accomplish some seemingly contradictory goals. It should generally be eye-catching and inviting for readers, yet it should also load quickly to avoid causing frustrated readers to go elsewhere. It should both highlight a few big stories and provide links to smaller ones. It should also be designed with both flair and simplicity, providing clear yet comprehensive links to the contents of the site.

Styles of home pages vary widely. Some online editions of print outlets try to copy the general look of the front page of the daily paper, featuring the same stories, photos and headlines but including teases with links to other stories and

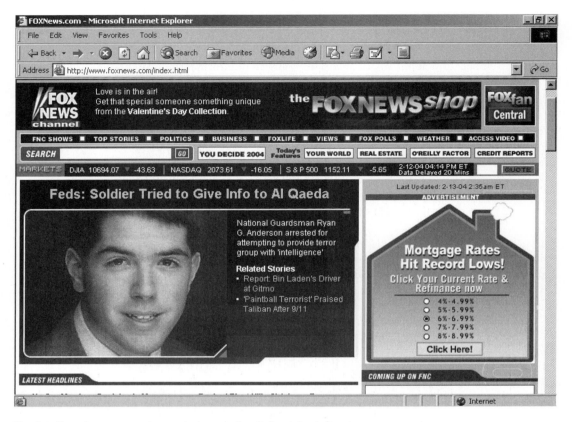

The Fox News home page does not place section links at the left as is common at many sites. The Fox site features a colorful lead story box with a yellow headline and a banner featuring navigation links, ads, stocks and a search function at the top of the page.

SOURCE: foxnews.com (accessed February 13, 2004). Used by permission of Fox News Network LLC.

sections. Some divide up the page and list the top stories in each section, while others include links to every story from that day. One way or another, there are two main goals of the home page—to attract readers and to provide them with the easiest and most intuitive path to a day's news coverage.

As with sections in a newspaper, there is generally a home page for each section—local news, business, sports, features and the like. However, unlike the home page, at many outlets the section pages link to stories from several previous days. This is usually done to allow readers to browse recent stories and to make the day's local, business or sports news look a bit less sparse. Whatever the reason, this gives users an opportunity to catch up on coverage of continuing stories.

Almost every online news site's main home page contains photos, logos, ad-

Rather than using a standard text headline, the MSNBC home page features a lead headline superimposed on a photo and saved as a graphic. The page also includes section links at the left, story links at the right and below, and video links immediately below the lead story.

SOURCE: msnbc.com (accessed August 14, 2003). Used by permission.

vertisements and dozens of links. The task facing those who design such pages is daunting. They must strike a balance between style, substance and simplicity—between a page that is eye-catching, exhaustive and loads quickly. The more you try to attract readers with photos or other graphical elements, the longer it will generally take for the page to load, which puts you at risk of losing users. It's a difficult balance to strike. It's true that your main goal is to hook the reader and to get your information across, not just to dazzle. Most editors say that it's more important to create a home page that's functional than one that's beautiful. However, the same editors would also tell you that the page had better not be downright ugly or hard to read. Even great news organizations can't make people read an unreadable, visually unappealing page.

The CNN home page features some fairly standard layout traits, including section links at the left, story links at the right and below, and video links near the top. It also includes a search box as part of its banner at the top of the page.

SOURCE: cnn.com (accessed August 14, 2003). Used by permission.

LINKS AND MARGINALIA

Links are clearly one of the most distinctive features of the online medium. You need to think of them a little differently when looking at layout. In addition to being an element sometimes included within stories, links also frequently appear grouped outside the text. While some online outlets choose not to place links within the text of stories, almost all of them include some links at the end of stories or within the margins of pages. Some common layout styles have emerged, but there's still no one accepted place to put links on a news page.

Often the placement of links depends on their function. On home pages, links primarily take the user to a particular story within the site. On the story pages themselves, however, links often have a different function. On story pages, news outlets generally want to make it easy for the user to return to the home page or to section pages, and they employ various methods to do this. Almost every news outlet these days places a logo at the top of the page that can be clicked to return to the site's home page. In addition, daily outlets will frequently place links to the day's sections in the left margin of the page. However, some organizations want the user to be able to do more. Some outlets place small section links across the very top of the page—usually competing for space with advertisements. Sometimes these will appear as small "tabs" to be clicked, and other times the outlets will employ drop-down menus that allow the user to go directly to a section. This then frees up space in the margin to include links to other stories from the same section (local news, city/state, sports, features and so on).

Many outlets provide story-specific links—that is, links to stories or sites related to the subject of a given news story. The most common placement for these is at the end of the story, which seems logical—if a user has finished the story and wants to read more about the subject, it's a simple matter to read the headlines of related stories and click on one that looks interesting. Like so many things in the online world, however, this is far from a universal practice. Some sites take advantage of their search functions by allowing users to click a single button to perform a preformatted search for stories covering the same subjects. In addition, in the case of a major story, some sites will create a special archive page devoted to the outlet's coverage of the story. This allows readers who want to immerse themselves in a topic to do so, and it removes long lists of links from the bottom of each story on the subject.

Links to related sites—Web sites of companies, organizations and people related to the story but with no ties to the news organization—are a subject of some disagreement within the industry. Some see such links as a service to readers, a way to help people read more about a story and learn about the people, institutions and issues involved in an issue. Others take a more pragmatic approach, noting that such links actually take readers away from your site, thus completely contradicting the central goal of attracting readers. In many cases off-site links are designed so that, when clicked, they open a new browser window for the off-site page. This is easily accomplished with HTML code (it just requires the TARGET=NEW switch within the link tag) and creates at least the possibility that when readers are finished with the new page they'll close it and return to your site. Links from within the text of a story (see Chapter 11) also frequently open new windows.

Since it's become common to place links, advertisements and other peripheral material in the margins of Web pages, items on the perimeter of pages have become known as **marginalia.** This is appropriate not only because items appear in the margins but because they're seen as peripheral or marginal to the content of the story.

As with so many other aspects of online journalism, certain items are commonly found in margins, but there is no set standard of what items should be placed at different locations. The closest thing to a standard is the notion that readers look for links to sections or other articles in the left margin, but even that is not a universal. While most commercial sites place banner advertisements across the top of the page, some place smaller ads within the left and right margins as well, in addition to links and other material.

Placing ads or other items in the right margin is a relatively new phenomenon online. As consumers have bought more powerful computers with bigger monitors, many Web sites have moved away from the standard screen resolution of 640 × 480 and toward the higher resolutions of 800 × 600 and 1024 × 768. Since this allows for more information on the screen, it gives site designers room to add material to the right of where their pages used to end.

From a layout point of view, margins are often differentiated by color as well as by content. As with paper layout, online news outlets generally adopt certain colors and graphic features throughout their sites. It's common for an outlet's dominant color to appear in its left margin, whether as a background or on buttons or other navigation items.

TEMPLATES, SCRIPTS AND STYLE SHEETS

In certain isolated corners of the Web, there are still a few online news outlets that remake their pages from scratch for every edition. More often than not, these are very small outlets, either school papers or small-town weeklies, which are simply trying to get a product online without really understanding how the medium works best. In some cases, to create each new edition, editors simply overwrite the previous one. Not only does this eliminate the possibility of keeping an archive, it also creates a lot of repetitive extra work for layout personnel. There are smarter ways to approach the day-to-day operation of creating an online news product.

In many ways, the problems these outlets are having in learning to put news online are similar to the difficulties many old-school news editors have had in adapting to computer layout programs for their print outlets. Until the last 15 years or so, virtually all newspaper editors were trained to lay out their pages using blank paper dummy sheets. These sheets—usually produced on 8 ½ × 14-inch paper for a standard broadsheet page—were basically small-scale models of pages, with marks corresponding to the inches on a page. Editors would mark up these dummies to show the size of each story and where the photo should be on the finished page. Dummies then became the blueprints for pasting type and photos onto the full-sized pages that were later photographed and turned into printing plates.

What does this have to do with misunderstanding the production of online news? Well, in the old system, while section headers and other elements would generally stay the same, at some level editors became accustomed to starting with a blank slate every day. When computer layout programs for print newspapers came along, such as QuarkXpress, PageMaker and others, suddenly dummies became much less necessary. Editors could now create master page files (templates) for all their pages. These would include all the graphical and editorial elements for which they'd previously allotted space on a blank dummy sheet every day. With template files, editors could simply save a copy of the file, then modify that copy to fit the day's news. They could abandon paper dummies entirely and simply allot space for stories right on the screen. Still, tried-and-true methods die hard, so many news editors—even those who work with computer layout programs—still use dummies as guidelines for laying out their pages.

This blank-slate mentality is feasible in print, but it's not a good fit with the characteristics of the online medium. In print, the appearance of the page is all that matters—it's relatively easy to set aside the top three inches of a dummy for the Sports page's section header, or the whole left column for a daily columnist. With online news pages, however, editors have to worry about both the page's appearance and all its interactive elements. Various links, assorted buttons and advertisements appear daily, and the often complex coding that makes them work must be perfect every day. This is the reason all major Web news outlets use templates to create news pages.

Web templates can be relatively simple or dizzyingly complicated, depending on the needs of the editors and readers and the skill of those who create the pages. Every outlet contains different types of pages—the home page, section pages and story pages, among others—so every outlet creates templates for each kind of page. Each template contains the elements that appear on every page of its type—it acts as sort of a mold into which editors pour story content or section content. At major outlets, most writers and editors don't worry about templates on a daily basis—the top editors and management generally work with professional Web design firms to determine their content. However, at smaller operations—particularly online outlets at colleges and universities—you'll need to know the basics of how templates work.

When designing an online news site, many hours of work are put into designing templates because every element must both look right and work right. Every item must be placed correctly, coded accurately, then tested on as many different machines, browsers and platforms as possible, with as many different settings as possible. All of this is to assure that most users will be able to navigate through the site quickly and easily, with no dead ends or formatting glitches. In general, most templates provide preformatted headlines, bylines and cutlines for writers and editors to fill in. This assures both consistent appearance and functional coding on all pages.

Many HTML editing programs make using templates very easy—most allow you to save any page as a template, which locks the original document to keep it from being overwritten. When an editor calls up the template file, this automatically creates a new file identical to the template. Changes can be made to the original template, but the program generally warns the user before saving changes to avoid accidental alteration of the template file. The simplest templates use straightforward HTML code for all formatting, including placement of images, links and backgrounds. On story pages, text is generally either imported or pasted onto the page from the original story. There are often separate templates for stories with photos, sidebars or other design elements to assure consistent formatting of those elements.

Importing stories from a word processor program is a problem still faced by most college outlets and many professional news organizations. In most instances, editors for print outlets make last-minute corrections within their layout programs,

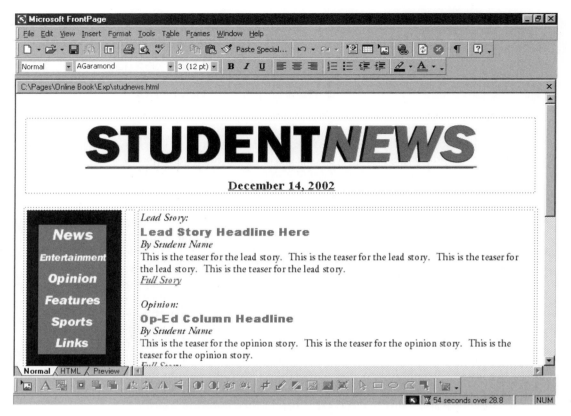

Templates help create consistency across pages on a Web site. Here a page template in Microsoft FrontPage provides many different kinds of formatting for headlines, subheads, bylines and link text. Editors can then simply plug copy into the appropriate areas throughout the page.

but there's no truly convenient way for those changes to be easily transferred to the online version. Many online editors still go to completed print pages in QuarkXpress or Pagemaker, copy story text and paste it back into a Microsoft Word file. Software makers have promised improvements on this, and a few top-level professional organizations have developed systems where reporters' stories are written as source files that are automatically imported into both print and on-line layout programs. Still, right now importing stories is a bit of a hang-up at most online outlets, but stay tuned.

For the average college online news outlet, simple HTML templates can produce excellent results. The language can accommodate a rainbow of colors, endless images, dozens of type styles and a multitude of different layout choices. Students often want to go crazy with bells and whistles at college outlets, but they frequently run into trouble when adding more complicated elements that don't immediately work properly across platforms. This is why it's a good idea to start out by creating a site that uses basic HTML in its templates—HTML is easy to use, even to its fullest capacity, and causes a lot fewer problems than when you try to build more complex templates. You have to walk before you can run—it doesn't matter how many cool features your site has if they don't work.

Once you've put together a solid, dependable site using HTML, you can dabble in some of the more advanced items that can increase a news site's functionality. These often involve using **Java** applets, **JavaScript** or **Flash.** Both Java and JavaScript are supplemental programming languages that work with HTML to produce sophisticated effects. The main difference between the two is that Java uses separate small programs ("applets," as in small applications), and JavaScript functions entirely through code written into an HTML document. These two features are at the root of a number of popular items at online outlets, such as news tickers, time and date functions, dynamic menus, and dozens of other interactive features. Flash works more like a Java applet, where a separate file is created and read by the browser to produce graphical effects.

There are pluses and minuses about using these languages. The benefits basically all center on functionality and creativity—they allow you to do all sorts of interesting things on your pages, many of which are popular with readers. This is why most professional news organizations make use of these technologies on their sites. The down side is that putting these things together can be complicated, and various computers, browsers and platforms sometimes interpret such coding differently. You could take a full-semester class on Java, JavaScript or Flash and still run into problems when putting new content of this type on your site. At the heart of the problem is that many current HTML layout programs still don't work well with Java, JavaScript and Flash. They generally require the user to know all necessary code and make sure it's formatted correctly. Furthermore, some HTML programs simply don't respond well to certain commands within these languages or use formatting that conflicts with functions within the scripts or applets.

This doesn't mean you should never use scripts or applets—it just means that you'll need to learn a lot about their code and how they work before you commit to using them regularly on your pages. Fortunately, this is possible with some dedicated study of Web technology. One of the great things about the Internet is that so many talented programmers are willing to share their work for free. You can find scripts and applets that will do practically anything yet are offered free of charge on the Web, along with instructions on how to use them. Often the only thing these programmers ask in return is that you acknowledge that you used their code on your site. This is a matter of honesty and common courtesy—they've helped make your site more appealing or functional, and the least you can do is thank them by acknowledging them. This is one of the things that makes Web technology so unique. Never before has so much valuable information been made freely available.

Another advanced technique for designing templates involves the use of **style sheets.** These are sets of commands that can be used to give certain types of pages the same characteristics, such as fonts, links, colors, images, backgrounds or other page elements. By using style sheets, you can set headlines, cutlines and the like to one size and color for all your story pages or home pages or whatever—you can have a different style sheet for each type of page. The effect is the same as making new pages from standard HTML templates every time you need one, but it can replace many lines of formatting code with a single line pointing to the appropriate style sheet.

For major news sites that post hundreds of similar pages per week, style sheets are a way to cut down on the storage space occupied by page after page of text. Perhaps more important, however, style sheets allow for quick changes to huge volumes of pages. If you want to add a button or link to all of your archived stories, you simply change the original style sheet rather than modifying each archived page. This is tremendously helpful during major redesigns of news sites. The coding gets complicated, but many people in the business believe it's worth the effort.

SUMMARY

Designing a news outlet for the Web is a very different process than for any other medium. It requires a lot of patience and a deep understanding of what your outlet is trying to accomplish, both visually and editorially. It also helps to know how HTML works and how to take full advantage of its assorted quirks and characteristics. It's always best to first design a site that works and is easy for readers to follow. Only then should you dip your toe into the more murky waters of scripts and applets. The payoffs in terms of appearance, functionality and possibly even readership are great, but it's awfully easy to get in over your head. Remember—when in doubt, keep it simple.

RELATED WEB SITES

Mindy McAdams' Web page design overview
http://www.well.com/user/mmcadams/online.newspapers.html

Yahoo's JavaScript listings
http://dir.yahoo.com/Computers_and_Internet/Programming_Languages/JavaScript/

What are style sheets?
http://www.herts.ac.uk/lis/ltdu/technology/style_sheets.html

Protocols for Cascading Style Sheets
http://www.w3.org/TR/WD-css1

The Browser-Safe Color Palette, by Lynda Weinman
http://www.lynda.com/hex.html

EXERCISES

1. Go to a favorite Web page of any sort (news, sports, entertainment or whatever) that you believe is visually interesting. Write a paragraph on why this site appeals to you—what is it that catches your eye or otherwise makes you want to interact with the page? Next, print out a copy of the page (the printout may run through several printed pages), then with a pen note *every* design element you can find. This includes images, backgrounds, tables, links, unusual fonts, colors and anything else you can identify. Turn in both the paragraph and the marked-up Web page printout.

2. Choose any two news Web sites and print out their home pages. Then write a one to one and a half page summary describing the differences in how the two are laid out, and how those differences might influence a user's behavior on a site. Does one page's layout attract the reader to the day's lead story while the other highlights many stories? Does one page lead a reader to particular stories or to sections within the day's publication? Where are advertisements placed, how large are they, and how many are on the page? Answer these and similar questions.

3. Look at several news outlets on the Web and select one whose home page you believe is poorly laid out. Print the page and write a one to one and a half page summary of what you dislike about the page's layout and what you would change about the page to make it work better.

||||||

PART IV

Standards, Laws
and Ethical Issues

Part 4 deals with big-picture issues involving what should and should not be published online. While you may be aware of basic journalistic standards, most students—and many professional reporters—are unfamiliar with and unaware of the nature of standards and laws governing online material. The chapters in Part 4 introduce you to these concepts and help to prepare you for the consequences that can result from online publishing.

14 Online Standards versus Journalistic Standards

A lot of people think that neither journalism nor the Internet have any standards whatsoever, but in this chapter you will learn that this is a misconception. The chapter looks at both the longtime standards of newsrooms and "netiquette," the politeness customs of the Internet, and examines where they diverge and intersect.

15 Legal Issues Online and Offline

A mind-boggling variety of laws relate to both journalism and the Internet. This chapter examines such thorny issues as libel, invasion of privacy and fair use as applied to news as well as to discussion groups, chat rooms and the like. The chapter also looks closely at recent court cases and legislation dealing with online content.

16 Ethics in Cyberland

The emergence of the Internet has created all sorts of new ethical questions, and many of them bear directly on online journalism. This chapter examines many ethical cases from recent history that relate to everything from advertising to privacy to obscenity, and asks an important question: To whom does a journalist owe moral duty?

17 The 21st Century Journalist

What will the job of journalism look like in 2015? The evidence presented throughout this book highlights the traits and skills journalists will need as technology advances further. This chapter presents some thoughts and opinions on these issues from the professionals interviewed for this book.

14

||||||

Online Standards versus Journalistic Standards

The Internet is often seen as an untamed frontier of free expression, yet online journalists are bound by many of the same standards and laws as their print and broadcast counterparts. This chapter looks into the long-held, often unwritten rules of journalism, superimposes them on the Internet and discusses where these standards intersect with and diverge from "netiquette."

"Standards? What standards?" This is what an average person might say about the notion of guidelines as to what is acceptable or unacceptable on the Internet. People have heard so much about pornography, racism and hate mongering on the Web that they're likely to think that the idea of online standards is laughable. On top of this, the concept of ethical online behavior isn't helped by the huge quantities of junk e-mail received by Web users, hawking a thousand new ways to make money or telling another worn-out joke or begging you to pass this message on to 10 more people. The Internet may be a lot of things, but most people don't see it as a bastion of integrity. Of course, many people also observe similar problems in mainstream journalism. Some seem to think news has been reduced to the race to find the next two-headed baby or high-profile sex scandal.

In spite of these perceptions, people who work within traditional journalism or on the Internet will tell you that each contains definite customs and courtesies that should be followed. This chapter examines some of these practices, discusses how they diverge and intersect, and looks at how online journalists can operate in ways that live up to both sets of standards.

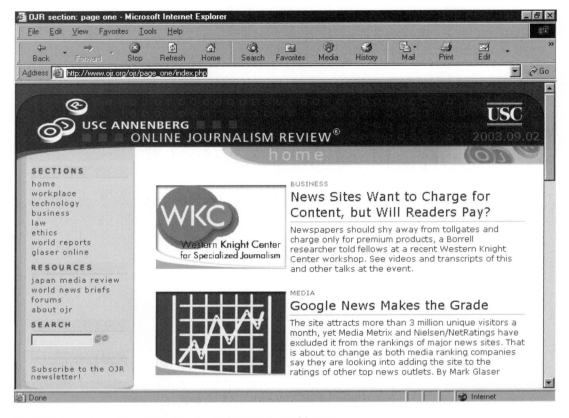

The USC Annenberg School's Online Journalism Review addresses
many issues of journalistic practices and standards in the online world.

SOURCE: ojr.org (accessed September 2, 2003)

JOURNALISTIC STANDARDS

In many ways, standards are higher within the profession of journalism today than
they were in the first few decades of this century. "Anything for the story" was
the motto of this earlier time, and this often manifested itself in dubious ways. In
his 1993 book *Making News* (Boston: Harvard Business School Press), Martin
Mayer quotes veteran newsman Bob Casey on the subject of journalism ethics in
the 1920s.

> The journalistic profession in Chicago was just about as clean as it was any-
> where else. It had its own peculiar system of ethics. Numerous reporters
> would have looked upon burglary in quest of photographs as an extremely
> venial sin. Nobody thought it much of a crime to represent himself over the
> telephone as the coroner or the Governor of Illinois. It was perfectly all right
> to tap a telephone wire, or read private mail, or steal evidence or bribe any-

body who would accept a bribe. Nobody thought the worse of a reporter because he occasionally kidnapped the leading character in an important story. But all of this was justifiable only in behalf of an undefinable, somewhat nebulous service to a public that had only halfheartedly asked for it—the discovery, extraction and presentation of THE NEWS. . . . It was, and is, the unspoken Hippocratic Oath of the newspaperman that, though he may sell out everything and everybody else in the world, he will never sell himself. (p. 59)

Things have changed dramatically since those days. Virtually any journalist caught engaging in burglary, bribery or kidnapping would not only be fired but also probably be arrested. Regardless of the weight of a given story, such behavior is now seen as abhorrent. While other aspects of this seem a bit less serious, such as impersonating the coroner (or the governor) to get some information, such activity would still be seen as unethical today. Indeed, about as far as most journalists will go in this regard is to pose as an ordinary citizen in a public place while they're researching a story. Still, some reporters even feel it's necessary to identify themselves as journalists if they stumble on news during off-work hours.

There is no single set of rules or guidelines for journalists—no "Hippocratic Oath"—but there is a fairly coherent notion of what is right and wrong. Many journalism organizations have their own ethics codes, and these tend to overlap quite a bit. In their 1996 book *Hold the Press: The Inside Story on Newspapers* (Baton Rouge: Louisiana State University Press), John Maxwell Hamilton and George A. Krimsky identified 10 rules that writers and editors follow within most reputable news organizations. They have dubbed these rules "The 10 Commandments of News" and apply them to all journalists.

Thou Shalt Not:

1. Lie in print or on the air (this also means not using new technology to alter photos).

2. Lie to or threaten a source.

3. Report rumors or other unverified information.

4. Suppress or omit opinion with which one disagrees.

5. Show favoritism or personal bias in one's reporting or writing.

6. Misrepresent oneself or use deception to get a story (without having very powerful reasons to do so).

7. Plagiarize words or ideas (journalists can use the words with attribution).

8. Tap or tape telephone conversations without permission.

9. Use one's position for personal gain (for example, accept gifts from sources).

10. Do anything that may be construed as a "conflict of interest" (for example, write political speeches for the candidate being covered in an election). (pp. 106–107)

These may seem obvious, but each of the 10 rules deals with situations common to journalism. Let's look at them a little more closely.

1. Thou shalt not lie in print or on the air.
2. Thou shalt not lie to or threaten a source.

Rule 1 generally extends beyond simply lying—any clear attempt to mislead the audience is dealt with harshly in any self-respecting newsroom. This rule has been extended to computer alteration of photos, which has gotten *Time, Newsweek* and other news outlets into trouble. Likewise, lying to or threatening a source is seen as a distortion of the news process. In the past reporters boasted of their techniques at squeezing information from sources, but this often caused people to change or retract their stories later.

3. Thou shalt not report rumors or other unverified information.

Online journalists are particularly vulnerable to accusations of violating this rule. Due to the proliferation of gossip online, sometimes readers aren't sure where gossip ends and news begins, and occasionally reporters are tempted to blur the lines. Due to increased time pressure from the continual news cycle, increased competition from the hundreds of online news sites and perhaps lured by the ease of updating, some online outlets have published insufficiently verified stories. Most notably, on February 28, 1997, the *Dallas Morning News* Web site broke the story that Timothy McVeigh had confessed to his lawyers that he built and delivered the bomb that blew up the Oklahoma City Federal Building and killed 168 people. When this turned out to be based on flimsy evidence, it reinforced the perception that online media were not trustworthy, even when connected to a respected paper such as the *Morning News*. The perception is that online reporters are so desperate to get a scoop that they'll risk their professional credibility to do it. Yet while there are examples of this every year in traditional media as well, many online journalists point out that somehow examples of bad online journalism get a lot more publicity.

4. Thou shalt not suppress or omit opinion with which one disagrees.
5. Thou shalt not show favoritism or personal bias in one's reporting or writing.

Rules 4 and 5 are closely related, and they're also a source of trouble for online journalists. Anyone can create a Web page on behalf of any cause, and for the sake of democracy and ongoing public discourse, that's probably a good thing. However, this trait also creates the impression among much of the public that the Web is full of nothing but slanted news. Online reporters must be extra careful to include both sides of an issue fairly when writing straight news stories.

6. Thou shalt not misrepresent oneself or use deception to get a story (without having very powerful reasons to do so).

This rule is strongly related to Rule 2, and it indicates that things have changed since the 1920s. This rule often requires more explanation to students than any of the others, largely because of the proviso about "very powerful reasons." To be sure, this caveat dilutes the effectiveness of the point, but the rule remains a good one overall. Your sources are much less likely to complain about the content of your story if you've been honest with them from the beginning of the process. By "very powerful reasons," reporters generally mean a situation where the stakes are high—where lives, jobs, public health or similar important matters are at stake. The question reporters have to ask themselves is, "Does the weight of the story justify the deception?" Usually the answer should be "no." Ironically, in spite of the oft-cited anonymity of the Internet, you might have difficulty posing as someone else if you're an online reporter. If your e-mail address ends with "nytimes.com" or "chicagotribune.com," you'll have a hard time passing yourself off as anything but a journalist.

7. Thou shalt not plagiarize words or ideas.

This is the most ironclad rule in journalism. For reporters, being caught using someone else's words is cause for immediate firing. Very likely, you'll never work in the profession again. In a recent case, a longtime entertainment columnist for the *Indianapolis Star* was suspended when it was discovered that one of his articles bore a striking resemblance to an article on another paper's Web site. When his previous work was examined and a pattern of similar instances was found, he was fired immediately. Finding no work in journalism in spite of nearly 20 years of experience, he had to take a series of menial jobs to pay the bills. Paradoxically, the Internet both makes it easy for reporters to find other authors' material and also makes it easy for editors to catch plagiarists.

An addendum to this might be "Thou shalt not fabricate stories." This has unfortunately also become an issue because the Internet makes it easy to learn about faraway places and events without leaving your office. The notorious case of *New York Times* reporter Jayson Blair in 2003 underscores this problem. Under intense competitive pressure to crank out stories at the *Times,* Blair discovered he could fake in-person reporting by doing research on the Internet. He subsequently took this to absurd extremes, filing expense reports for trips he never took and making up details about stories out of thin air. When Blair was caught, it had a huge, wide-ranging impact on the profession of journalism. Blair's ethical violations cost him his job and made him unemployable for life in the journalism industry and resulted in the resignation of several top editors at the venerable *Times*. But beyond that, it's essentially turned Blair into the face of evil in the industry because of the harm he did to the reputation of journalism as a whole and the *Times* in particular.

8. Thou shalt not tap or tape telephone conversations without permission.

In this media-saturated age this rule might seem outdated, but it's generally the law. You can tape a phone conversation only when everyone involved in the conversation agrees to it on tape—this is not the law in every state, but it is considered common courtesy. Journalists generally ask permission as part of arranging the interview, or at the very least shortly before getting started. Once permission has been received, the general practice is to start the recording and reconfirm the permission, which then gives you proof of the interviewee's compliance. An

||||||| **FROM THE FIELD**

Scott Woelfel
Co-Founder, CNN Interactive
President and CEO, Armchair Media

When Scott Woelfel began to assemble the team that would make up CNN Interactive, he didn't worry about any differences between traditional journalistic standards and online standards. As a veteran CNN newsman, he simply adhered to the standards of the esteemed cable network.

"We followed the same rules as CNN does," says Woelfel. "We wouldn't just go off and, if we see something on a Web site, say, 'That must be OK, let's go ahead and print it.' That hasn't changed."

Woelfel spent 15 years with CNN, more than five of that online. "I was executive producer for CNN on the television side," he says, "and I started to do interactive projects on the side. It was mostly in the early days of CompuServe, early CD-ROMs, things like that. I just got more and more interested in it as time went on and decided I wanted to do it full-time."

Woelfel attributes CNN Interactive's unique character to its policy of hiring people from many different media. "When we first started," he says, "we intentionally tried to hire people from a broad range of backgrounds, knowing that together something new would emerge if all these people brought their skills and experience together. So we had people with television experience, broadcasting experience; we had newspaper, wire service, magazines, a little bit of everything. And I think that from that, you did see a new form of journalism start to evolve."

oft-overlooked facet of the Bill Clinton–Monica Lewinsky scandal was that Linda Tripp's tape recordings of her conversations with Lewinsky violated Maryland law.

9. Thou shalt not use one's position for personal gain.
10. Thou shalt not do anything that may be construed as a "conflict of interest."

These final two rules are often closely linked. Journalists sometimes find themselves being offered gifts or money by people who might eventually be the subjects of stories. There are endless accounts of everyone from public officials to corporate and sports figures trying to cozy up to a reporter, particularly at major news outlets. Reporters must resist this urge—some of them will accept nothing at all, whereas others draw the line at a cup of coffee. The point is to avoid being beholden to anyone but your news organization and your audience. Rule 10 basically requires that reporters not engage in any personal activities that could compromise the fairness of their coverage. The most famous case of this in recent years

According to Woelfel, a critical point in that evolution came with the release of the Starr Report online. "It was our single biggest day ever on the Web," he says. "For one thing, it was the first major story where if you weren't online, you felt like you were missing part of the story, because of the way the report was released online. For much of the first day, while reporters were still trying to digest it for turnaround for broadcast or for publication in print, you could go to it online and get to it directly yourself. That sort of primary source information works so well on the Web, and with a story that generated so much interest like this, that really clicked in people's heads. We had about 35 million pages served that day, and I think it was for a very good reason."

For Woelfel, the hybrid product that is online journalism seems to be erasing many traditional boundaries for journalists. "I think the idea of being a print reporter is starting to become obsolete. If you're a reporter for the *L.A. Times,* is your story going to end up online? Almost certainly. Are you going to do something differently, knowing it's going to be online? I think more and more people are thinking that. That may mean two versions, or it just may mean you look at the one version a little bit differently, and you're augmenting it in different ways."

Woelfel says this is starting to change reporters' approaches to the job. "These days you're seeing print reporters go out with a camera," he says, "to either get a photograph or get some video or record some audio of an interview subject, and that's happening more and more. The labels that we've given ourselves in the past were basically caused by the way our products were distributed. And now that the online area is breaking down some of those walls of distribution, I think we're starting to see some of the skills come together."

Of course, just because online journalism is having such a tremendous impact doesn't mean it's fully developed. "We still hear from our users when something doesn't work well," says Woelfel. "We still hear that it's a pain to do this certain thing, and what if we tried it this other way? That's still happening. It's still an evolving process five years later."

was when political commentator George Will helped prepare Ronald Reagan for his 1980 debate with Jimmy Carter, then analyzed Reagan's debate performance on national TV. Will later admitted the wrongdoing, was reprimanded and has since steered clear of such conflicts. However, these days this sort of thing is seen as a firing offense by many news organizations. Ultimately, this is one area where Casey's quote about the 1920s still rings true—to preserve their integrity, journalists must never sell themselves out.

By and large, the overwhelming majority of working journalists adhere to the "10 Commandments of News." Those who do not are subject to discipline within their news organizations and throughout the industry. The industry effectively polices itself—various trade publications regularly report on unethical behavior, making it hard to hide from ethical lapses. Perhaps the best-known example of this is *Columbia Journalism Review's* "Darts and Laurels" column, which both praises excellent reporting and condemns instances of poor judgment. Journalism may not have one set of written rules, but it does have its own etiquette, which must be understood by reporters.

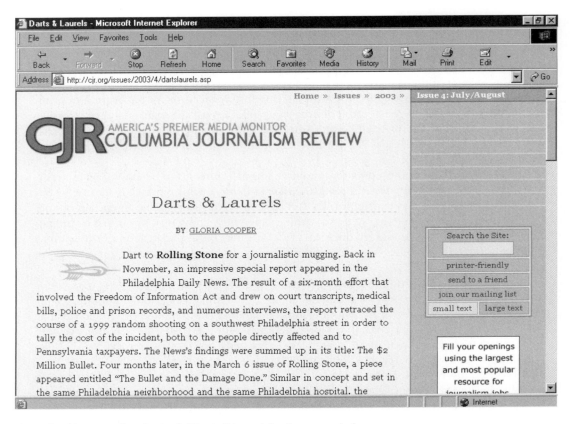

The Columbia Journalism Review's "Darts & Laurels" column regularly passes out praise to those who adhere to journalistic standards and scorn to those who do not.

SOURCE: cjr.org (accessed August 23, 2003). Used by permission.

ONLINE STANDARDS

In journalism there's etiquette. On the Internet there's **netiquette.** There are certain rules that all Web users—not just journalists—are generally expected to follow online.

While journalism has its "10 Commandments," in her 1994 book *Netiquette* (San Francisco: Albion Books), author Virginia Shea introduced 10 "Core Rules of Netiquette." Here they are:

1. Remember the human.

2. Adhere to the same standards of behavior online that you follow in real life.

3. Know where you are in cyberspace.

4. Respect other people's time and bandwidth.

5. Make yourself look good online.

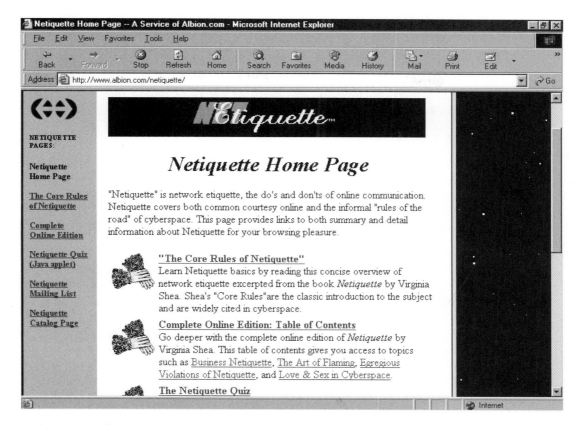

Author Virginia Shea's concept of "Netiquette" gained popularity and importance as the Internet became more and more of a mass medium.

SOURCE: albion.com (accessed September 25, 2003). Used by permission.

6. Share expert knowledge.

7. Help keep flame wars under control.

8. Respect other people's privacy.

9. Don't abuse your power.

10. Be forgiving of other people's mistakes. (pp. 32–45)

Not all of these rules immediately make sense to the inexperienced user, so let's examine them individually.

1. Remember the human.

Essentially, this means to remember that the Internet is not just made up of pages and messages but of the people behind them. It is easy to forget that all of this material isn't simply text and pictures—it's been put together by a human being. Too many Internet users seem to forget this judging by some of the blisteringly mean-spirited messages you'll sometimes see in discussion groups or in e-mail. A simple rule holds here—would you say this to a person's face? It's so easy to hide behind the anonymity afforded by the medium that sometimes we forget we're dealing with fellow human beings here. Just because people disagree with you does not automatically mean they're evil.

2. Adhere to the same standards of behavior online that you follow in real life.

This is closely related to Rule 1 but deals more with ethical and legal standards. Just because you're online doesn't suddenly make it legal or morally acceptable to send chain letters or to defraud, threaten or stalk people. Lots of Web users seem to believe that the anonymity of the Web somehow makes it OK to violate obscenity, privacy and copyright laws. No matter what you may have heard or read, breaking the law is bad netiquette. (Of course, this assumes that you follow such standards in everyday life, but that's beyond the scope of this discussion.)

3. Know where you are in cyberspace.

You should recognize that not all communication is the same online. You can say all sorts of things in a private e-mail message to a friend, but when you place inflammatory comments on a publicly available Web page, it can cause all sorts of problems. The situation gets stickier with online discussion groups because even though they're essentially a forum for expressing opinions, they're also a frequent breeding ground for rumors that are later treated as fact. The most important point here is to understand the environment in which you're operating—know its rules and customs before you start posting things.

4. Respect other people's time and bandwidth.

This has a lot of implications, but it mainly refers to the tendency of some users to send out huge amounts of e-mail messages to large lists of people. Too often once you get on someone's mailing list, you'll receive a daily stream of the latest tired jokes, sob stories and mundane chatter. The result is that the term "mailing list" has become a dirty word to many users. The point here is that messages carry a lot more weight if they're only sent when you have something to say, and if they're only sent to people to whom they're relevant. Cluttering up other users' mailboxes with unwanted messages only serves to lessen the importance of your e-mails and generally results in an instant delete.

5. Make yourself look good online.

No, this has nothing to do with your physical appearance. People come across better online if they appear literate and well informed. This is why all Web users, journalists or not, should learn to write well. If you spell poorly, use bad grammar or swear excessively, you'll look ignorant regardless of your true intelligence. Likewise, if you pop off about a subject you don't know much about, you'll look like a fool. Making yourself look good also extends beyond putting together sentences. If you engage in chat or post to discussion groups, you've undoubtedly noticed that certain users seem to revel in making outrageous statements simply to invite negative responses (known as "flames"). This wastes time and bandwidth that could be used to promote serious discussion.

6. Share expert knowledge.

Shared knowledge is at the heart of the Internet culture and has been for years. It's seen as a democratizing factor—anyone who can get online can learn about nearly anything without taking a training course or spending hours in a library. If you know a lot about a particular topic, chances are there's someone out there who could use your help. One warning, however—you should not claim great knowledge where it doesn't exist. Deliberately misleading people about your expertise also constitutes a violation of netiquette. After all, how would you feel if you based a term paper on erroneous information from someone else's site? (Of course, you should engage in a little fact checking beforehand, but that's another issue.)

7. Help keep flame wars under control.

Flame wars—the seemingly endless heated exchanges between people who disagree in chat sessions, forums, discussion groups and other areas of online discourse—are simply a waste of time and bandwidth. Online veterans recognize that a certain amount of flaming will take place but will frequently step in when things get out of hand. While discussion groups don't occupy as much of the online landscape as they did a few years ago, they continue to thrive.

8. Respect other people's privacy.

How would you like it if someone read your e-mail? Probably not very much, which is why you should extend some respect toward other people's private messages and files. We're always hearing about security breaches on the Internet, yet the majority of hackers who go after large businesses and government entities simply crack the codes to prove they can do it, not to browse through individuals' inboxes. On a more basic level, just because someone gets up and leaves a lab computer without logging off doesn't give you the right to sit down and browse through his e-mail. It's rude and disrespectful.

9. Don't abuse your power.

This can be interpreted in several different ways. First, the medium of the Internet gives you the power to create a Web page that can be seen anywhere in the world. Whether you realize it or not, this is an amazingly powerful thing to do. Your page can be read by literally millions, yet many people post all manner of garbage on their Web sites, oblivious to what impact it might have. Another interpretation is that since some users are more experienced and may know the ins and outs of the Web better than others, those users have a certain power. Taking advantage of others' inexperience—through sending them anonymous e-mails or viruses, toying with their machines while they're gone, or any number of other things—is considered a breach of netiquette. It's simply not a nice thing to do.

10. Be forgiving of other people's mistakes.

This last rule is related to Rule 9. One of the most common practices of Internet veterans is complaining about "newbies"—people new to the Internet or to a given site who are just beginning to figure out how everything works. One of the things that scares people away from interacting on the Web is the fear of being humiliated when something goes wrong. This remains a common problem, unfortunately. It may seem to you like everyone's on the Web these days, but there are still plenty of people who are just now taking the plunge. If you spot an egregious mistake on the Web and decide to tell someone about it, you shouldn't send a fire-breathing e-mail with the subject line "YOU SUCK!" or post something about it on a public page. This still happens, largely because a lot of Web users are very young and tend to show their immaturity in this way, but it's fundamentally counterproductive and mean. Try to be polite and informative when you find a mistake, and keep your response private. After all, even experienced Web users were newbies at one time.

While Virginia Shea's book was written in the mid-90s, these principles are still adhered to by most veteran users of the Internet. At the heart of all of these rules is one simple principle—be a decent human being.

COMMON GROUND

On the surface, comparing journalistic standards and online standards may seem like apples and oranges. One involves professional writing and the other deals with the less formal process of sharing information online. Yet for online journalists it's just as important to understand the accepted practices of the medium (the Internet) as those of their craft (journalism).

Understanding Web culture is important in part because it can affect the way readers think of the online news product. There is a lot of information on the Web—on personal and group home pages, in discussion groups and chat and so forth—that has little or no credibility. All sorts of rumors and "urban legends" get passed off as news online, and they proliferate without any sort of substantiation, fueled by discussion groups, chat and e-mail. Unfortunately, people often superimpose these dubious ethical standards onto legitimate Web news sites.

In spite of this, when you apply netiquette to journalism, many aspects of it are quite appropriate. Some elements are more obvious than others—for example, the act of publishing a news product is essentially an act of sharing expert knowledge. You've gone out and learned about the subject, and now you're sharing it with readers. Similarly, by getting permission before taping phone calls, you're respecting others' privacy.

However, there's even more overlap than at first glance. A number of journalistic principles fall under the heading of adhering to the same standards as you do in real life. Blatantly lying in your coverage, misrepresenting yourself, and several other "commandments" apply here. A less obvious example of this ties in to plagiarism and proper citation and attribution. In Web news, it's very common to refer to information from other sites and to link to them. Just like in college term papers, reporters need to be sure to attribute these references properly. While blatant copying of other people's work appears regularly on the Web, to run a professional site, you need to stay clean. If someone else has a good idea that you want to use, just cite it! Give credit where it's due.

A more legalistic interpretation of adhering to high standards involves copyrights. This is always a hot issue online, and if reporters have any doubt at all about

---

THE JATO ROCKET: A WEB LEGEND

A major part of Internet lore—one that dates to long before there was a World Wide Web—are the tall tales that users have passed around to amuse each other. Sometimes they've been represented as real events, and sometimes they're correctly identified as just stories. These tales often have some sort of odd, horror-movie quality to them, involving things like gang members harvesting body parts or killers hiding in back seats of cars.

The worst of these often end up in a seemingly endless loop of chain letters. The best, however, still attract a certain reverence because they're entertaining stories. Probably the most famous of these involves an intrepid driver who got a bit carried away with trying to make his car go fast. The story is reprinted here in its most well-worn Internet version. Please note that this story, while entertaining, is completely fictional.

> The Arizona Highway Patrol came upon a pile of smoldering metal embedded into the side of a cliff rising above the road at the apex of a curve. The wreckage resembled the site of an airplane crash, but it was a car. The type of car was unidentifiable at the scene. The lab finally figured out what it was and what had happened.
>
> It seems that a guy had somehow gotten hold of a JATO (Jet Assisted Take Off—actually a solid fuel rocket) unit that is used to give heavy military transport planes an extra "push" for taking off from short airfields. He had driven his Chevy Impala out into the desert and found a long, straight stretch of road. Then he attached the JATO unit to his car, jumped in, got up some speed and fired off the JATO!
>
> The facts as best as could be determined are that the operator of the 1967 Impala hit the ignition at a distance of approximately 3 miles from the crash site. This was established by the prominent scorched and melted asphalt at that location. The JATO, if operating properly, would have reached maximum thrust within 5 seconds, causing the Chevy to reach speeds well in excess of 350 mph and continuing at full power for an additional 20 to 25 seconds.
>
> The driver (soon to be pilot) most likely would have experienced G-forces usually reserved for dog-fighting F-18 jocks under full afterburners, basically causing him to become insignificant for the remainder of the event. However, the automobile remained on the straight highway for about 2.3 miles (15 to 20 seconds) before the driver applied and completely melted the brakes, blowing the tires and leaving thick rubber marks on the road surface, then becoming airborne for an additional 1.4 miles and impacting the cliff face at a height of 125 feet, leaving a blackened crater 3 feet deep in the rock.
>
> Most of the driver's remains were not recoverable; however, small fragments of bone, teeth, and hair were extracted from the crater and fingernail and bone shards were removed from the steering wheel.

the right to use something online, they need to ask permission, just as they would in the print world. One common problem with online outlets is the use of wire service material. While most newsrooms have agreements in place with wire services, many online outlets do not yet assume they can use wire material freely. In fact, this is generally not true (see Chapter 15).

Reporting rumors, threatening sources or otherwise breaking commandments violates the tenet to remember the human behind the story. An extension of this might be to remember where you are online—if you publish rumors about someone in a news story, it's very different from talking about them in a discussion group. While journalists should never be in the habit of speaking publicly about unsubstantiated rumors, they should at least recognize the difference between public and private forums.

Another rule of netiquette that all journalists (online or off) should follow is not to abuse power. This aligns closely with several of the commandments of news. Suppressing information, showing favoritism in reporting or using your position for personal gain are all abuses of power. These actions are less obviously destructive than e-mailing someone a virus, but they are nonetheless examples of journalists trying to exert undue influence on the public. Taking a position on an issue is perfectly acceptable on a personal Web page, but when delivering straight news coverage, the rules are different.

One last rule of netiquette relates to journalistic credibility. As companies, organizations and people on the Web get to know HTML and its related languages better, Web pages as a whole tend to look more and more professional. This keeps raising the standards higher and higher for what is acceptable. Web news audiences are sophisticated these days, and they're rightly suspicious of unprofessional-looking sites, even if they have reliable content. It is expected that a respectable news outlet will be cleanly formatted, easy to navigate and contain quick links to the major stories of the day. Those stories are expected to have photos and to provide links to any related stories. If your news site doesn't live up to these online standards, you'll hear about it.

For online journalists, the consequences of not following both journalistic standards and online standards can be disastrous. In many ways, they have a tougher task than print journalists. In addition to following traditional journalism standards to the letter, they now have a whole new series of rules to learn and abide by. A helpful thing for online journalists to remember is that at the heart of netiquette lies a simple principle—be a decent human being and treat others as you'd like to be treated. While the hard-nosed standards of journalism initially sound like an odd fit with such a sunny philosophy, in fact they work splendidly together.

SUMMARY

Is it possible that two media with such lurid reputations as journalism and the Internet could reach a harmonic convergence of high standards with online news? It is, but it takes some understanding of the core doctrines of each medium. Journalism's strengths are a series of straightforward, no-nonsense rules based on truth, fairness and disclosure. The Internet's overall philosophies tend toward the reinforcement of the notion that we're not all robots, and that the medium should operate as an arena of mutual respect, shared knowledge and understanding. Online reporters need to be aware of the philosophies, strengths and customs of both media to use it to its fullest.

RELATED WEB SITES

Netiquette home page
http://www.albion.com/netiquette/

Columbia Journalism Review
http://www.cjr.org/

CNN Interactive
http://www.cnn.com

CNN Interactive's special page on the Starr Report
http://www.cnn.com/SPECIALS/multimedia/timeline/9809/starr.report/frameset.html

USC Annenberg Online Journalism Review
http://www.ojr.org

EXERCISES

1. Compare what Bob Casey said at the beginning of the chapter on the topic of journalism ethics in the 1920s with the 10 Commandments of News. Discuss the ways in which the system Casey describes violates the 10 Commandments. Then address this question: How would you defend the system Casey depicts? Does it have any redeeming qualities? Or is it indefensible?

2. Visit a chat room, discussion group or other forum on the Web (choose your own subject matter). Don't participate—just examine the discussions. Look at 10 to 20 responses on a particular topic. Then write a one to one and a half page summary of the degree to which various users adhere to or violate the 10 Core Rules of Netiquette. Is there respect shown here, or is there constant flaming of fellow participants?

3. A political candidate's Web site is touting the results of a public opinion poll that seems to you to have skewed results. Nonetheless, it's getting a lot of attention in the news. You decide to try to get a look at the poll's questions to see if they're slanted to produce a certain result. You've heard that other reporters' requests for these questions were turned down, so you e-mail the site's manager from your private account and ask for the poll questions, posing as an interested citizen. You don't say you're a reporter, but you also don't say you're *not* a reporter. The manager sends you all the poll information, and you discover that, as you suspected, the poll was full of one-sided questions. You publish a story about it. Does this violate Rule 6 of the 10 Commandments of News? Why or why not? In your opinion, is this acceptable behavior? Explain your position.

 4. Using InfoTrac College Edition, find an example of a case where a reporter has been disciplined or fired for improperly using information from the Internet. You can look for material on the examples mentioned in this chapter or find your own up-to-date examples. Write a one and one half to two page report detailing what the reporter did wrong, how it violates specific rules discussed in this chapter, and why you believe the punishment received by the reporter was appropriate or inappropriate.

15

||||||

Legal Issues
Online and Offline

Just because journalism revolves around a set of unwritten rules doesn't mean there aren't written laws that govern different aspects of the job. As the only type of private business afforded constitutional protection, legal issues are a central concern to all journalists. By entering the online world, however, journalists open themselves up to a whole new realm of legal questions. This chapter looks at such traditional issues as libel and invasion of privacy and explains how they apply to various aspects of online news. The cloudy areas of Internet regulations and laws, public figures versus private citizens, copyright laws and recent legislation dealing with online content are also addressed.

Let's get one thing straight right from the beginning: Online publishing isn't e-mail. Please do not confuse one with the other. One is public, and one is private. One operates under the standards of journalism, and the other doesn't. Perhaps most important, online publishing has all sorts of legal implications that e-mail does not.

Maybe this is an exercise in stating the obvious, but for those who have grown up with the Web, there's a tendency to forget that placing something online does constitute publishing. The line between making snide comments in a discussion group and putting the same comments in Web publications is frequently blurred. It's so easy to post Web pages containing any silly thing that we sometimes treat online publishing lightly. In fact, in many ways online publishing is a much more powerful act than traditional publishing, and one that leaves you open to all sorts of potential legal problems if you don't take it seriously. This chapter briefly examines some of the traditional legal concerns of journalists and how they apply to online publishing. It also looks at some laws specific to the Internet that might have an impact on online news. Please note that scores of books have been published about the legal aspects of journalism—you should consult them to get further details about these subjects.

TRADITIONAL PROTECTIONS AND LAWS

It's true that the First Amendment guarantees freedom of the press in the United States, but it's also true that this freedom has never been absolute. All sorts of laws exist across this country that address the ways news media go about their business. In our haste to understand laws and protections pertaining to online publishing, don't forget that traditional laws often apply to the online world too.

All reporters and most journalism students are familiar with the concept of **libel**—it's usually defined as a published (or broadcast) false and defamatory statement that damages the reputation of an individual. The fact that it's published or otherwise disseminated by the media distinguishes it from slander, which usually involves speaking rather than publishing. The key word within this definition is *false*—most libel cases involving private citizens hinge not on whether a statement is defamatory but on whether or not it's true. This is why reporters who publish articles that cast someone in a negative light need to be particularly careful to back up their statements and attribute any interview material carefully.

Two aspects of libel law need to be immediately noted. The first is that, unlike First Amendment rights, libel laws are not federal statutes—every state has its own unique set of libel laws. Though they tend to be similar in character, they're not identical. Your news organization should be familiar with the particular quirks within your state. Second, the inclusion of the phrase "private citizen" highlights the most important distinction in libel law. Most state libel laws distinguish between public and private records—public records can generally be published—and between public figures and private citizens. They generally allow for "fair comment and criticism" of public officials and other public figures.

The Supreme Court's biggest contribution to libel law came from its decision in *New York Times v. Sullivan* (1964). This decision mandated that to claim libel, public figures had to prove that the news organization demonstrated actual malice toward them, published knowing falsehoods, or showed reckless disregard for the truth. The notion behind it was that public officials and public figures are simply the subject of much more comment and criticism than private citizens, and thus that the media (and the public) should be given more latitude in discussion of their actions. Because of this, public figures have a tough time suing journalists and news organizations for libel. Without internal memos, e-mails or other documents proving malice or other punishable offenses, they generally don't have a case. This protects journalists from frivolous lawsuits by grandstanding public figures.

STATES WITH SHIELD LAWS AS OF 2000			
Alabama	Florida	Minnesota	North Dakota
Alaska	Georgia	Montana	Ohio
Arizona	Illinois	Nebraska	Oklahoma
Arkansas	Indiana	Nevada	Oregon
California	Kentucky	New Jersey	Pennsylvania
Colorado	Louisiana	New Mexico	Rhode Island
Delaware	Maryland	New York	South Carolina
District of Columbia	Michigan	North Carolina	Tennessee

SOURCE: Student Press Law Center (http://www.splc.org/legalresearch.asp?id=31).

Another way that journalists are legally protected is through **shield laws.** These laws protect journalists from having to divulge their sources. As mentioned earlier in this book, source confidentiality is often vital to the professional survival of journalists. If sources confide in you off the record and you subsequently give up their names, you'll likely see your pool of sources dry up quickly. Shield laws protect journalists from being forced to name sources or turn over notes. Like libel laws, these are state statutes, but while every state has libel laws, as of 1999 only 30 states and the District of Columbia had shield laws. All reporters should know if their state has shield laws and should be familiar with their stipulations.

The other side of the coin for journalists is invasion of privacy. Generally, laws state that privacy is invaded when one intentionally intrudes, physically or otherwise, upon a person's solitude or into his private area or affairs. Sometimes this gets called into question in cases of trespassing, publication of private facts, creating unwanted offensive publicity or portraying someone in a false light. Again, this is a case where state laws predominate. Nearly every state has laws recognizing the right of privacy—most try to strike a balance between people's right to privacy and the public interest in freedom of the press. Unfortunately, this can cause conflicts, which is why reporters need to know their state's privacy laws. A good rule of thumb is simply to consider whether reporting the information is fair—are you taking advantage of someone or not? Are you using information that really should remain private? And what are the costs and benefits to publishing the information? Usually the answers to these questions will steer you in the right direction.

Another legal issue that traditionally crops up in journalism is **prior restraint**—the act of a person or organization stepping in to prevent publication before it happens. Usually this is in a case where the person or company will look bad in an article, and often the individual or the corporation will file suit claiming invasion of privacy, illegal acquisition of information or the possible publication of classified or otherwise protected material. The Supreme Court has solidly stood with journalists against attempts to censor the media in this way, with the exception of one order barring publication of the movement of troop ships during wartime. This doesn't mean that people, agencies and companies won't try to do it, but if your organization is armed with the facts and prepared responses, it's more likely to be able to ward off time-consuming lawsuits.

While these are some of the traditional legal concerns of journalists, the technological environment of the past few years has opened up a Pandora's box of new issues and forced the rethinking of some long-standing issues.

INTERNET-RELATED LEGAL ISSUES

The Internet has operated for more than 30 years, yet the legal status of much Internet communication is still largely unclear for three main reasons. The first is that it's a truly international network, with no central headquarters in one nation and no organizing authority. Second, it has radically changed the nature of intellectual property. Third, the explosion of the Web in the last few years has brought an exponential growth of commerce to the Web, with all its accompanying legal issues. Each of these has implications for journalists.

A large part of Internet mythology is based on its lack of central authority. Because it doesn't reside in one single country, the notion is that it stands apart from most governmental regulation. While this is debatable (as will be discussed later), for journalists this borderless realm is both a blessing and a curse. The freedom of information embodied within a structure like this seems absolute, allowing exchange of all kinds of material instantly across international borders. If information is your business, as with journalists, this is pretty close to heaven. However, for U.S. journalists, it also creates lots of potential problems. All of the legal protections discussed previously are U.S. protections—they don't necessarily apply anywhere else. When you're writing for the Internet and your stories can be read anywhere in the world, this creates all sorts of potential problems, particularly if you're covering international issues or reporting from a foreign country.

For example, if you're in Libya as a foreign correspondent for a U.S. news organization, you might submit a story describing Libyan leader Col. Moammar Gadhafi as "nutty." In the United States we can call our leaders far worse names than this without worrying about libel or other repercussions. However, if your report is published on the Internet while you're in Libya and Gadhafi sees it and disapproves, U.S. rules will not likely apply. It might be a U.S. publication, but on the Web English-speaking people in Libya can read it, and it thus becomes a very hazy legal issue. Beyond that, if you're tossed into a Libyan jail, it might take means beyond legal wrangling to free you. This is a somewhat extreme example, but it illustrates the difficulties journalists can face.

Even in the United States, with different libel laws in every state this can be a sticky issue. A story that might be considered libelous under the strictures of Indiana law might not be in California. As of this writing, the language in many states' libel laws is fairly specific and rarely relates directly to online material. This leaves it wide open to interpretation, which offers little comfort to journalists. In addition, a feature unique to online journalism—the ability to quickly publish corrections and retractions—raises a whole host of new issues related to libel.

Printing a retraction is often a key element in libel cases—in some states an organization can't be sued for libel unless it refuses to print a retraction. In others, this isn't the case. State laws, however, don't yet distinguish between a piece of information that is published online and remains there for months versus something quickly corrected or inadvertently posted and quickly removed. (This is at the heart of the *Blumenthal v. Drudge* case, which is discussed later in the chapter.)

A long-standing issue in publishing of any kind is obscenity. In the United States there are several legal precedents dealing with this issue. In *Roth v. United States* (1957) the Supreme Court ruled that obscenity was not protected by the Constitution, and subsequent rulings helped establish parameters for obscenity. Most notably, in *Miller v. California* (1973) the Court made it into a local issue by ruling that material should be judged according to the standards that prevail in a given community. While this is most commonly associated with pornography, it has implications for online journalism as well. For example, the Starr Report on the Clinton–Lewinsky scandal contained sexual details that many communities might find obscene, yet it was published online by many news organizations. Did this leave them open to lawsuits? It's hard to say. Other possibilities exist with different types of story content, and certain news photographs might be deemed obscene in certain communities because of depictions of death, carnage, nudity or other situations. In addition, none of this deals with different standards in other nations.

A related issue is the use of software filters. Due to the pornography available online, many software manufacturers have created filters that purport to block out such material while allowing access to all other items online. However, none of these filters is perfect, and many have been shown to block out all kinds of useful information. In fact, many people believe this technology could be used for purposes beyond protecting minors. Several commentators have noted that software companies and other organizations can easily design filters to block access to competitors' sites or other locations they deem undesirable. As an example, a report in April 2000 indicated that America Online's youth filters allowed access to conservative sites (the Republican National Committee, the Libertarian Party, the National Rifle Association) but blocked access to liberal ones (the Democratic National Committee, the Green Party, the Coalition to Stop Gun Violence). Journalists see this as censorship and have waged numerous fights against it.

The issues of intellectual property and copyrights are hugely important online. They have grabbed headlines due to actions by software and music corporations to protect their property against piracy. These issues are also tremendously important to journalists because they deal with access to information, whether it be material for news stories or the stories themselves.

Copyrights are a major issue for journalists of all kinds, and they're particularly important on the Web. Like every other kind of information, news articles can be circulated quickly and easily on the Web. For journalists, this cuts two ways. Reporters and news organizations could lose out on their rights because their articles could be copied and illegally distributed all over the world with no compensation whatsoever. Obviously, this can be prosecuted, but with all the traffic on the Internet, it's very hard to trace. As such, cases of news organizations suing over

---

NETSURFER'S SIMPLE GUIDE TO COPYRIGHTS

Since copyright law is such a major issue online, users are justifiably concerned with understanding how it works. Many sites have posted a brief synopsis that boils down U.S. copyright law into five simple rules. It's hard to give credit for this list—it's generally credited to nothing more specific than "a lobbying group in Washington." Regardless of its origins, however, it's a handy tool to have at your disposal.

- If you didn't create a written work, art, photograph, or music, or obtain distribution rights to it, you don't own it.

- If you don't own it, you can't copy or distribute it.
- The author or owner must explicitly relinquish rights for a work to be placed in the public domain.
- Fair use allows copying of small portions of a work without the owner's permission, but only for criticism, education, and news reporting.
- When in doubt, ask for permission to use a work.

---

copyright violations are rare. Plus, many news sites keep free archives of old articles, preferring to make them available for the public to read, though unauthorized copying remains illegal. The positive side of the unfettered flow of information on the Web is that, when used legally, it creates a market for past news articles, which might otherwise have been largely forgotten. With user-friendly searchable archives, it becomes easy for users to find and gain access to articles in an organization's back catalog. This can prove lucrative, as many news organizations charge fees for the privilege of viewing archived articles.

Less obvious is the effect copyright laws might have on reporters' gathering of information. Journalists and others have long had access to all kinds of material through **fair use** provisions of the federal Copyright Act. When a work is being used for journalistic purposes—or for activities such as research, teaching or criticism—the use is not legally considered to be an infringement because of its noncommercial or incidental character. The intent is generally to provide information to the public and to promote discussion, as when books or movies are reviewed or works of literature are discussed in classes. However, some recent proposals aimed at curbing online piracy would also restrict fair use. While these proposals would not necessarily prevent journalists and others from gaining access to such material, it would make them pay for the privilege, which goes against the notion of the free flow of information. Again, journalists and others have protested against this type of legislation.

Another troublesome area for journalists stems from the anonymity that many Web users regard so highly. When a reporter contacts a source via e-mail or looks at his Web page, the assumption is that the person is who he says he is. But with minimal technical skill and the right software, anyone can fake an identity in an e-mail message. Indeed, many e-mail-based computer viruses of the past few years have circulated rapidly because they bore the name of a friend as the sender. Similarly, just because a name is on a Web page doesn't mean the named individual really created it.

||||||| FROM THE FIELD

Denise Caruso
Internet Commentator/Analyst
Former Technology Columnist, *New York Times*

The laws and legal issues surrounding the Internet are numerous and perplexing. Denise Caruso has done her best to try to clarify them for the public because she believes they're vitally important and rarely known or understood.

"If the Web and the Internet and computer communication is going to become as integral to our lives as we say," Caruso states, "we need to know what these laws are."

In her years as technology columnist for the *New York Times,* Caruso wrote about these issues in an effort to raise awareness among the *Times'* huge audience. "There are a lot of really important, interesting problems that are being looked at now," she says, "that will absolutely dictate the level of discourse, the level of free speech, and the quality of journalism in the next 20 years."

Chief among these, in Caruso's opinion, is the nature of software code. "How software code is written is law," she says, "and it dictates how we behave online. If we aren't paying attention to how the software is made, our behavior is being changed without our permission."

She cites an example of how, in the past, users of online services banded together to force changes in policies. However, a simple change in rules can forbid such online democracy. "On America Online," Caruso notes, "they don't have a main bulletin board where all users can post, and the limit to how many people can gather in a chat room is 23. That means there is

While this is fraud and can generally be prosecuted, it nonetheless creates some uneasy scenarios for journalists. If you base a news report on information from someone who turns out not to be who he claimed, it could make your organization liable for damages against the impersonated person or other affected individuals. Even if the information is true, misidentifying or misrepresenting the source casts all your information in a questionable light, which can damage your organization's reputation. If a reporter engages in a little fact checking, this shouldn't happen, but it remains a grim possibility nonetheless.

Beyond these issues are security questions that affect all users. While many people believe that the Internet is beyond regulation, there are ways in which the software and protocols that make the network run could infringe on the security of users, in effect regulating the Web. Harvard professor Lawrence Lessig made this argument in *Code and Other Laws of Hyperspace* (New York: Basic Books), which had the online community abuzz upon its release in late 1999. Lessig, who later served as a Special Master in the *Department of Justice v. Microsoft* trial, maintained that changes to the network to facilitate online commerce and government tracking of crime could actually threaten the core American values of privacy and freedom of information.

no way on AOL to instigate a mass uprising of the 5 million people who are on that service. They're all on AOL, but they have no way to all be in the same place at the same time. That is a perfect example of how software code dictates how we assemble online, the things we can do online, how we can communicate online."

Another legal issue that concerns Caruso is fair use—the provision of the Copyright Act that allows journalists, educators and others to use copyrighted works for noncommercial purposes. This has been threatened by recent Internet legislation. "It could completely stop the flow of information," she says. "The Internet is the opposite of that. It has always been about facilitating open, free discourse."

In spite of these concerns, Caruso remains optimistic about communication in the 21st century. "The really cool thing about technology is that it's very decentralized power," she says. "The means of production are in the hands of the people, in terms of media. The more corporate media that there is, the more independent people there are going to be, with their little digital video cameras. They're gonna be uploading stuff from their laptops, moving around from cell to cell, and they're gonna be impossible to catch. There's going to be a real underground media that's going to be very exciting, and that's probably going to be really healthy for this culture."

Caruso sees this as a potentially great thing for democracy and discourse, but only to the degree that people are determined to make it so. "Where it all ends up is so dependent on how we move from where we are now to where we're going next," says Caruso. "It depends on how much attention we pay to credibility, to context. It depends on how much attention we pay to making sure that people who need to get the tools in their hands can get them. We need to look at the Web as a means of providing democratic discourse, and not just paying lip service to it, but making sure that happens and engineering that in a way so that it happens."

Lessig uses examples to illustrate how freedoms could be eroded. He discusses how a "worm"—a piece of computer code that works its way through networked machines—could on one hand be used by intelligence agencies to sniff out breaches in national security, but on the other hand it could also snoop on individual users to create profiles of individuals' online behavior. He examines how the use of encryption technology, of the kind used to create secure credit card transactions online, could actually allow tracking of individuals in the process of authentication of those transactions. Gradually, Lessig argues, this could result in a loss of online anonymity in favor of an "architecture of identification." Ironically, he maintains, most of this would happen as users voluntarily submitted information in the process of making purchases and conducting assorted business online. This gradual disclosure of all manner of information could have all sorts of nightmarish consequences.

How might this affect journalists? Aside from turning much of the information that is their lifeblood into a heavily guarded, top-secret commodity, it could also hamper their ability to do different types of research anonymously. When learning about different institutions or agencies, journalists often must work behind the scenes to get at the truth, studying all sorts of documents and records.

This might compromise that ability, and it could get them into legal trouble depending on the nature of the information they're seeking or the subjects they're covering (see the Larry Matthews case described later in the chapter). Rather than acting as a fly on the wall, journalists might well be relegated to taking whatever sugarcoated information institutions gave them. In addition, it might compromise their ability to use unnamed sources—if everyone can be tracked, sources might not want to run the risk of being identified, thus eliminating reporters' ability to get at information only known by people who work within large companies or government agencies.

These are some, but by no means all, of the legal issues that face online journalists. Of course, new legislation is constantly being introduced that might change the equation even more. The final section of the chapter examines some recent court rulings and legislation that have influenced the legal status of online journalism.

LEGISLATION AND COURT CASES

The Internet has operated for more than 30 years, yet the legal status of much Internet communication is only now being debated and addressed legally. The explosion of the Web has brought all kinds of unforeseen issues to light in the courts and Congress—and, critics argue, much resulting legislation has quietly eroded important freedoms. Let's take a look at a few of the laws, rulings and other actions that have an impact on online journalists.

Freedom of Speech and Libel

Cubby v. CompuServe (1991)

CompuServe, which was one of the earliest and largest providers of online services, carried a daily journalism forum called "Rumorville USA." Within this forum appeared an electronic gossip magazine called "Skuttlebut," which posted a comment about Cubby, Inc., a company that was then developing a journalism news database of its own. Cubby saw the comment as defamatory and sued CompuServe, alleging that the article libeled Cubby and its owner. United States District Judge Peter K. Leisure dismissed the suit, ruling that even if the Skuttlebut article defamed Cubby, CompuServe could not be held responsible. Leisure saw CompuServe as a distributor of information, an "electronic, for-profit library," that had no reasonable duty or opportunity to review the content of its holdings before they were published.

This is generally recognized as the first major case on Internet libel. It was crucial to the future of online speech and online media because it established online services as carriers rather than originators of information. This relieved them of the near-impossible task of monitoring all posts.

Stratton Oakmont v. Prodigy *(1995)*

Prodigy, another early online service provider, carried a financial forum called "Money Talk." An anonymous Prodigy user posted negative statements about Stratton Oakmont, an investment securities firm, and its president, Daniel Porush. Porush sued Prodigy, claiming the service was responsible for the poster's claims. Prodigy defended itself as a distributor of information, using the precedent of *Cubby v. CompuServe,* but Stratton Oakmont argued that Prodigy should be more correctly classified as a publisher because, unlike CompuServe, it maintained editorial control over its content. New York Supreme Court Justice Stuart L. Ain ruled that Prodigy was different from CompuServe in that Prodigy made clear to all users that it retained the right to edit, remove and filter all messages on its site to ensure a "family" atmosphere online. Because Prodigy had editorial control over the messages in the Money Talk forum, Ain concluded it was a publisher and not merely a distributor. Thus Ain ruled that Prodigy was liable for the content of those messages and awarded damages to Stratton Oakmont.

This case established boundaries for online services in allowing for free use of bulletin boards and other forums. Some argued that while this case might have appeared to be a blow against free speech online, in fact it ensured unfettered free speech by discouraging online services from exercising any kind of controls on the speech of their users.

ISPs and Editorial Content

Zeran v. America Online *(1996)*

In this case, an individual user, Kenneth Zeran, sued the America Online service provider over a fraud perpetrated by another user. This anonymous user somehow obtained Zeran's home address and phone number and posted them in advertisements throughout AOL selling T-shirts and other souvenirs hailing the 1995 Oklahoma City bombing. Zeran received death threats and relentless harassment due to these ads and sued AOL for negligence in allowing them to be posted. AOL claimed immunity as a distributor of information rather than a publisher. U.S. District Judge T. S. Ellis III ruled in favor of AOL, maintaining that Internet service providers may not be held liable for defamatory statements posted on their ISPs by third parties. This decision was upheld on appeal one year later.

This decision refined some of the earlier rulings and is now regularly cited as the precedent for cases involving Internet service providers and traditional editorial functions, such as deciding whether to publish, withdraw, postpone or alter content.

Blumenthal v. Drudge and America Online, Inc. *(1998)*

On September 11, 1997, Internet columnist Matt Drudge published a story quoting an unnamed source as saying that White House aide Sidney

Blumenthal had a history of spousal abuse that had been effectively covered up. One day later, Drudge retracted the allegation and pulled the item from his Web site. However, Blumenthal and his wife sued Drudge and AOL, which carried his columns, for defamation, seeking $30 million in damages. While AOL was dismissed as a defendant in April 1998, as of this writing the case against Drudge remains unresolved.

This case addresses several issues vital to online journalists. First, by dismissing AOL from the suit, the court ruled that service providers are not responsible for damages from articles written by content providers. Second, it raises questions regarding the degree to which First Amendment protections extend to "citizen journalists" online, who sell their articles to service providers. This could also extend to writers for any other online outlet, from small operations all the way up to CNN or MSNBC. There is a lot that remains unclear here—how the law might affect freelancers versus full-time employees, for example—and many of these issues may not be addressed when a decision is handed down in this case.

Privacy and the First Amendment

United States v. Matthews *(1998–99)*

Reporter Larry Matthews of National Public Radio said that in September 1996 he was researching a freelance article about child pornography on the Internet. In the process of doing research, he sent and received images of kiddie porn. One of these images was sent to an undercover FBI officer. Matthews was arrested on two counts of trafficking in child pornography. Matthews argued that he had done a similar story a year earlier and was simply updating the story. He said that he had talked with editors about selling the story, and he pointed out that while he had no written contract this isn't unusual for a freelancer. However, he also had no notes, story drafts or evidence of interviews, which left him legally vulnerable. Federal District Judge Alexander Williams Jr. refused to let Matthews use the First Amendment as a defense, and though he acknowledged that Matthews was a respected veteran journalist with no history of sexual issues, Williams sentenced Matthews to 18 months in federal prison and fined him $4,000. Matthews appealed the ruling, but lost his appeal in April 2000 and began serving his sentence in November 2000.

The implications of this ruling are widespread—reporters go undercover to find out information regularly, and the Web has proven tremendously valuable in that regard. This ruling could imperil that freedom, though Matthews did leave himself unprotected by not documenting his research or getting anything in writing from editors. A lesson for future journalists might be to thoroughly substantiate any assignments or projects that might involve legal risk.

Ford Motor Co. v. Lane *(1999)*

Nursing student Robert Lane ran a Web site devoted to news about the Ford Motor Co., its products and employees. When Ford employees provided him with internal memos, agendas, engineering blueprints and photographs in October 1998, he posted them on the site. When Ford threatened legal action, Lane posted 40 more documents. In August 1999, Ford filed suit against Lane and was granted a temporary restraining order, which said that Lane was restrained from "using, copying or disclosing any internal document of Ford Motor Company." However, in September Federal Judge Nancy G. Edmunds threw out the lawsuit, asserting that First Amendment restrictions of prior restraint applied to the Internet just as they do to traditional media.

This ruling could clearly set a precedent for applying the First Amendment to Internet publications, as well as establishing guidelines in the battle between editorial and business concerns. It establishes the primacy of freedom of speech over protection of economic interests and trade secrets, guarding online journalists' rights to report on the internal workings of corporations and other institutions.

Freedom of Information and Copyrights

Digital Millennium Copyright Act (1998)

Signed into law by President Clinton in October 1998, this bill's central focus was to protect online service providers whose servers are used to transfer copyrighted material without their knowledge. However, it also contained a provision that made it a crime to circumvent copyright protection mechanisms built into software, even if using the underlying material would constitute fair use. It also criminalized the manufacture of software that would crack these codes.

Though this is actually a somewhat tamer version of a previous bill, the World Intellectual Property Organization Copyright Treaties Implementation Act, it still has journalists howling. It basically means that journalists might now have to pay for information that they have the legal right to possess under the existing Copyright Act. This is still being fought by First Amendment advocates and journalists' organizations.

Telecommunications Act and Communications Decency Act of 1996

The Telecommunications Act was a sweeping communications law, affecting virtually every communications industry, which included a set of provisions called the Communications Decency Act (CDA). This law required broadcasters to rate the violence in their programming and to develop and implement the "V-chip," a device that would allow for the automatic blocking of TV stations based on criteria for sex, violence and other material deemed inappropriate for minors. The bill also made it a crime to use the Internet or any other communications device to transmit indecent or obscene material with the intent to annoy or harass the recipient. It invoked the "community standards" provision in criminalizing the use of the Internet to transmit any offensive content.

The CDA was declared unconstitutional by a federal court four months after it passed, but the gist of the law alarmed many journalists. According to the letter of the law, journalists could be prosecuted for publishing all sorts of material that would ordinarily be considered acceptable as news. In fact, after the law was overturned, the Clinton–Lewinsky scandal illustrated the shaky ground on which the law was based. Many informed observers agreed that the Starr Report would have been considered obscene under the CDA. Ironically, many of the same legislators who worked hard to get the CDA passed found themselves working equally hard to make sure the Starr Report was available far and wide.

A&M Records, Inc. v. Napster, Inc. *(2001)*

The Napster computer program allowed computer users to download copyrighted sound recordings over the Internet through a process known as peer-to-peer file sharing. Rather than storing any of these files on Napster's own computer servers, the process allowed users to search for music files stored on other users' computers and download them. Napster claimed that because the company itself did not store files or share them, it could not be held responsible for any copyright infringement that might take place using its software. The recording industry (represented by A&M Records) claimed that Napster was liable for allowing known copyrighted material to be copied using its network. The U.S. District Court of Northern California ruled that Napster was guilty of "contributory copyright infringement" by encouraging and assisting the infringing activity. Napster was forced to shut down its operation and ultimately declared bankruptcy.

While this doesn't directly relate to online journalism, it was the most high-profile Internet-related legal case of the early 21st century. It also established a precedent regarding intellectual property that has far-reaching implications throughout news and entertainment media. While file sharing and other forms of copyright violation (including plagiarism) still take place, there is greater awareness of the legal culpability of those who don't take such matters seriously. There's also more of a widespread belief that such cases can be fought and won by the rightful copyright owners, which can embolden journalists (online and offline) whose work is used without permission.

Media Protections

APBnews.com v. Committee on Financial Disclosure *(2000)*

The 1979 Ethics in Government Act made the personal financial disclosure statements (listings of gifts, free travel, investments and other financial information) of all federal judges publicly available. Any citizen has had the right to request them. However, a 1998 amendment to the law gave the judiciary the right to temporarily withhold information for security reasons. Online news outlet APBNews.com requested these documents in late 1999, planning to make them available through a searchable online database. On December 14 the U.S. Judicial Conference disclosure committee denied the request, saying it feared for the safety of the judges, though it had approved

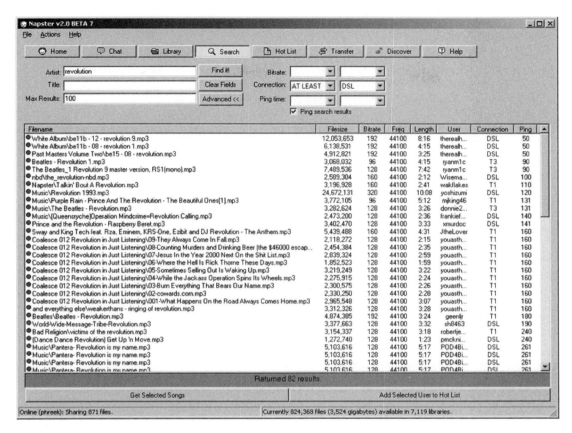

The Napster music program started the file sharing revolution and made MP3 a household word.

SOURCE: Screenshot courtesy Roxio Inc./Dave Winer.

similar requests by traditional media outlets. The committee argued that federal law required citizens to make written requests to the federal bench. If the disclosures appeared on the Internet, then anyone could see the public documents. On December 22 APBNews filed suit against the committee, seeking the release of the statements. In March 2000 the committee reversed itself and agreed to release the documents after being advised to do so by U.S. Supreme Court Chief Justice William Rehnquist.

This is an important case because it fended off an attempt to impose a double standard. While there are plenty of laws governing the release of assorted public records to print and broadcast news outlets, there is much less written into law regarding online journalism. When this is coupled with the fear some people have of the Internet and its global scope, instances like this one can result. For online journalists, any precedent that extends traditional media protections to include online news is a victory.

SUMMARY

Clearly, online journalism can be a minefield of potential legal troubles. Part of the reason for this is the very public character of publishing anything online, from personal Web pages to international Web portals. While you might think your small publication couldn't be of interest to anyone beyond your tiny readership, in fact it's just as potentially visible online as the *New York Times*. This is why it is vital for beginning online journalists to understand these legal issues. The laws, cases and other material discussed here are just a small portion of the mind-boggling sets of regulations that can relate to online publishing, but if you learn from them and work with others to better understand the legal playing field, you can steer clear of lawsuits.

RELATED WEB SITES

Drudge Report
http://www.drudgereport.com

"Online Fair Use of Copyrighted Material," by Gerard Martin
http://www.ncsa.uiuc.edu/SDG/IT94/Proceedings/Pub/martin/WWW-Online-Essay.html

"The Law and the Internet: Beware," by Denise Caruso
http://www.cjr.org/year/98/3/ilaw.asp

"AOL's 'youth filters' protect kids from Democrats," by Brian Livingston
http://www.news.com/Perspectives/Column/0,176,421,00.html

Definition of libel
http://192.41.4.29/def/1032.htm

Freedom Forum's pages on freedom and technology
http://www.freedomforum.org/technology/welcome.asp

First Amendment Handbook
http://www.rcfp.org/handbook/viewpage.cgi

EXERCISES

1. Do you think the ruling in the *U.S. v. Matthews* case was fair? Why or why not? How do you think it might affect the job of reporters in the future? What if the subject matter was just pornography rather than child pornography? Do you think that should have made a difference? Explain your position.

2. Do you see the Digital Millennium Copyright Act's fair use provisions as a threat to freedom of information or a necessary step against the rampant piracy of copyrighted material on the Internet? Discuss your position, and provide some examples.

3. After reading this chapter, how would you propose to deal with issues of libel, obscenity and copyrights across state and international borders? Would you use the laws of the country where documents originated, where Internet server computers are located, or where users have objected? Provide some examples and explain your reasoning.

4. Using InfoTrac College Edition, locate more information on any one of the cases mentioned in this chapter. Write a one and one half to two page report on the case and include the arguments on each side, the final ruling, and why you think the ruling was either appropriate or inappropriate.

16

||||||

Ethics in Cyberland

Drawing the line between what is legal and illegal in online journalism is a somewhat complicated task. Deciding what is right and wrong can be even more complex. The emergence of the Internet has created all sorts of new ethical questions, and many of them bear directly on online journalism. This chapter examines many ethical cases from recent history and discusses them in terms of moral duty, conflicts and ethical principles.

Every new medium ever created has brought along its own new ethical questions and concerns. However, because of its combination of worldwide presence, instant updating, multimedia and near-universal ability to publish, the Web may pose more questions and raise more issues than any other news medium in history. Virtually all of its strengths are also potential weaknesses, and there is little agreement on exactly what should be done about or how to prepare for future problems.

This chapter looks at some traditional approaches to media ethics, then examines some of the many ethical concerns shared by many within the business of online journalism. The chapter closes with some examples of cases where different factors combined to create ethical dilemmas for online journalists.

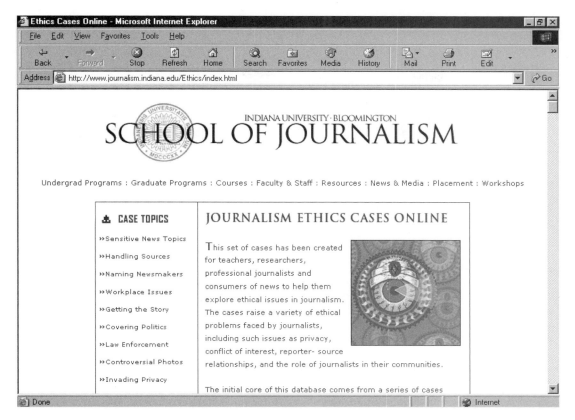

Indiana University's School of Journalism has an archive of journalism ethics cases online for use by students and others interested in ethical questions.

SOURCE: journalism.indiana.edu (accessed September 3, 2003). Used by permission.

TRADITIONAL ETHICAL APPROACHES

At the heart of any discussion of ethics in journalism, online or offline, is the issue of *values*. It's become common to associate this word with assorted political or religious points of view, but everyone has values of one sort or another. People adhere to their own principles or standards of what is right and wrong, what is desirable or undesirable, what should or should not be. Values are inherently stronger than simple attitudes, beliefs or opinions. You may have all kinds of opinions—that a particular flavor of ice cream is the best, or that a given politician is incredibly misguided—but you probably have a few core values that guide your decision-making processes. The things you find most important, that you

SOCIETY OF PROFESSIONAL JOURNALISTS CODE OF ETHICS

PREAMBLE

Members of the Society of Professional Journalists believe that public enlightenment is the forerunner of justice and the foundation of democracy. The duty of the journalist is to further those ends by seeking truth and providing a fair and comprehensive account of events and issues. Conscientious journalists from all media and specialties strive to serve the public with thoroughness and honesty. Professional integrity is the cornerstone of a journalist's credibility.

Members of the Society share a dedication to ethical behavior and adopt this code to declare the Society's principles and standards of practice.

SEEK TRUTH AND REPORT IT

Journalists should be honest, fair and courageous in gathering, reporting and interpreting information.

Journalists should:

- Test the accuracy of information from all sources and exercise care to avoid inadvertent error. Deliberate distortion is never permissible.
- Diligently seek out subjects of news stories to give them the opportunity to respond to allegations of wrongdoing.
- Identify sources whenever feasible. The public is entitled to as much information as possible on sources' reliability.
- Always question sources' motives before promising anonymity. Clarify conditions attached to any promise made in exchange for information. Keep promises.
- Make certain that headlines, news teases and promotional material, photos, video, audio, graphics, sound bites and quotations do not misrepresent. They should not oversimplify or highlight incidents out of context.
- Never distort the content of news photos or video. Image enhancement for technical clarity is always permissible. Label montages and photo illustrations.
- Avoid misleading re-enactments or staged news events. If re-enactment is necessary to tell a story, label it.
- Avoid undercover or other surreptitious methods of gathering information except when traditional open methods will not yield information vital to the public. Use of such methods should be explained as part of the story.
- Never plagiarize.
- Tell the story of the diversity and magnitude of the human experience boldly, even when it is unpopular to do so.
- Examine their own cultural values and avoid imposing those values on others.
- Avoid stereotyping by race, gender, age, religion, ethnicity, geography, sexual orientation, disability, physical appearance or social status.
- Support the open exchange of views, even views they find repugnant.
- Give voice to the voiceless; official and unofficial sources of information can be equally valid.
- Distinguish between advocacy and news reporting. Analysis and commentary should be labeled and not misrepresent fact or context.
- Distinguish news from advertising and shun hybrids that blur the lines between the two.
- Recognize a special obligation to ensure that the public's business is conducted in the open and that government records are open to inspection.

fall back on to help you deal with moments of indecision or uncertainty, are your values.

Because of the nature of the job, journalists frequently have to decide what really matters to them. The central ethical concerns of journalists outlined in the "10 Commandments of News" should give you a good idea of what journalists believe to be ethically important (see Chapter 14). At this point, though, it's useful to stop and reflect on a few of the values behind the standard practices of jour-

SOCIETY OF PROFESSIONAL JOURNALISTS CODE OF ETHICS, *continued*

MINIMIZE HARM

Ethical journalists treat sources, subjects and colleagues as human beings deserving of respect.

Journalists should:

- Show compassion for those who may be affected adversely by news coverage. Use special sensitivity when dealing with children and inexperienced sources or subjects.
- Be sensitive when seeking or using interviews or photographs of those affected by tragedy or grief.
- Recognize that gathering and reporting information may cause harm or discomfort. Pursuit of the news is not a license for arrogance.
- Recognize that private people have a greater right to control information about themselves than do public officials and others who seek power, influence or attention. Only an overriding public need can justify intrusion into anyone's privacy.
- Show good taste. Avoid pandering to lurid curiosity.
- Be cautious about identifying juvenile suspects or victims of sex crimes.
- Be judicious about naming criminal suspects before the formal filing of charges.
- Balance a criminal suspect's fair trial rights with the public's right to be informed.

ACT INDEPENDENTLY

Journalists should be free of obligation to any interest other than the public's right to know.

Journalists should:

- Avoid conflicts of interest, real or perceived.
- Remain free of associations and activities that may compromise integrity or damage credibility.
- Refuse gifts, favors, fees, free travel and special treatment, and shun secondary employment, political involvement, public office and service in community organizations if they compromise journalistic integrity.
- Disclose unavoidable conflicts.
- Be vigilant and courageous about holding those with power accountable.
- Deny favored treatment to advertisers and special interests and resist their pressure to influence news coverage.
- Be wary of sources offering information for favors or money; avoid bidding for news.

BE ACCOUNTABLE

Journalists are accountable to their readers, listeners, viewers and each other.

Journalists should:

- Clarify and explain news coverage and invite dialogue with the public over journalistic conduct.
- Encourage the public to voice grievances against the news media.
- Admit mistakes and correct them promptly.
- Expose unethical practices of journalists and the news media.
- Abide by the same high standards to which they hold others.

SOURCE: http://www.spj.org/ethics_code.asp

---

nalism. These are common to most journalists and are part of many journalism organizations' stated ethical guidelines. Within the industry, the most widely accepted code of ethics is the Society of Professional Journalists (SPJ) code (see box).

Nearest and dearest to journalists are *accuracy* and *completeness*. Reporters and editors must make sure their stories are as accurate and complete as possible. Without accuracy, you lose all credibility with the public, and your reputation as a news organization is really all you have to sell. If people don't believe you, they'll find another news source. Furthermore, if you only report part of the story, you're misleading the public, which is why completeness is a necessary part of the equation. A phrase often used in conjunction with these concepts is "Seek the truth and report it as fully as possible," which illustrates several related points. It assumes journalists actively go out and find facts rather than simply waiting for the phone to ring; it assumes that journalists are only interested in the truth; and it assumes that journalists will report the whole story, not just carefully selected bits of it.

Closely associated with this is the notion of **balance** or fairness. To tell the whole story, you must make sure to represent as many sides of the issue as possible. It's common to assume there are two sides to every issue, but in fact there are usually many more than that. You'll find that on major issues that affect lots of people, dozens of different groups and individuals will have different interests and things at stake in the matter. Wherever possible, this should be represented in your stories. A journalist's job isn't just to report on the most popular arguments on an issue—it's to reflect the whole range of points of view whenever possible. As noted earlier, you'll sometimes hear the term "objectivity" used when discussing this issue, but many journalists believe that no one can be truly objective about an issue that might affect them and thus prefer to think of it as being fair.

A similar issue is *independence*—the notion that journalists are not beholden to anyone but their readers. While most media outlets accept advertising, journalists insist that advertisers should never have any say in what is or isn't published, or in the content of stories. This is often at the heart of conflict between upper management and the newsroom, but on occasions when the rule is broken, it's always a major issue within newsrooms. It gets back to the issue of credibility—if a news organization is to remain credible in the eyes of the community it serves, it should not allow outside agents of any sort to influence the content of the news product. This also goes for local officials, public figures, corporations or any other individuals, groups or companies. For virtually everyone in the news business, a journalist's independence is sacrosanct.

Accountability is also an important issue for both journalists and audiences. Many journalists see their role within society as policing the institutions—keeping the government, corporations, law enforcement and other agencies on their toes so they don't abuse their power. The role of exposing wrongdoing within social institutions—often called the "watchdog" role—basically boils down to making sure that public and corporate officials are held accountable for their actions. Most journalists see part of the role of a free press as to provide information to the public in an effort to hold institutions responsible for their actions. What is often overlooked is that there is a flip side to this—journalists should also be accountable for the facts that they report. Good reporters and editors recognize this, which is why they're such sticklers for accuracy.

Another take on the ethical questions of journalism is to look at the profession in terms of *serving the public interest*. This is a long-stated goal of journalism, yet it's a fairly complex topic because the public isn't some single monolithic group. Sometimes serving one segment of the public hurts another. Sometimes serving the interests of the masses puts you at odds with other important people and in-

---

ONLINE ETHICS RESOURCES FOR JOURNALISTS

For journalists, the online age has brought tremendous resources for story information. In addition, it has brought the ability to peruse ethical standards and case studies from a huge variety of sources. Here are a few useful sites for journalists interested in ethics:

Society of Professional Journalists (SPJ): http://www.spj.org
This journalism organization has probably the most widely known code of ethics in the business, and an entire section of its site covers ethical issues.

American Society of Newspaper Editors (ASNE): http://www.asne.org
This long-standing newspaper organization devotes several pages to ways of building credibility and trust in newspapers.

Radio-Television News Directors Association (RTNDA): http://www.rtnda.org
This site addresses ethical issues unique to broadcast news with codes and guidelines, as well as results from workshops and signups for upcoming events.

American Society of Magazine Editors (ASME): http://asme.magazine.org
Under the heading of "Guidelines," this site offers principles for magazine journalists as well as advertisers.

Journalism.org: http://www.journalism.org
This site is the joint Internet presence of the Project for Excellence in Journalism and the Committee of Concerned Journalists, two journalism advocacy groups working toward the common goal of higher standards in journalism. The site offers ethical codes and other material for journalists in the online, print and broadcast fields.

Poynter Institute: http://www.poynter.org
The Poynter Institute is a school for journalists, future journalists, and teachers of journalism. Its online site contains codes, links, case studies and articles that deal with a variety of ethical issues.

Indiana University: Journalism Ethics Cases Online: http://www.journalism.indiana.edu/Ethics/index.html
The Indiana University School of Journalism has put together an archive of ethical cases for journalists and students to peruse. The cases cover a huge range of subjects, from sensitive news topics to handling sources to invading privacy and many more.

---

stitutions. Sometimes serving the public means publishing something that embarrasses your news organization or a colleague. It's not an easy task.

Journalists have always had to analyze the costs and benefits of a story—the question of who will be helped or hurt by its publication. In *Media Ethics: Cases and Moral Reasoning* (6th ed., New York: Longman, 2001), Clifford Christians and colleagues have addressed this issue by asking an appropriate question—"To whom do you owe **moral duty?**" As a journalist, do you answer primarily to your readers, your editor or whom? With whom do your primary loyalties lie? If serving one conflicts with serving another, which one comes first? Christians describes five audiences or agencies that a journalist should feel obligated to support (pp. 22–23):

- *Yourself.* Theoretically, journalists are decent human beings with consciences. They have to look themselves in the mirror every day and feel good about themselves, and this certainly keeps many journalists from ethical lapses.

However, Christians points out, the need to advance one's career sometimes clouds judgment toward the effects actions may have on others. In other words, conscience sometimes takes a back seat to careerism.

- *Subscribers or readers.* This is an audience most journalists would cite immediately. These are the people who, at least indirectly, pay the salaries of journalists, which is at the heart of the ethical arguments most journalists make on behalf of informing the public. The trouble is that subscribers or readers generally aren't homogeneous and passive. Not everyone in the readership wants the same thing, and not everyone appreciates some of the other news values that journalists hold in high regard. This can lead to all sorts of conflicts.

- *Your news organization.* If subscribers and readers indirectly pay journalists' salaries, news organizations pay them directly. This is why news organizations can inspire loyalty among employees (at least ones who are paid adequately). This goes beyond simply being a "team player." Like any other business, news organizations employ lots of people who don't directly influence the final product. People who sell ads, people who answer phones, people who sort mail are all fellow employees. If a reporter harms the organization's reputation and readership plummets, it can affect lots of people, not just reporters. (Of course, some reporters are perpetually at war with their organizations, which changes the ranking of loyalties considerably.)

- *Your colleagues.* There is generally a certain amount of camaraderie among fellow reporters and editors. When joining a news organization, most reporters exhibit a measure of professional pride in trying to uphold their colleagues' standards. One of the lowest blows in journalism can be to let down your colleagues. But what if a colleague is at the center of a problem that threatens to compromise the integrity of your organization? How deep are your professional loyalties?

- *Society.* Some reporters might ask why society in general—that is, beyond your readership—is included on this list. The answer is that news reports frequently have ripple effects far beyond their core audience. For example, if you break a story locally and then a national media outlet picks it up, it can have far-reaching implications, and if you've done your job well, you can inform a much larger public. In addition, the social responsibility model of journalism holds that regardless of your target audience the ultimate goal of journalism is to serve society. As an individual journalist, then, you should consider the overall impact on society as well as on these other parties when making decisions.

Clearly, there have long been plenty of ethical concerns for journalists to address. With the coming of online journalism, however, the ethical dilemmas have multiplied exponentially.

The Poynter Institute has an online collection of ethics-related material ranging from examples to critiques and histories.

SOURCE: poynter.org (accessed May 14, 2003). Used courtesy The Poynter Institute, St. Petersburg, FL.

ONLINE ISSUES AND CONFLICTS

All of the issues just discussed also matter in online journalism—in fact, some would argue they matter more than ever. On the Web, however, certain aspects of these issues are magnified, reconceptualized and modified due to the medium's characteristics. Almost every issue must be dealt with in a completely new light.

For example, accuracy and completeness would seem to be issues on which there is no compromise, for the reasons previously stated. Yet with online news there is a new factor—speed. A breaking story can literally be known worldwide in seconds, so there is now constant pressure to crank out stories quickly. It's become harder to scoop your competitors, so getting something online 10 minutes before they do has become a measure of journalistic success. While broadcast news has been going live for years, the core of its coverage is often live footage

James Lattanzio

|||||| **FROM THE FIELD**

Jon Katz
Media Critic, Author and Novelist
Contributing Editor, *Rolling Stone*
Former Lead Columnist, *HotWired*
Former Producer, CBS News
Former Reporter, *Washington Post, Boston Globe*

When the *Dallas Morning News* Web site broke the story that Timothy McVeigh had confessed to the 1996 Oklahoma City bombing, then had to retract the story, the traditional media used the event as an example of how the immediacy of online news allowed for a slippage of standards.

Jon Katz doesn't buy that. "The *Dallas Morning News* is a very responsible organization, online and off," he says. "They don't run a lot of erroneous stuff. I mean, the *New York Times* runs corrections almost every day. So should they be put out of business because they run five corrections a week? Are they a dangerous medium because they sometimes make mistakes?"

In traditional media, you hear a lot of horror stories about Web outlets putting half-baked information online. According to Katz, however, for a real horror show, many traditional journalists should look in the mirror.

"Traditional journalism's approach to the rise of the Internet and other new media technologies has been almost uniformly reactionary, wrong, phobic and exploitative," says Katz. "They're constantly throwing reasons at you why the online culture is dangerous or different or strange or menacing."

While these are harsh words, Katz can back them up with a résumé that few in journalism can match. After many years with prominent newspapers, Katz worked as a producer for CBS News, then spent several years as media critic for *Wired* magazine and its online outlet,

as opposed to detailed reporting involving fact checking and full-blown story write-ups.

The pressure to crank out polished stories immediately flies in the face of the notion of "get it first, but first get it right." Some have argued that the ease of correcting stories online provides an all-too-convenient crutch that makes it somehow OK to mislead the public by publishing mistakes for a short while. Most analysts have argued that the speed factor is the single greatest threat to the credibility of online journalism.

An argument related to this has to do with *authenticity*—conveying not just the on-the-spot facts but the background behind those facts that paint a more complete picture of the story. Many journalists argue that this gets abandoned entirely with the lightning speed of the online medium. They argue that without the proper context the audience can easily misunderstand the meaning and signifi-

HotWired. He's since gone on to become a successful novelist as the author of the Suburban Detective mystery series, but that doesn't mean he has ignored what's going on in today's media.

"Journalism has basically viewed pop culture or technology as a dangerous virus to be protected from," Katz says. "They say it's addictive, it's de-civilizing, it's dangerous, it causes violence, it's a medium for sexual predators. The list of phobias journalism has passed on about pop culture and new media is just insane. So younger people see journalism as the sort of bovine and clueless institution that it is. Journalists have become sort of the temperance ladies of our culture—all they do is run around and cluck about time moving on."

Katz believes that many print and broadcast journalists don't understand the Web or interactivity and are threatened by them. "It's a fearful, backwards-looking way of viewing new media that has paralyzed journalism," he says. "They're so busy running around looking for reasons that it's dangerous or destructive that they don't come to understand it."

Katz says that traditional journalists need to open their minds and realize that the online world is not some menacing underground subculture but rather an inviting new way to tell stories and attract readers.

"The Web is a very journalistic medium because it's so continuous," says Katz. "You can break a story any second of the day on the Web, as opposed to once a day in a newspaper, or once a week in a newsmagazine, or only on the evening news. It's a wonderful medium for breaking stories, but since it's continuous, verifying stuff is more important because it's very easy to transmit erroneous information. But isn't that what journalists are supposed to do anyway? Online and off, a journalist has to be responsible for the information he or she gathers, is supposed to be factual, is responsible for being fair-minded and for bringing in different points of view."

In fact, Katz says, the Web might raise standards because it's so easy for readers to point out mistakes. "I think that I'm held very accountable for what I write online," he says. "People respond to me very instantly and quickly. If I make a mistake, it's very visible. Hundreds of people correct me immediately. And they have no trouble reaching me."

cance of the facts. It should be noted, however, that this has long been a problem in journalism. For years, commentators have correctly argued that daily journalism too often answers the first four basic questions (who, what, when and where) at the expense of the last two, more analytical questions (why and how). In particular, broadcast journalism has been criticized for this. It should be noted, however, that broadcast journalism has always battled the clock, and while it's had its share of ethical problems, it has certainly proven its worth over the years.

The question of *fairness* is also at issue in the online world in ways not imagined before the Web. Writers can still prepare reports that are scrupulously fair, but does that mean that readers won't be influenced in a particular direction by other aspects of the Web presentation? The online medium is particularly ripe for influence beyond the content of a story. It's true that newspaper readers or TV viewers can leave a report in the middle. Yet unlike the others, the online medium actively encourages readers to abandon ship. With advertisements running down the margins, a reader can be distracted at any point and leave the story before all sides have been presented. Furthermore, if there are links embedded within the text, readers might click on one and go to one side's Web site and never be exposed to the message on an opposing site. How might this characteristic of the medium influence what a reader takes from a story? It's hard to say.

Closely related is how the Web environment influences the notion of journalistic independence. Commercial media have long had to sell advertisements to pay the bills, but the Web exerts different sorts of commercial pressure on sites. The ways in which ads are placed on Web pages make them functionally very different from those in newspapers or on TV, and potentially more influential. In a print newspaper, advertisements are not part of a story's presentation; on TV, ads occupy their own time separate from stories. However, in online news, a story almost always occupies its own page, and ads are almost always part of that presentation. Studies have shown that users often don't know when they've stopped reading editorial content and started reading a commercial message. Ads on Web pages are also clickable, so at any point they can be clicked and immediately take precedence over editorial content. In addition, it has become common for online news organizations to form partnerships with various companies. This might give users access to different types of materials, but it also raises issues about journalists' freedoms to report accurately on partner institutions.

The use of links and ads on story pages also raises the issue of accountability. If a reporter's story appears on a page that contains links to advertisers' sites, how does the reporter know whether or not any linked pages contain accurate information? Readers have been known to click on ads and end up at a site that looks much like a news site yet presents information designed to make a corporation look good. This is even thornier when sites use link text within stories. Let's say, for example, that you make a reference to defects in machines made by Bangzoom Computers, Inc. If a user clicks on the name before getting the gist of the story and ends up at Bangzoom's Web site, it might very well contain misleading information about the quality of Bangzoom's products. If a reader buys a Bangzoom computer and it falls apart, the reader might believe your news organization has misinformed him. Even if you link to seemingly responsible sites, who's to say when they might publish something inaccurate? If you've linked to it, there's an implication that you've vouched for its accuracy, even if your site states otherwise. Beyond inaccuracy of linked sites, there's also the question of the character of the content on the other end of a link. You can link to a respected news site and then discover it contains a feature that offends your readers.

Control of information can be a problem even if you don't link to other sites. One of the great benefits of online journalism is its inherent interactivity—readers can respond quickly and easily to online content. Nevertheless, there can be a downside to it as well. Discussion forums and chat rooms are often very popular elements of news sites, but the news organization seldom maintains any control over the information in them—that would be seen as censorship. But that means that users can say anything they want about anyone. They can make libelous statements, they can guess at the identities of rape victims or unnamed sources, they can use foul language and even incite riots, all on a site sponsored by your news organization. While many reporters might think this is simply part of what happens in a true democracy, this prospect often horrifies publishers and other management personnel.

Another issue that seems like an undeniable positive for news organizations is the posting of database information and background archives online. Usually this is done to back up a major story—posting the raw material behind a story relating to increases in cases of spousal abuse or material about an ongoing trial. It seems to take advantage of one of the strengths of the medium by offering raw material and letting readers judge for themselves. Yet raw numbers can be misleading to the inexperienced reader, which can lead to misunderstandings and complaints. Such material also inevitably omits something—a different database, another article that could have been included, and so on. Since you can't publish everything, you run the risk of being accused of bias through selective omissions to support a point of view.

Online news outlets have dealt with many of these issues for years. In most cases, procedures have been developed that help to deal with some of the twists and turns of these issues. Some are simple—for example, when correcting stories, many online outlets have made it a policy to note that a correction was made and list the date and time of the correction. Most news outlets that link to outside sites place disclaimers on their pages indicating that external sites are not endorsed by them, and many outlets program their links so that they open the linked page in a new window. Still, it's hard to plan ahead for every circumstance, and Web news is still new enough that not every scenario has been foreseen or experienced.

ETHICAL CASES

Clearly, there are many issues for online journalists to keep in mind. An effective way to prepare for such decisions is to examine scenarios that have occurred at other news organizations over the years and to think about how you might address them. Let's look at a few cases that have arisen involving different online news organizations and consider some questions that these cases pose. These examples are all based on real cases, although some represent circumstances from more than one case.

Profiting from the News

In an effort to make some money from its unprofitable online site, in October 1997 the *New York Times* reached an agreement with bookseller Barnes & Noble. At the end of every book review on the *Times'* site, a link would appear that would allow readers to buy the reviewed book from Barnes & Noble. The *Times* stressed that this would in no way influence the content of its book reviews, but critics pointed out that readers were not informed that the *Times* would receive a transaction fee from Barnes & Noble from each click on the link. Once this practice was established at the *Times,* many other news outlets followed suit, placing context-specific ads on news pages. Detractors maintained that this blurred the line between editorial content and advertising.

Commercial news organizations have to make a profit to survive, but they're also expected to remain independent. Do you think this is simply a necessary step for the survival of the newspaper, or do you believe it compromises the integrity of the news organization? Do you believe such partnerships are just part of surviving in the marketplace, or are you concerned at possible effects down the road?

Providing Links to Suspect Sites

Your news site regularly places links at the end of stories to Web pages related to subjects in the story. Usually these connect to company, agency or assorted personal sites. However, you've written a story about a popular computer program that makes it easy for Web users to trade files. This program is under heavy fire from the recording and software industries, which claim it encourages copyright violations and could cripple their industries. There are legal threats pending that could make it illegal to use the program, but for the moment the software is legal. Your usual procedure would be to place a link to the program's home page at the end of the story, along with links to the Recording Industry Association of America, the Software and Information Industry Association and assorted other parties mentioned in the article. You know that placing a link to the program's home page is legal, but you're unsure about whether it's right or wrong.

Would you include a link to the program's home page at the end of your story? How would you defend your decision? Do you believe that since it's a legal product you can link to it; or would you argue that since it might encourage piracy you shouldn't? In a different situation, would you link to the Web site of a religious cult if you wrote a story about it? To a site that tells people how to defeat a popular car antitheft device? To an adult magazine site?

Walking the Line between Content and Ads

You're running the online site of a print news outlet and struggling to pay the bills. Staff cuts may be necessary if you don't start making more money from advertising. Then you get a message from a member of your advertising sales force. A leading manufacturer of computer printers wants to place a lucrative series of eye-catching ads on your site's section front pages promoting its new line of color printers. You respond positively but insist that nothing about your site's stories will be compromised by advertisements. The company's representative agrees but presents this scenario. The pages, which are normally colorful, would appear entirely in black and white when first loaded. Only when the user clicked on the ad would the page suddenly appear in full color. All story and link text would remain the same regardless.

The company's representative mentions that, among others, USAToday.com and HotWired.com have already run these ads.

Given all the factors involved, would you run the ads? Why or why not? What do you see as the costs and benefits? Do you believe it would compromise your site's journalistic integrity or not? What other issues are at stake here?

Defining the Limits of "News"

The *New York Times'* Web site was one of the first major newspaper sites to include Web-only content and features, and the site has long been allowed certain latitude to publish things that might not otherwise appear in the *Times*. The *Times* site reached an agreement in 1998 with author Joe Hutsko to publish installments of his upcoming novel *The Deal*. Hutsko, who had written for the *Times'* technology section and for other respected news outlets, based the book on his own experiences as an employee of Apple Computer, Inc. The book included two main characters that strongly resembled longtime Apple bosses Steve Jobs and John Sculley. Just days before the installments were to begin, the project was suddenly shelved. *Times* officials said they had concluded that serializing a novel drifted too far away from the mission of the newspaper. Critics argued that the *Times* might have backed away fearing repercussions from Jobs or Sculley.

Under the circumstances, would you have published the excerpts on the Web site? Do you believe it would have detracted from the site's news content? Why or why not? Do you believe that the subject matter should have anything to do with your decision to publish? What about the potential for controversy among high-ranking corporate officials?

Dealing with Sex Stories in Online News

One of the watershed days in the history of Web news was the day in September 1998 that the Starr Report was released on the Web. Prosecutor Kenneth Starr's report on President Clinton's affair with Monica Lewinsky contained graphic descriptions of sexual conduct that would not normally have appeared in a family newspaper. In spite of this, many publishers eagerly posted the entire Starr Report on their Web sites, or linked to sites with the full text, arguing that the weight of the story overshadowed the character of the content. Some editors chose not to do so on moral grounds. Regardless, the day remains one of the busiest in the history of Web news.

There are several choices editors could make here. One is to download the entire report and place it on their Web site. A second choice is to run excerpts of it, carefully labeling them as such. A third choice is not to run the report but to place links to the report on their site. Finally, editors could opt not to link to it at all. Which of these choices would you make, and why? Who would you serve with the choice you've made? What might you give up in the process?

Considering the Public's Right to Know

A major security flaw has been discovered in a popular e-mail program. The flaw would permit an intruder to send a message containing a virus that could make a computer crash, destroy data, or even retrieve personal information and copy it to the intruder's own machine. The company that makes the program is providing a fix on its Web site, yet company employees have told you privately that the fix will not fully correct the problem. In fact, they say that the entire program might have to be rewritten from scratch—a hugely time-consuming and expensive process. Unless it happens, however, the program will remain vulnerable. You know that this is valuable information, and if you don't publish it, many people's personal files might remain needlessly endangered. From your own research, you also know that hackers are passing the code that cracks the program all over the Internet. If you publish this information, forewarned readers could stop using the program and protect their files. However, you're also concerned about the response of the manufacturer, and about your article possibly encouraging more hackers to go online and crack the program.

Would you publish this information? Why or why not? Should you be concerned with the repercussions of the article or focus instead on the public's right to know? What other actions might you take?

Posting Targeted Ads Online

A concern of Web advertisers is that people rarely click on banner ads. While simple exposure to an ad might encourage buying, clicking on an ad indicates true interest, which is why advertisers pay sites for every time a user clicks on an ad. Accordingly, Web sites have an interest in encouraging people to click on ads. One way to do this is with "ad targeting," which involves tracking the content of the user's favorite sites and creating user profiles based on that information. Based on these profiles, a program calculates the types of ads the user might be interested in, then places that type of ad on the screen. Users' names and other personal information are never gathered. On one hand, it provides users with advertisements for products they're likely to be interested in, thus making them more likely to click on the ads (and making your site more money). On the other hand, the process does raise privacy concerns, particularly because part of the process involves personal IP addresses, which could be tracked at a later time.

Would you agree to place targeted ads on your site? What arguments would you make on behalf of your decision? Does the potential good of increased ad revenue outweigh the potential harm of privacy concerns? Do you believe users would voluntarily exchange anonymous demographic information for the type of ads they might welcome?

SUMMARY

The ethics of online journalism is at once a fascinating and horrifying topic. Ethical questions have puzzled journalists in the traditional media for years, yet the online venue seems to add more layers to both the types of dilemmas and the repercussions for actions. Many journalists believe that the best approach to these questions is always based in traditional news values—accuracy, integrity, balance and independence. Yet the realities of the medium and the marketplace can sometimes put these core values—and the sheer need for survival—at cross purposes.

RELATED WEB SITES

"Preserving Old Ethics in a New Medium," by J. D. Lasica
http://www.well.com/user/jd/coldec97.html

Guidelines for presenting advertising online
http://www.ojr.org/ojr/business/1017969389.php

Society of Professional Journalists (SPJ)
http://www.spj.org

American Society of Newspaper Editors (ASNE)
http://www.asne.org

Committee of Concerned Journalists (CCJ)
http://www.journalism.org

EXERCISES

1. Choose three of the ethical cases discussed in this chapter and write a paragraph or two about how you would act in each case. Be sure to address the questions following each case summary as well as the question of moral duty—to whom would you owe primary moral duty in each case? What are the conflicts?

 2. Using InfoTrac College Edition, look at stories from a major news outlet and select one that you believe would face some sort of ethical question—whether to publish particular information or photos, whether a journalist behaved ethically and so forth. Then apply some of the ethical standards discussed in this chapter to that story. Write a one to one and a half page summary.

17

||||||

The 21st Century
Journalist

After all this, what does the future hold for journalists? Will other forms of journalism disappear in favor of the online product, or will current forms simply change to adapt to the challenges of the 21st century? This chapter examines these questions and includes the opinions of experts from the field. The chapter also looks at the prospective nature of newsrooms in the 21st century.

It's easy for students looking toward the online world to get caught up in the technology that makes it seem so appealing. If you can learn a certain amount of Flash or JavaScript or DHTML, you can create all sorts of interesting effects on your Web page. And if your primary goal is to dazzle, you can certainly accomplish that mission.

"Dazzling" isn't this book's primary goal, however, nor is it the primary goal of online journalism. Before you learn how to make your pages look Cooler Than Thou, you need to know how to interview people, how to structure stories, and how to prepare them for publication. This book, first and foremost, is about journalism—as a student, you must understand the underlying craft of journalism before you attempt to work as any kind of reporter or editor. This is the central theme to which this book always returns. If you can't grasp or work within the fundamental principles and precepts of journalism, you should find another line of work.

To become a successful online journalist, however, does require some fresh thinking. It requires you to think seriously about some subjects that would have made reporters of 20 years ago roll their eyes (and reporters of 50 years ago blow their tops). Attention to presentation—to audio, video and the usability and look of the page—is a simple necessity given the nature of the medium and its primary audience. It's true that this doesn't really have anything to do with the actual nuts and bolts of a story, but it can tell that story in a unique and engaging way. To succeed in online journalism, you must be able to hang on to the values of traditional journalism without getting bogged down in some of its resistance toward new ideas.

THE CYBERJOURNALIST IN 2015

A reporter walks into a newsroom in the year 2015. He works for what is now referred to as a news portal, which produces news for a variety of media, including handheld devices, television, computers and print. As he walks in to sit down at his desk, flat video screens here and there throughout the room show live news footage from other online and broadcast outlets.

He checks to see whether a photographer will accompany him to shoot a video standup, or whether he'll have to shoot raw footage of the event himself. One way or the other, he'll need to take his DRN with him—his Digital Reporter's Notebook. This device can record audio and video and can access databases and the Web using a wireless modem. (The DRN can also translate recorded interviews into text, but it makes too many mistakes for this reporter's tastes, so he still transcribes most of them when he gets back to the office.) If a big event occurs, he can use the DRN to send live audio and video to the portal's servers to be streamed online, but the quality is not as sharp as when it's recorded and edited with a professional digital video camera. Still, it's important for him to be able to provide some sort of live coverage until a photographer arrives. Then the reporter can track down interviewees and put a professional package of audio, video and text together that will give his audience a more complete picture of the event's causes, dimensions and consequences.

Providing this sort of detailed coverage is what separates professional reporters in 2015 from individuals with their own transmitting equipment and home-brew news portals. These people, referred to derisively as "One-Man Bands" or "Ambulance Chasers" by professionals, periodically get footage or interviews that the pros don't, but most of them seldom provide anything of value beyond simple curiosities. In a few cases, however, individuals have proven prolific enough to eventually get hired by professional news portals.

Professional or amateur, in 2015 all news reporters need to be able to gather and verify information using all the technology available and present it in a multimedia format so that it offers value to users of many technologies. The best reporters will be the ones who consistently provide truth and insight and deliver it in ways that make people understand the subjects better.

If the core mission of the 2015 cyberjournalist sounds familiar to you, it should. The central goals are generally the same, but the means of gathering and presenting information will most likely be radically different. We're already seeing examples of that as print media outlets add multimedia elements to their Web sites.

CNN Interactive founder Scott Woelfel has seen this firsthand. "You are seeing print reporters go out with a camera," says Woelfel, "to either get a photograph or get some video or record some audio of an interview subject, and that's happening more and more. If you're a reporter for the *L.A. Times,* is your story going to end up online? Almost certainly. Are you going to do something differently, knowing it's going to be online? I think more and more people are thinking that. That may mean two versions, or it just may mean you look at the one version a little bit differently, and you're augmenting it in different ways. So yeah, the walls are breaking down."

T. J. Sullivan of the *Ventura County Star* is participating in this change. "We're doing it, and it changes the way that you think about reporting," Sullivan says. "We haven't always needed to know how to pronounce things, for example, because we were writing for print, and we didn't think like television or radio reporters thought. And now we do need to think that way because we're able to get audio and video and put it on our Web site. Some print journalists are having to get used to the idea of actually being on camera on the Web."

Just like today, reporters in 2015 will still be primarily interested in the facts of a story, but they will also need a deep understanding of the structure and presentational aspects of their stories. "They'll need to think versatility," says Stan Austin of the *Kansas City Star*'s kansascity.com. "Certainly you must learn to become a competent writer, with all the skills and course work involved in that, but you'll also need to get some editing experience and some exposure to page composition. Some of those skills are transferable to the Web. I know good paginators on the print side who are also good at packaging information for online. They've learned to think presentation, which is important. Get some basic understanding of how a page is put together, and how the Web works."

MAKING DIFFERENT MISTAKES

Many of the online journalists interviewed for this book believe that the online medium has not yet fully developed but likely will within the next few years. Part of this process involves simple trial and error—as more and more news organizations invest more and more of their resources in the online medium, customs will emerge out of the ideas that work. Unfortunately, this means that there are still an awful lot of errors yet to be made, and those of you reading this book will undoubtedly make a few of them. Experimentation inevitably leads to some failures.

Owen Youngman of the *Chicago Tribune* has been through this process in combining the resources of the *Tribune* newspaper and the radio and TV resources of WGN, also owned by the *Tribune*. "We made mistakes," says Youngman, "but as the users voted with their feet, or their thumbs, we shifted resources away from things they weren't interested in seeing. Early on we devoted a lot of resources to doing stories on the Web that didn't appear in the paper in any form, and there was just no payoff. Instead we saw that people valued information that enhanced their use of the newspaper—a lot of breaking news and things that change during the day."

There are some things to remember about failed experiments as new technologies and procedures develop. First, you must learn from them, both in terms of your own observations and user response. Second, and perhaps more important, while you might be inventing new ways of telling stories and attracting readers throughout your career, you're not reinventing the wheel entirely. By operating from the basic journalistic principles outlined in this book, you can avoid making the same mistakes other journalists have made over the years. You might be inventing the medium of the future, but don't forget to learn from the accumulated knowledge of the past.

"They need to hone their basic, fundamental journalistic skills," says Rich Jaroslovsky, managing editor, of the *Wall Street Journal*'s WSJ.com and president of the Online News Association. "You should become a solid news person. And beyond that, be flexible, be a quick study, be willing and eager to learn new tricks and new things, because the way that online journalism is practiced today is not the way it's going to be practiced tomorrow or five years from now. So the most important thing is that you remain flexible and adapt to the new technology as it comes along. But first and foremost, develop your most basic news skills."

This means adhering firmly to the "10 Commandments of News" as well as maintaining a reputation for honesty and integrity. The surest way for a journalist fresh out of college to fit in with new colleagues is to uphold (and sometimes raise) the standards of his colleagues. While veteran news personnel might still scoff at the presentational aspects of Web news, you can win them over with solid reporting and editing skills. This, in turn, can open some eyes to the possibilities of the Web—and also gain you some room for making the errors inevitable when working in a new medium. You need to make sure there's substance behind the style.

This doesn't mean there won't be new challenges, as Retha Hill of BET.com explains. "It's a different experience in the sense that it's faster," Hill says. "It's much more akin to working on a wire service, where you're just getting that news up as quickly as you can. You're taking digital photographs and you're getting that information on the site as soon as you can. In the meantime, someone else working with you would do this discussion area where people can interact, there might be someone doing a quick poll just to get a sense of how the users are coming down on a particular issue. So, for example, if you have a shooting at a high school, then somebody might create a poll, which is unscientific, on whether or not more stringent gun laws would have prevented the tragedy. It's a quick snapshot, but it gives people an opportunity to react. So you're moving quickly, the story is evolving."

The more solid your traditional reporting and editing credentials, the more likely you can win over non-online colleagues and get them to share material with you for the online side of the operation. In many newsrooms, gaining the approval of your print or broadcast colleagues is the toughest aspect of working for the online site.

"Part of our role has always been to educate the newsroom at large," says Stan Austin. "That's the first step in getting them to actually help you. This is something I tell students and educators all the time, people who are interested in this side of the business. We would love it if we had a person who does rewrite for the Web on every originating desk—in fact, that's something I'm proposing and trying to get formalized here."

Fostering cooperation among your colleagues not only can get you more material for the online site, it often gets you advance notice of the types of stories you might be able to share. This gives you a chance to assemble interactive or multimedia elements specific to that story. Without such cooperation, you often receive stories at the last minute, giving you no chance to prepare anything extra to accompany the story.

THE WORLD WIDE WORKPLACE

The discussion of fitting into a traditional newsroom raises one of the most fascinating questions related to online journalism. What will the online newsroom of the 21st century look like? How will it operate? What customs, procedures and machinery will operate there?

Right now most online outlets are shoehorned into corners of traditional newsrooms, and those that are lucky enough to have separate facilities are generally cramped for space. As resources committed to online outlets increase, what is likely to happen is the emergence of a true multimedia workplace—something of a cross between a TV and a print newsroom.

Brock Meeks of MSNBC may be closer to living this reality than most due to MSNBC's ties to the Web, cable and broadcast TV. "Let's say I'm covering a trial," Meeks says. "After the courtroom proceedings at the end of the day, both sides would come out and do a standup on the courthouse steps, which would be taped by the folks at CNBC, a sister cable station. Instead of taking down everything verbatim during that question-and-answer, I can just make notes about particularly salient questions and good answers. Then I can tell my video folks to grab that piece of video, and I would just allude to it in a couple of short sentences in my story and provide a link to the video rather than having to write 200 words about that question and answer dialogue. That saves me space and time in a story, so then I can go on and get to other things."

Streaming audio and video facilities will be necessary, yet the written word will likely continue to dominate the field for the next few years. The reasons are both economic and logistical in nature. Online users consistently agree that they appreciate the depth of reporting on the Web—they enjoy being able to read more about a subject. The most efficient way to keep huge archives is not through video but through text. There will almost certainly be archived video of major events, but for a deep archive, text simply works better—it eats up far less storage space and requires less bandwidth for transmission.

Some might ask when full-time video news will come to the Web, yet the sheer economics of such a prospect currently point to cable and satellite TV rather than the Web. Simply put, TV does video better than the Web. "We've experimented with doing a lot of online video," says Youngman, "and didn't really see that people (from other disciplines) did it very well. So at the *Tribune* the editors of the various media—radio, TV, print, Internet—confer on who might be best to cover a story at that given time, given what the deadlines are and the kind of story it is. Sometimes it'll be a print person, sometimes it'll be a radio or Internet person nominally, but it's all about gathering the news and getting it back and out to the viewers, the readers, the users."

With the relative lack of expense of broadcasting via cable and satellite, for the foreseeable future any news organization aiming to provide full-time video news in anything more than experimental fashion will likely go with cable. In addition, until the technologies merge completely, there will probably be better advertising support for cable because Web advertising is currently notorious for its low success rates.

What does this mean for the working reporter in online journalism? As noted at various points throughout this book, it means that versatility is likely to be the most prized trait a journalist can have in the developing new medium. Because of the disparate technologies involved in producing the advanced broadband multimedia that everyone anticipates, and because of the unpredictable nature of news, organizations that are well stocked with adaptable journalists will be at a competitive advantage. To put it plainly, it's not going to be enough anymore just to write well or design pages well—you'll need to possess exceptional skills in three or four areas and adequate abilities at the rest. While other corporate pursuits might reward specialization, in online journalism you'll need to be as well rounded as possible (which isn't a bad trait in the rest of your life either).

One trait most professionals agree is useful is simply a strong knowledge of the Internet, both as a news medium and as a source of information. "I would say, learn how to use the Web really well," says Mindy McAdams, former content developer for the *Washington Post*'s Digital Ink site and now Knight Chair Professor in the University of Florida's Department of Journalism. "Use it a lot for missions—use it like a tool. Go out and look stuff up and become really good at finding things. Check your e-mail more than once a day. Really immerse yourself in the environment—not to become addicted but to understand in a deep way how it actually works. You need to learn all the standard journalism skills, but in addition to that, you need to understand the Web thoroughly and deeply. If you have that, you're far ahead of most of the people that I ever interviewed for any kind of online jobs."

Having said this, the skill that will almost certainly help you the most is the ability to write well. Whether you're producing a written story, writing a script for a video package or reporting live from a scene, putting sentences and paragraphs together skillfully will do nothing but help you. News will always be based on information, and at some level you'll always need to recount an event using your skills with words.

Even if you're not writing a report or script, the simple ability to develop a narrative structure can help you. In creating timelines, slide shows or other visual narratives, the ability to put together information so it flows well and makes sense to the reader will be vital. The principles behind these different ways of telling the story are based on the same questions. How will the user best understand the essence of this information? How can I get it across in a way that will prove most stimulating within my given context? An open mind plus an understanding of narrative will take you a long way in the online world, no matter what it looks like 20 years from now.

TRANSPORTING THE USER

Few if any online journalism professionals consider their medium to be a finished product. Because of its interactivity, it has the potential to go beyond any previous medium in giving news consumers a truly engrossing experience—to "transport" them to a site elsewhere in the world or into a huge, easy-to-use realm of information about their chosen topic. But due to a combination of still-developing technologies and practices, it's not there yet.

"What's missing is something that I acknowledge is very hard to do, and very time consuming," McAdams says. "That is that kind of complex structure that makes it so I can go into a set of information and lose track of how much time has passed, because I am just so into it. I'm in there, and I'm clicking and I'm reading and I'm viewing, and I'm gathering information without having to search intently with a lot of keywords. I'm traveling through a space that's well constructed. And that hasn't happened to me yet."

"A true Web story takes into account that some readers want to plunge deeper into every paragraph that you offer," says Patricia Sullivan of the *Washington Post*. "Most readers want to interact with the information they're getting, whether it's interacting with the writer by e-mail or by chat or by video or audio, or they want to interact with the information by putting their opinion in, taking quizzes, discussing it with others. I think there's going to be some kind of interface we don't even imagine yet. And that is the real challenge of working on the Web—keeping your mind open all the time to these unknown applications."

The one facet of the online medium that is more of a departure than any of its other traits, the one that comes closest to truly transporting the user to another place, is the link. In the words of author and *Feed* magazine co-founder Steven Johnson, a link is like a "three-dimensional punctuation mark."

"I think that's a really good way to look at it," says Internet commentator and analyst Denise Caruso. "The link is a punctuation mark that actually has dimension—it takes us somewhere else. It's why I think of the Web as a real living document. I really do think that article that gets written to be published online should be thought of as a Web—it should be thought of as links to other things, as providing pathways to other things."

In many ways, this is a magical thing—at what other point in history could we essentially visit another place on Earth and interact with it instantly? This is something to be savored, not just by journalists but by everyone.

Even when applied to standard news stories, the link retains a certain measure of magic. On one hand, it allows journalists to let readers visit some of the places that they got their information, in effect letting them in on part of the journalistic process. This lets users verify the authenticity of the information for themselves, thus reinforcing the legitimacy of the story. On the other hand, journalists can provide links to stories, sites and archives related to the general topic of the story. This, in effect, allows interested readers to immerse themselves in topics on the spur of the moment, learning in an hour what it might have taken a day or two to learn doing traditional research. The journalist becomes not only a storyteller but a tour guide, pointing out sites along the way that might interest the user, letting the user step away to pursue a special topic for a while and then rejoin later.

An online journalist's job, then, should involve structuring information in such a way as to make it easy and rewarding to navigate. "It's all a matter of the information structure," says McAdams. "You need to think of it in terms of the possibilities that the readers might want to pursue, and what directions of pursuit would make sense. As an example, in certain houses or buildings, you'll walk through a certain doorway, and you're faced with a wall, and you suddenly need to turn right or left, and it seems odd. Like, why did they put a wall right here in front of the doorway? Sometimes the flow inside a building—or even a park, some kind of public space—is messed up. And sometimes, you're in a certain mood, and it strikes you. And you think, 'What was this architect doing? This is not a sensible flow within this space.' And that's how editors online need to think, but it's about information. Things need to be labeled, pathways need to be inviting and clear, and the structure needs to make sense."

The desire to create sensible paths for users to follow is an extension of one of the Internet's traditional strengths—the desire to share information freely with others. The interactivity of the medium creates more of a feeling of an information community than does traditional journalism. Rather than Edward R. Murrow or Walter Cronkite becoming a single trusted voice passing along wisdom, hundreds of users share their information back and forth.

"You can be a big-time newspaper reporter and used to writing your stories and think you have the world by the tail," says Patricia Sullivan, "but when you get on the Net, all of a sudden you find out that there are people who are smarter than you, who are better informed than you, and who don't mind telling you about it. Now, you can use that as a writer and a reporter as another resource, and make your reporting and writing better, or you can fold up and hate e-mail and hate reader interaction, which some people unfortunately do."

Across the centuries, media of all kinds have metaphorically transported people to faraway lands. Whether it was through books, news, movies or TV, the media have long served to inform, entertain, and make people look differently at the world. The medium of online journalism can do all of these in ways no other

|||||| **FROM THE FIELD**

J. D. Lasica
Senior Editor, Online Journalism Review

J. D. Lasica is one of the most familiar voices in the online world. As a veteran of the WELL, Newslink and many other online outlets, he's as familiar with both the potential and the realities of online journalism as anyone. And while he's optimistic about the online medium, he's not without concerns.

"A lot of mainstream journalism today is too timid," Lasica says. "It can stifle expressions of creativity and ignore the concerns of young people. These new avenues of online journalism expression are refreshing and should be welcomed by old-line journalists as well as the mainstream public. But I think they do so at their peril if they want to abandon all of the values and standards of journalism, because there's a lot that we've learned over the past 100-plus years that still applies to the brave new world of cyberspace."

As a newspaper reporter for 18 years prior to moving his work online, Lasica can see how online reporters interact differently with their readers than traditional print reporters do. "Having worked in newsrooms over the years," Lasica says, "I can probably count on two hands the letters that I've gotten over the years. For the most part it's always been a mentality of a one-way, top-down structure, where readers don't even expect to be able to talk to a reporter and editor. So it's very patriarchal and hierarchical in that sense. Not only myself, but most of the online journalists I've talked to have expressed wonder and awe, they revel in the fact that readers are part of the equation now."

Having said this, Lasica says he's beginning to see elements of the top-down model emerging in larger online outlets. "At a lot of the large online publications," says Lasica, "you're not even given the e-mail address of the reporters who have written about a subject that you might

medium can match. It can convey stories in a multiplicity of ways, but they all ultimately depend on the skills and convictions of the people who report, write, edit and present those stories. Sure, an online journalist could approach the task just like a print or broadcast reporter, and probably communicate the message in a satisfactory fashion. But when you're watching TV news, are you fully satisfied when there's no video to accompany a story? Are you fully satisfied when a newspaper has pictures of an event but no analysis to go with it? Responsible and effective journalists recognize the strengths of their medium and do their utmost to tailor their reporting to those strengths. We might not yet know what all the strengths of the online medium will be as it develops throughout the 21st century, but we do know this—the journalists that succeed in the medium will be the ones skilled enough and open-minded enough to adapt their methods to the strengths that emerge.

care passionately about. There's no way for you to follow up to ask questions of the journalist, to interact with him or her in any meaningful way. So there's still that kind of barrier, that wall that goes up. Journalists think that, 'OK, I've written my story, now I can move on to the next thing.' Well, the fact is that the public online wants to engage in a two-way dialogue. Maybe they're not ready for you to move on to the next thing until you're done discussing the subject in a forum or an e-mail or some other thing."

Lasica believes that while online outlets should take advantage of their speed and interactivity, they should not lose sight of the standards upheld by the best established news organizations. "When traditional journalism publications—the Washington Posts, the New York Times, the CNNs of the world—have gone online," Lasica says, "they've brought the same sorts of journalism traditions and values, of fairness and balance and accuracy, making sure they get both sides of the story without rushing things onto the Internet. Having said that, there are certain instances where they have sort of gotten away from those kinds of values, and when they've done that, they've invariably gotten burned by it."

So what does this mean for individual reporters looking to start careers in online journalism? Lasica says they can express their creativity online, but not at the expense of understanding what readers want. "There are different styles of journalism," says Lasica. "If you want to do analysis or opinion or commentary, that's fine. But most people in this country are still used to going online and looking at news and expecting the reporters to tell a story, present the facts, instead of engaging in a diatribe with an agenda."

Above all, he says, reporters should embrace the interactivity and far-reaching nature of the Web. "I've gotten e-mails from people all over the world from columns or articles that I've written months ago," Lasica says. "It still touches these people's lives in really personal, extraordinary ways. If you're writing for an online publication, you really know when you've hit a vein of interest in the public. The outpouring of feedback and response you get both ways is amazing. You're going to get a lot of criticism, but whether it's positive or negative feedback, it's still a really great thing to know when you've struck a nerve."

"The technology's all going to change," Caruso says. "Journalism is journalism. If you learn to practice good, honest, hardcore journalism, it doesn't make any difference what medium you're in. Learn how to think, man."

SUMMARY

We can't know precisely what journalism will look like 10, 20 or 50 years from now. It's fun to speculate, but even the experts—professionals who work daily in the online field—are unclear exactly what the job of reporter or editor will entail as this century unfolds. The one thing about which they do agree is that qualities such as curiosity, thoroughness, accuracy, fairness and a commitment to good writing are the core elements of an outstanding journalist. In the 21st century, however, you can add one more useful trait—a willingness and an ability to adapt to ever-changing technologies in the gathering, processing and dissemination of news. If you display these qualities in your work, you will be a credit to the field of journalism, period. It shouldn't matter if you're on paper, on a Web page, on streaming video, a PDA or a cell phone. Good reporting is good reporting.

RELATED WEB SITES

CNN Interactive
http://www.cnn.com

Ventura County Star
http://www.insidevc.com

Kansas City Star
http://www.kansascity.com

Chicago Tribune
http://www.chicagotribune.com

Wall Street Journal
http://www.wsj.com

Online News Association
http://www.onlinenewsassociation.org

BET.com
http://www.bet.com

MSNBC.com
http://www.msnbc.com

Washington Post
http://www.washingtonpost.com

University of Florida College of Journalism and Communication
http://www.jou.ufl.edu

EXERCISES

1. Given the technological breakthroughs of the past few decades and what you know about technology of the current day, write a two-page discussion of your take on a day in the life of a journalist in a distant future year of your choice. How will journalists gather information, what means will they use to distribute it, and how will audiences receive it? Be as specific as possible about the roles that current technologies (such as television, radio, the Web) will play at that time for journalists and news consumers. Will those technologies still be around and thriving, will they converge, or will they disappear?

2. Find a news site that you believe presents news in an innovative and useful way and write a one-page summary on what you believe this site offers readers. Be as specific as possible about the benefits of this site's presentation, and discuss how you think sites of the future might learn from the one you've examined here.

3. Think of the features that current technologies (computers, databases, cell phones, PDAs, digital recorders and so forth) offer today's reporters. Then put them together and come up with a description of your own ideal electronic reporting device of the future. What features should it have or not have? What elements would be the most important for a reporter covering a breaking story? What compromises might you make to keep the device portable enough to be useful?

||||||

Glossary

accountability   In the news business, the necessity for journalists to be responsible for the information they report.

active voice   Writing technique in which the subject acts rather than responds to others' actions. Considered more engaging to readers than passive voice, this style is preferred in journalism and most forms of writing.

advance story   A news story written about an upcoming event.

AVI   (Audio Video Interleaved) A video format created by Microsoft for its Windows PC operating system and often used as a raw format for capturing video. It is the precursor to the Windows Media streaming video format.

balance   In journalism, the presentation of differing sides of controversial issues without slanting coverage to favor or discredit any side.

bandwidth   Technically, the range of frequencies a network can use, but more commonly used to mean the volume of data that can be sent through a given network connection.

blog   (short for "Web log") Web page that allows individuals to raise issues on any topic and encourages readers to post responses for all to see. Structurally identical to message boards, but much more commonly used by individuals with their own Web pages and much less formally structured.

broadband   Literally, a network connection with enough bandwidth to support multiple channels of high-quality video, voice and data. Informally, any high-speed home Internet connection.

browser   A software program that translates hypertext code into graphical "pages" of information. This enables readers to view Internet content on the World Wide Web and to navigate among pages on different sites.

chat room   Web page that lets readers submit questions to notable persons, who then answer those questions live online at a predetermined time. In online news, these individuals are generally reporters, editors or newsmakers. Most often found at larger news organizations.

chronology   News writing structure that recounts events in the order in which they occurred; sometimes called a narration.

content producer   Job at many online news outlets that not only involves writing but also frequently entails copyediting, researching, headline writing, layout and many other functions.

courtesy titles   Formal titles, such as Mr., Mrs., Dr. and the like, added to the beginning of people's names. These days most news outlets tend to avoid using them.

cyberspace   A term coined by author William Gibson describing the "world" of all communication using computers and computer networks.

database   A collection of information on a particular subject, usually in an electronic form, that allows users to search, access and sort the data.

dialogue   In news writing, the technique of alternating quotes from different sources to create a more diverse and compelling narrative.

domain name   A Web address (for example, "www.domainname.com") using letters and an extension (such as ".com" or ".edu"). Contrasts with an IP address, which uses only numbers (such as "12.345.678.9").

fair use   The right to use copyrighted materials for journalistic purposes, or for activities such as research, teaching or criticism. Such use is not legally considered to be a copyright infringement because of its noncommercial or incidental character.

feature lead   A lead that uses storytelling techniques rather than hard facts to engage readers. Used most often on features, profiles and other less "serious" stories.

feedback page   Web page that allows readers to make comments and suggestions using submittable online forms. Comments are private and are not generally posted for public viewing. In online news, these generally invite readers to comment on news coverage and suggest story ideas.

Flash   A popular animation format for Web pages that can incorporate audio, video and animation in an interactive window. Developed by Macromedia Inc., it enables users to interact with audiovisual elements.

follow-up story   A story that provides new details about a previously reported story and serves two main functions—to provide new information about the previous story and to bring readers who didn't see the earlier story up to date.

GIF   (Graphics Interchange Format) Image format common on the Web that allows for 256 colors. Used most often for illustrations and graphics rather than for photos.

home page   The "front page" of a Web site, to which other pages are linked. Also occasionally referred to as a splash page or index page.

HTML   (Hypertext Markup Language) A text-based cross-platform computer language used to create graphically rich pages of information on the Internet.

HTML tags   Small pieces of code within an HTML document that dictate page or text formatting, insert images, create links and perform other functions.

interactivity   For journalists, the process of establishing a two-way, reciprocal relationship with the audience through the use of online technology, in contrast with the traditional one-way notion of simply publishing stories and moving on. For readers, the process of making choices in navigating Web content and responding in various ways using assorted online tools.

Internet   A global network of computer networks made popular in the 1990s with the introduction of a hypertext-driven graphical user interface called the World Wide Web. Originated in the 1960s in the United States as a Cold War command and control network.

inverted pyramid   A technique of writing news stories in which facts are arranged in descending order from most to least important.

Java   A programming language used to create online programs (called "applets") that provide assorted interactive effects and features on Web pages. Developed by Sun Microsystems.

JavaScript   A popular scripting language that enables Web programmers to include a variety of interactive features on their pages. Allows page designers to write scripts directly into HTML code rather than creating separate programs. Developed by Netscape Communications.

JPEG   Image format that allows high-quality images to be compressed for quick download. This is the most common format for photos on the Web. JPEG stands for Joint Photographic Experts Group, which developed the format.

lead   In news writing, the first sentence or two of a story, often reporting the most important elements of the story. (Pronounced "leed," not "led.")

libel   A published or broadcast statement that is false and defamatory and damages the reputation of an individual. Different legal rules apply to statements about public figures.

linear   In news writing, a technique where information is assembled using a logical order, with a central story thread to guide readers in a clear single path from start to finish. Can be applied to story structure and also to page layout.

link   On Web pages, text, photos or other elements formatted with hypertext to act as pointers to other pages. Activated by clicking with the mouse cursor.

link text   Text formatted with hypertext code to be clickable as a link. In online news, frequently a headline used to attract readers to a story on another page.

marginalia   Items such as links, advertisements or logos placed along the edges of Web pages. Usually considered of secondary importance to the main content of the page, they offer opportunities for readers to drift away to another item of interest.

message board   Web page that invites readers to post comments and opinions for all users to read and allows readers to post responses to others' messages. Similar in structure to discussion groups and blogs.

moral duty   In journalistic ethics, a reporter or editor's allegiance to various people and agencies affected by his news coverage, such as the news organization, colleagues, subscribers and society at large.

MP3   Audio format that compresses CD-quality audio to a fraction of its original size. Popular for downloading music. Short for Motion Picture Experts Group, Audio Layer 3, it is a descendant of the MPEG video format.

MPEG   Video format that digitizes and compresses broadcast-quality video into files that can be viewed on computer screens. Short for Motion Picture Experts Group, the organization that developed and set standards for the format. Descendants include MP2, the video format used to created DVDs, and MP3, the popular downloadable audio format.

multimedia   In the online world, elements of Web pages that provide motion, audio, video, animation and other stimulating features.

netiquette   General rules of online behavior that Web users are encouraged to follow.

news hole   The amount of space on a page to fill with news content after advertisements and other non-news elements have been placed.

nonlinear   In online news writing, a technique wherein a story is broken into chunks containing links, which the reader can follow in various directions at his choice. Structure is far less logical than linear storytelling, but it fits with characteristics of Web pages.

official sources   People working in companies, institutions or agencies whose job specifically involves providing information to the press.

ombudsman   In the news business, a liaison between journalists and the public who solicits feedback from the outlet's audience and from the community in general.

pacing   Writing technique in which sentences of varying lengths create a rhythm within a story.

passive voice   Writing technique in which the subject responds to actions or is acted upon. Generally believed to be less compelling to readers than active voice.

pixels   Short for picture elements, the tiny dots of color that make up a graphical image on a computer screen.

plagiarism   Labeling another person's work as your own, or using it without giving proper credit to the original author.

plug-ins   Small programs that work within Web browsers to allow users to access different types of multimedia and other content.

prior restraint   A person or organization stepping in to prevent publication of a news story before it happens.

prominence   In news reporting, the degree of notoriety of a person or persons involved in a story.

proximity   In news reporting, the nearness of the site of an event to the location of your outlet's audience.

QuickTime   Video format created by Apple Computer that is common on both Macintosh and PC computers.

RealAudio/RealVideo   Streaming audio/video format common to PC and Macintosh machines. Allows users to watch and listen to content as it downloads rather than waiting for the complete file to load.

repurposing   Taking news stories from a print or broadcast medium, reformatting them for the Web and using them as the basis for the online product.

resource   In news reporting, any publication, database or other source of information a reporter can use for a story.

rolling deadline   The notion that, because online news can be updated at any time, reporters must write and update stories immediately. This contrasts with the print news tradition of a single daily deadline for stories.

search engine   A Web site that allows users to search the content of other Web sites using keywords.

sense-making journalism   Concept of journalists providing not only information about an event or subject but also the context needed for users to fully understand it. The term was coined by journalists Bill Kovach and Tom Rosenstiel.

shield laws   State laws protecting journalists from having to divulge their sources.

shovelware   Derisive term for simply "shoveling" content from a print or broadcast outlet onto the Web with little regard for taking advantage of the strengths of the online medium.

sidebar   A secondary news story that expands on one aspect of a major story and appears nearby for readers who want more information.

six basic questions   Six essential aspects of an event—Who? What? When? Where? Why? How?—that journalists are expected to report in their stories.

source   In news reporting, a person who shares information with a journalist.

source networking   The process of a reporter using one source to lead him to other people who have information on a topic.

story flow   In writing, the degree to which one element follows from another; logical structure and clear writing that allows readers to follow easily.

story package   An in-depth assortment of news stories and other information about a particular subject that allows interested readers to dig deeply into the details of that subject.

style sheets   Sets of commands that can be used to give certain types of pages the same characteristics, such as fonts, links, colors, images, backgrounds or other page elements. For online pages, the most common type is Cascading Style Sheets (CSS).

style   In journalism, accepted sets of spellings, grammar rules and other guidelines followed by news organizations.

summary lead   A lead that summarizes the most important basic facts of a news story in its first few sentences. Most often used on fact-driven hard-news stories.

timeliness   In news reporting, the speed with which breaking news is verified and reported to the public.

transitions   In news writing, points where a story shifts its focus or otherwise moves from one section to another.

unofficial sources   People working in companies, institutions or agencies who provide information to journalists in less formal capacities.

update   An addition to a preexisting story to provide new information, usually reserved for breaking news. Not a complete rewrite of the original story.

URL   (Uniform Resource Locator) The address that points browsers to a particular Web site, often known simply as a Web address.

Wall Street Journal structure   News story structure featuring a long, descriptive lead, followed by a transition that ties the lead to the main details of the story. This term is derived from the structure commonly used at the *Wall Street Journal* newspaper.

Web directory   A searchable index of other Web sites' material, usually organized by subject, geographic area or other traits.

webcast   A broadcast of information over the Web, most often audio or video, of an event streamed live as it happens.

Windows Media   Streaming video format developed by Microsoft for its Windows PC operating system. Allows users to watch video without waiting for long downloads.

World Wide Web   A system using hypertext to create graphically rich "pages" of information posted on the Internet and viewed using a browser program. Emerged in the 1990s as the system that brought the Internet to the masses.

Index